ELEMENTARY LANGUAGE ARTS INSTRUCTION

ELEMENTARY LANGUAGE ARTS INSTRUCTION

Arthur Ellis
Seattle Pacific University

Joan Pennau
Marian College

Timothy Standal
University of Washington

Mary Kay Rummel
Poet and *National Consultant for the Language Arts*

PRENTICE HALL, Englewood Cliffs, New Jersey 07632

Library of Congress Cataloging-in-Publication Data

Elementary language arts instruction / Arthur Ellis . . . [et al.].
p. cm.
Bibliography: p.
Includes index.
ISBN -13-258336-4
1. Language arts (Elementary) I. Ellis, Arthur K.
LB1576.E415 1989 88-30594
372.6—dc19 CIP

Editorial/production supervision: *Edith Riker*
Cover design: *20/20 Services, Inc.*
Manufacturing buyer: *Peter Havens*

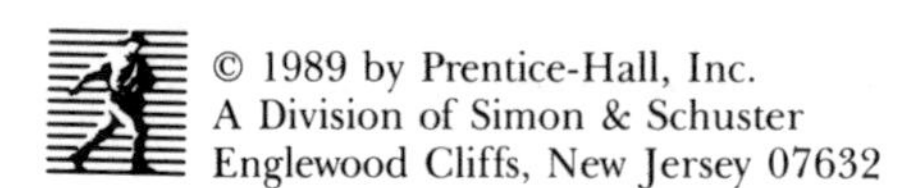

Printed in the United States of America

10 9 8 7 6 5 4 3 2 1

ISBN 0-13-258336-4

Prentice-Hall International (UK) Limited, *London*
Prentice-Hall of Australia Pty. Limited, *Sydney*
Prentice-Hall Canada Inc., *Toronto*
Prentice-Hall Hispanoamericana, S.A., *Mexico*
Prentice-Hall of India Private Limited, *New Delhi*
Prentice-Hall of Japan, Inc., *Tokyo*
Simon & Schuster Asia Pte. Ltd., *Singapore*
Editora Prentice-Hall do Brasil, Ltda., *Rio de Janeiro*

CONTENTS

PREFACE

This book is based on a simple premise: that theory and research can successfully inform practice. If the premise is useful, and if we have brought the worlds of theory and practice together, then all that is missing is a motivated, informed teacher who wants to see children develop a meaningful command of the language. We have attempted to make practical, day-to-day applications of research-based generalizations from the cornerstone areas of language: speaking, listening, reading, and writing. Those applications, put into the hands of a gifted teacher who loves language and loves to teach, will surely move the nation further along on the golden road to literacy.

The activities and rhythms of classroom life are demanding. They allow teachers little time for reflection and planning. Much of the teacher's time is spent reacting to situations that arise from the dynamics of thirty people in a classroom setting. Thus, the realities are such that teachers come to depend on their experience as a guide to what can be done with children of a certain age in a group setting, given certain resources. This book is meant to temper experiences, which as Leonardo Da Vinci wrote, "does not ever err, it is only our judgment, that errs." So if this book enables those who teach to sharpen their judgment, because their judgment will be strengthened with the knowledge of research, then it will have been successful.

We present the language arts as useful tools. To that end we have included a chapter on language and the total curriculum, a chapter that treats language as the core of interdisciplinary studies. We have also included chapters on planning, teaching strategies, and assessment techniques. Our desire is to help the reader develop and expand his or her sense of wholeness about the pervasive role of language in our society. Given that, we wish further to help the reader develop a sense of urgency toward our great national goal of literacy for all.

In this time of rapid technological change, it is not uncommon to find homes where 30 to 200 television channels are accessed. The range of programs is staggering. Even the concept of what is a library has changed. The average supermarket carries more than 500 magazine titles, upwards of 1,000 adult books from the classics to gothic romances, and hundreds of children's books, not to mention video and audio tapes, records, and compact discs. People drive to work listening to tapes that range from Jane

Austen to Wayne Dyer. And so on. We've come a long way from the days when Thomas Carlyle, recently moved from Scotland to London, lamented the fact that there was not a "library in every county town" because, after all, there were certainly a jail and gallows in every one. In fact, the library is everywhere.

This is a book about the power of language and about how to empower teachers to help children learn to appreciate and apply language in written and spoken form. The enduring power of language to illuminate the mind and spirit is often underestimated. When, in the eighth century, Charlemagne summoned the English bishop and scholar, Alcuin, to his court in France, to ensure that "grammar be taught and carefully corrected books be available," little did the great emperor know that that alone would be his enduring legacy. All his other wordly achievements have literally turned to dust. The alphabet you use today, derived from Phoenician, Greek, and Roman precursors, has come from Alcuin and Charlemagne virtually unchanged. It is the most versatile communication tool in history.

The children you teach, and will continue to teach, over the years will inherit that tradition. Their attempts to refine and improve its possiblities will be many and wondrous. And after all, that is what teaching is about: children and possibilities.

As you read this book, we encourage you to become involved in the possiblities. We invite you to think expansively about the potential for elementary-age children to develop a sense of respect and efficacy for the English language. The language you teach to young minds is representative of not only the rich cultural heritage of the past, but of the continuous process of addition and innovation as immigrants from other cultures take their place in the American mainstream. Historian Lynne Cheney reminds us to bear in mind the teacher, Julia Mortimer, in Eudora Welty's novel, *Losing Battles*, who "didn't ever doubt but that all worth preserving is going to be preserved, and all we had to do was keep it going, right from where we are, one teacher on down to the next."

1

INTRODUCING THE LANGUAGE ARTS

Two adults stand over a crib in which an infant lies on its back. The adults smile, make cooing noises, and speak words to the infant. The infant responds to their overtures by waving its arms wildly and making babbling sounds. It is clear that all three are having a good time. It is also clear that, for the infant, the process of speaking and listening is already in motion.

Long ago, prehistoric people began to communicate with each other through the spoken word. In a process which repeated itself many times, people, places, and objects were given names; Actions were labeled; Modifiers were used. This is how speech emerged. Perhaps centuries elapsed before someone connected spoken words to drawings. Centuries more elapsed before someone connected spoken words to symbols and writing emerged. Human beings embarked on an irreversible course which would lead in time to increasingly deeper levels of abstract thought and widespread communication beyond the moment in time.

In 1981 former Beatle, Ringo Starr, played in a movie called "Caveman." The film is set in the year One Zillion B.C.. Its main storyline is based on the premise that people in that day and age could communicate with each other only by grunting and pointing to things. The children and few adults entertained by the film were attracted to the novel idea that people at one time were forced to communicate without the benefit of conventional tools. The audience found such an unconventional (or preconventional) way of communicating inherently funny.

The tools of communication which were removed by the makers of "Caveman" are those which you use and perhaps take for granted every day of your life; speaking, listening, reading, and writing. You are, in a sense, an expert in the use of language. You have mastered its basic elements, such as meaning, structure, and style.

If this is so, you ask, then why are many elementary school teachers apprehensive about the teaching of language arts? For many teachers, this area of the curriculum, which you have been preparing for since you first listened to your parents from your crib, is as much a part of your culture as your food, clothing, and shelter. In order to bring this vast reservoir of information to a level of effective teaching, you will have to bring the language arts into focus. We will begin that task now.

BRINGING THE LANGUAGE ARTS INTO FOCUS

"Language arts" refers to speaking and writing, the expressive language activities in communication, and listening and reading, the receptive language activities in communication. Communication is at the heart of the language arts curriculum. The purpose of language arts instruction is to extend the language children bring to school so that they are able to communicate effectively in our technological society. This is a broader view than the traditional study of "English." "English" programs are generally limited to the study of written composition, grammar, and literature. Language arts, on the other hand, focuses on developing speaking, listening, reading, and writing skills.

The term "language arts" implies that effective use of language is an art. As with any art, the artist must master the basic skills and use them to create a product which reflects his experiences, thoughts, and feelings. Thereby, the language arts in the elementary school are aimed at developing language as a basic tool of communication and as an aesthetic form of self-expression.

In addition, the language arts are important to learning in all subject areas. It is virtually impossible to proceed in the sciences, the humanities, or the arts without language skills. Speaking, listening, reading, and writing, therefore, are at the core of learning.

LANGUAGE AND THINKING

Before proceeding it is important to address the relationship between language and thinking. The education literature is replete with discussions about their interrelatedness, but there are questions among theorists as to the nature of their relationship. From the Piagetian viewpoint, thinking comes first and is reflected through language. As Wadsworth explains, "only after achieving the capability to internally represent experience do (can) children begin to construct spoken language. When language develops, there is a parallel development of conceptual abilities that language helps to facilitate . . . " (p. 79) Vygotsky, on the other hand, concludes that language and thinking develop as a unitary process; for him, " . . . thought is born of language . . . " (p. 132)

Regardless of the differing viewpoints, there is a consensus that language and thinking spring from experience and support each other. This is a key point. It is of utmost importance to realize that language and thinking are vitally related. Learners receive information through language and their language, in turn, allows them to question and organize their thoughts. In the words of Bruner, language is " . . . a powerful instrument for combining experiences, an instrument that can . . . be used as a tool for organizing thought about things." (p. 105) Thinking is a basic element in all the language arts.

A GLIMPSE OF THE LANGUAGE ARTS CURRICULUM

The following is a brief overview of the language arts curriculum. Subsumed in the five headings are essential language components including vocabulary development, spelling, handwriting, dramatic activities, usage and grammar.

Speaking

Speaking is the process of orally expressing thought and feelings, of reflecting and shaping experiences, and of sharing information.

Ideas are the essence of what we speak and words are the vehicles of expression. We combine words to speak sentences and paragraphs and use a language style that is appropriate for the social context. Speaking is a complex process which involves thinking, language, and social skills.

Children enter school able to speak. They speak to express their needs, to question, and to learn about their ever expanding world. However, their language ability is incomplete. They are not capable of comprehending or producing complex sentences, nor do they understand that language style varies with the situation. Additionally kindergarteners have had different preschool experiences and different verbal opportunities. This results in a class with varied language abilities. It is the teacher's responsibility to build upon each child's language foundation, enriching and extending oral expression, and facilitating accepted usage in different settings.

Listening

The reciprocal relationship between speaking and listening (and writing and reading) may be likened to that of the chicken and the egg: you can't have one without the other. Communication involves both expressive and receptive activities. Speakers may speak (and writers may write) but unless someone listens (or reads) communication does not occur. Listening, the auditory receptive component of communication, is a conscious mental activity requiring the listener to perceive and interpret the speaker's words. This involves the thinking and language abilities—vocabulary knowledge, understanding of sentence structure, and organization of ideas in words—that are essential for all communication.

Listening is the primary mode of language learning. As children listen they experience language, from concepts, and acquire vocabulary and sentence patterns that they will use in speaking, writing, and reading. Effective listeners learn more. Developing effective listeners is the aim of listening instruction.

What is in the listener's head about any particular thing is known as the *schema* he/she holds about that topic. Schema is the result of background knowledge which the reader brings to the printed page (or any other source of information). You have a certain amount of background knowledge about the Civil War which you would bring to any passage you might read on that historical event. Research has shown that "differences in reading ability between five year olds and eight year olds are caused primarily by the older children's possessing more knowledge, not by differences in their memory capacities, reasoning abilities, or control of eye movements." (Hirsch, 1987, p. 47).

Reading

Reading is the visual receptive component of communication. It is the process of deriving meaning from the written word. Like listening, reading is rooted in the understanding of language.

Children use their total language ability when they read. Research has repeatedly demonstrated the correlation between oral language competency and reading achievement. Children who use complex sentences and mature vocabularies in their speech score high on measures of reading achievement. Children who are able to listen and understand speech also tend to be better readers, since listening and reading both require comprehension of language, whether it is written or spoken. Children's aural-oral abilities facilitate their reading abilities.

Reading comprehension also depends upon what is in the reader's head. When the content is beyond the reader's realm of experience, the person may have trouble understanding what is written. It is, therefore, important to develop proficiency in all the language arts to help children learn to read.

Literature

Literature is more than a subset of the reading program; it permeates every facet of the language arts curriculum.

First and foremost literature inherently enriches children's experiences with excitement and pleasure. We read to enjoy ourselves, to be carried away from the routines of life, to vent our emotions, to give us hope, and to try on different roles.

Through literature children have crossed America with Johnny Appleseed, fought Captain Hook with Peter Pan, and ridden in a balloon with Professor William Waterman Sherman. In their literary lives children have experienced the problems of growing up on the prairie with Laura Ingalls, they have identified with the characters in *Are You There God? It's Me Margaret*, and they have been transported through time in the *Green Knowe* books. These experiences expose children to their heritage, to differing ideas, values, and cultures, and help them to understand themselves, others, and the world in which they live.

Literature is a language experience. Just as literature enriches and expands children's experiential sphere, so does literature enrich and extend their language. A teacher points out and encourages children to notice words and sentences that convey impressions, heighten suspense, animate a character, or paint a scene. The words and sentence patterns met in prose and poetry will first appear in children's listening and speaking vocabularies and later in their reading and writing vocabularies.

Literature gives buoyancy to the language arts program. The feelings and ideas that it generates stimulate interest in reading. The content builds experiences and language.

Writing

Like speaking, writing is rooted in ideas and words. Children's experiences, firsthand and/or those lived through language, are the content of their writing. Written words, like spoken words, convey the emotions, knowledge, and perceptions of the writer.

Writing also differs from speaking in that written communication involves the mental and physical abilities of handwriting and spelling, and the conventions of usage, punctuation, and capitalization. Also, written language lacks the intimacy and intonational qualities of spoken language. To communicate these subtleties in graphic form one must use the imagery of words, written signs, textual organization, and language style.

Because of the complexity of the writing process, the teaching of writing often focuses on the product rather than the process. In subsequent chapters we will examine the steps involved in writing and provide examples for working with children at each stage of the writing process.

THE INTEGRATION OF THE LANGUAGE ARTS

As we have discussed in our curricular overview, the language arts complement one another. For example, the reception of language significantly affects the expression of language. The vocabulary and sentences that children use in speaking and writing are first experienced in listening and reading. This readily becomes evident in teaching specific forms of written expression. If we expect children to write description, they must have have heard and read descriptive passages; if we expect children to write poetry, they must have heard and read many poems.

Figure 1-1 depicts the interrelationships of the language arts. Speaking, listening, writing, and reading are shown to overlap because of their relationships. They are immersed in cognition, since thought provides the content of language and is important in the expression and reception of language. Language abilities, at the center, include vocabulary, sentence structure, and the organization of ideas in words. Because language ability is important for all communication, proficiency or deficiency in one area will have a positive or negative effect, respectively, on all the language arts.

Current emphasis on the theory of whole language in language arts instruction is supported by the work of many scholars. For further information consult the references at the end of this chapter. If the language arts are integrated in instruction with each other and with other curriculum areas classroom learning will build upon the way that children naturally learn language as a complex whole and not in segmented parts. This unity and the integration of instruction are the theme of this book. Even when the focus of a chapter is on a particular skill such as spelling, that skill is never isolated from the whole picture of the child as language user.

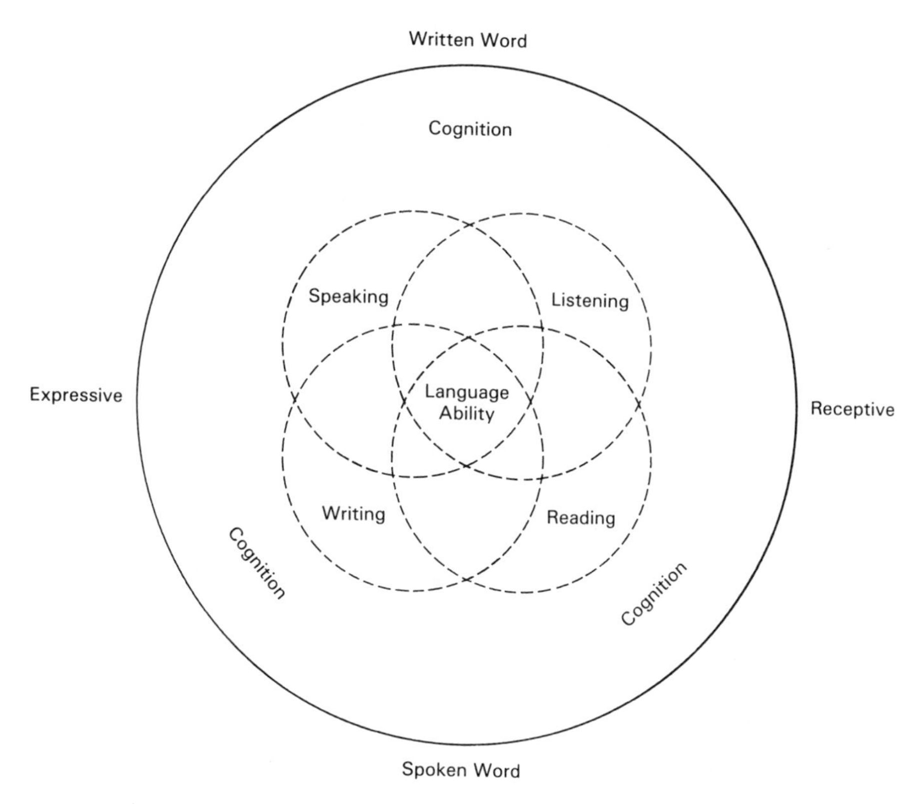

FIGURE 1-1

GOALS OF THE LANGUAGE ARTS CURRICULUM

The following are educational goals for the Elementary Language Arts Program (K through 6). They were adapted from a variety of sources including several state guides, district guides, and commercial publications.

Students should:

1. develop awareness of and appreciation for the importance of language to each individual and to society as a whole.
2. understand that oral language patterns vary and that language variations reflect cultural, regional, and individual differences.

Speaking

3. develop usage patterns which enable them to speak clearly and expressively about their ideas.
4. develop and be able to adapt speaking skills for varying situations and audiences, from one to one conversations to formal large group settings.
5. learn to participate productively and harmoniously in small and large oral discussion groups.

Listening

6. learn to interpret various kinds of oral communication including pitch, pause, volume, and gestures.
7. develop and be able to adapt listening skills for varying situations and audiences.

Writing

8. be able to use the writing process steps.
9. adapt their writing style for various purposes.
10. develop their writing skills to express themselves clearly.
11. recognize that precision in handwriting, punctuation, capitalization, spelling, and other elements of manuscript form are a part of the total effectiveness of writing.

Reading

12. understand that the purpose of reading is to obtain meaning from the printed page.
13. develop the necessary reading skills to comprehend a variety of written materials.

Literature

14. read for enjoyment and cultivate the lifelong habit of reading.
15. understand that literature is a mirror of human experience reflecting human motives, conflicts, and values.
16. identify with literary characters and thereby gain insights into themselves, others, and the world in which they live.
17. develop knowledge of various literary forms and techniques.
18. acquire a literary taste and be able to effectively discuss and write about various forms of literature.

Thinking Skills

19. use language to facilitate creative thinking—see new relationships, explore and express original feelings, perceptions, and ideas, and cultivate self-understanding.
20. use language to facilitate logical thinking—formulate hypotheses, understand conceptual relationships, and draw conclusions based on evidence.
21. use language to facilitate critical-evaluative thinking—to pose questions in order to discern meaning, to distinguish opinion from facts, and to evaluate the intentions and messages of speakers and writers, especially attempts to manipulate language in order to deceive.

LANGUAGE ARTS IN THE INFORMATION AGE

The twentieth century is marked as a time of increasing specialization. The knowledge base expands exponentially, forcing people to choose among highly concentrated, narrowly defined vocations. New jobs which require new skills and which have a technical language of their own appear almost daily.

It is curious that so much hope is invested in a 3,000 year old, little-changed invention: an arbitrary set of symbols called the alphabet. Technological change washes over it, leaving it in its ancient state. The printing press, the typewriter, and the computer take their places as tools of communication, but their place is secondary to this sturdy code. With all its shortcomings, the alphabet remains the best means of communicaiton for the largest number of people. There is considerable currency, therefore, in the widely accepted notion that our greatest national concern is to teach our people how to speak, read, write, and listen to the English language.

As you read these pages, you stand on a watershed of history and culture. The alphabet used to communicate the ideas of this book to you represents a stream which goes back 30 centuries in its present form and reaches even farther back in the form of its various precursors. As a basic tool, it has only one rival, the number system.

Listening, speaking, reading, and writing are the four most used of life's basic tools. The communication of ideas, desires, and feelings, however personal or general, rests on our mastery of these tools.

When you casually ask your students to "take out your language books," you have, without thinking about it, linked them in formal study to a tradition of learning that the editors of the 1770 *Britannica* called ". . . most copious, significant, fluent, courteous . . ." Your task is monumental. It is to mount a campaign on behalf of clarity of language. Though the task is simply stated, your opposition is formidable, and it is everywhere. Don't confuse your role with that of the hidebound purist who seeks to promote obscure grammatical and syntactical rules. You would render language dead by denying its dynamic function of change and expansion. Instead, your overriding concern must be with clarity. Clarity is the essence of good language expression. But the evidence of unclear language expression abounds. The hyperbole of advertising, the circumlocution of bureaucratic pronouncements, and the vapid commentary of sports announcers are cases in point.

The fact remains that in the arts, in education, in government, in business, and in our private communications, the ability to use language well is the best index of clear thinking. We intend to promote that idea, the relationship between clear thinking and good language, throughout this book.

SUMMARY

Language evolved to facilitate communication. As individuals we use language to communicate our thoughts and feelings and review the thoughts and feelings of others. As a society we use language to communicate knowledge, values, attitudes, and ideals.

Effective communication is the goal of language arts instructions. Each day's language experiences—creative drama activities, spelling exercise, reading assignments, group discussions, poetry writing, and all the rest—are designed to help children recognize the beauty and power of language and to develop their skills for effective speaking, listening, reading, and writing.

ACTIVITIES

1. As a class, or in small groups, brainstorm all the components that you think are subsumed under language arts. Based on your experience as an elementary student, which components tend to receive the heaviest emphasis? Which tend to receive little attention? Why? What do you think about this? Suggest ways of integrating the language arts components.
2. Observe an elementary classroom at a grade level of your choice. Note how the language arts seem to be taught.
3. Plan a lesson which integrates speaking, listening, reading, and writing. Base the lesson plan on another area of the curriculum, such as social studies, science, or art.
4. What questions do you have about how children learn language? Write them down now. See if they are answered as you continue through this text. If not, search other sources and/or ask your instructor.

SUGGESTED READINGS

BOORSTIN, DANIEL J. (1985). *The discoverers: a history of man's Search to know his world and himself.* New York: Vintage Books.
BRUNER JEROME (1960) *The process of education*, Cambridge: Harvard University Press.
BUTLER, ANDREA AND TURBILL JAN (1984) *Towards a reading writing classroom,* Portsmouth: Heinemann.
COGDEN, COURTNEY. (1988). *Classroom Discourse; the language of teaching and learning.* Portsmouth: Heinemann.
GARDNER, JOHN (1984). *The art of fiction: notes on craft for young writers.* New York: Alfred A. Knopf.
HIRSCH, E.D., JR. (1987). *Cultural literacy.* Boston: Houghton Mifflin Company.
HOLDAWAY, DON. (1979). *Foundations of Literacy.* Portsmouth: Heinemann.
NABOKOV, VLADIMIR (1980). *Lectures on literature.* New York: Harcourt, Brace Jovanovich.
NEWMAN, JUDITH. (1985). *Whole language theory and use.* Portsmouth: Heinemann.
VYGOTSKY, LEV (1962). *Thought and language.* Cambridge: MIT Press.
WADSWORTH, BARRY (1978). *Piaget for the classroom teacher.* New York: Longman, Inc.
WAIN, JOHN (1975). *Samuel Johnson: A Biography.* New York: Viking Press.

2

LANGUAGE ARTS AND THE TOTAL CURRICULUM

The term "language arts" is, of course, itself an interdisciplinary term. It is a holding property for the various subject areas which go together naturally to form that subject in the elementary school curriculum. But language arts ought to reside at the center of an even larger curricular picture: that of the entire curriculum. In this chapter we will explore a number of interdisciplinary strategies for developing curriculum themes which cross the often artificial boundaries among the separate subjects taught during the typical school day.

Interdisciplinary themes are easily constructed and carried out. To anyone who has worked with children, the idea of discarding a separate subjects approach to learning has a certain appeal. Children tend to view their world as a whole, and the idea of separate subjects is inherently foreign to them. Their early questions about numbers are not about mathematics as a separate subject any more than the stories which they hear when they are very young are about reading as a subject. Those distinctions come later and they must be learned.

We support interdisciplinary efforts wholeheartedly, but we also offer a word of caution. Not everything in the school curriculum should be integrated. Some skills and content are best taught and learned within the confines of a single discipline. The best balance between separate subjects and interdisciplinary is an issue which you must resolve for yourself.

WHAT IS INTERDISCIPLINARY TEACHING AND LEARNING?

Interdisciplinary teaching and learning represent an effort on the part of teachers and students to break down the walls that separate the subjects in the curriculum. This feat is accomplished through the vehicle of integrated studies, thematic teaching, or what is sometimes called the project method. No less a leading educational figure than John Dewey suggested that we "abandon the idea of subject matter as something separate from the child." Dewey thought of the child and subject matter as forming two ends of the same continuum. In that respect he encouraged problem solving and reflective thinking as a focus of learning (Dewey, 1910).

Dewey's ideas for a more intellectually engaged curriculum were expanded by William Kilpatrick (1918) who developed the project method as a means of having students' focus on a theme or project which would involve the application of skills, ideas, and content from various subjects. Examples of projects include "Our Community," "Consumerism," "Autumn," "Water," or any other theme which teachers and students might identify as being interesting and relevant. The very strengths of the project or interdisciplinary approach, that is, relevance of subject matter or topic, motivation on the part of teachers and students to learn, connectedness of subject matter and ideas, and so forth, highlight its perceived weaknesses: random selection of topics, breakdown in continuities provided by standardized scope and sequence, and failure to give a full measure of curriculum time to mathematics and other basic skills which often give way to arts and crafts and other hands-on activities.

In addition to the pedagogical problems which we have just identified, the project approach raises another "problem," one which concerns many administrators. That problem is one which we will call, in a global sense, management. Pre-set, textbook oriented curricula are, in fact, curricula of control. When the course of study is predetermined, it is much easier for an administrator to know approximately where a teacher and his/her class are or should be in the textbook and what content they will be studying. It obviously also makes for a quieter, neater room if all the students' desks are neatly arranged in rows and everyone keeps to himself or herself. Interestingly, one of John Dewey's first challenges in establishing his laboratory school at the University of Chicago was to search the warehouses of that city for tables and chairs that would allow him to break up the standard formation of rows and desks found at that time in almost all elementary classrooms (Ellis, Mackey, and Glenn, 1988).

In their book, *Interdisciplinary Methods: A Thematic Approach*, Humphreys, Post, and Ellis address the central issue of thematic teaching and learning:

> A school day is often divided into reading time, recess, more reading, spelling, lunch, arithmetic, recess, clean up, and go home. A child's day may be made up of thoughts of play, conversations, pretending, watching the custodian or the painter, contructing forts or making cookies, and looking forward to family sharing time. The former seems efficient and logical, the latter disorganized and illogical.
>
> The heretical thesis of this book is that the latter day, the child's day, may be a better model on which to develop thinking abilities, problem solving abilities, and conceptual structures. If children are to learn how their world works, they must interact with it. And their world is not like an assembly line. An integrated theme begins within the child's environment and expands to include elements of reading, arithmetic, science, social studies, and many others. You, the teacher, build the theme around the child's interests and slowly facilitate conceptual development through the challenges you offer, the questions you pose, and the investigations you initiate (1981, p. 19).

The best way to learn about interdisciplinary teaching and learning is through experience, because this method uses an experience-based approach. We encourage you to find a partner who is also interested in this method (someone in your class, perhaps) who can help you process the information in this chapter. After the two of you have worked your way through the ideas presented here, try developing one of the themes which we will suggest at the close of this chapter. Or, come up with your own theme, one which really interests you.

Let's begin by identifying a possible interdisciplinary theme. For purposes of illustration, we have chosen the theme of "Night." We begin by doing some brainstroming about things that happen at night. A popular brainstorming approach in thematic teaching is that called "webbing." To do a webbing, you place the thematic term, in this case *night*, at the center of a chalkboard or large newsprint page, and begin developing rays of ideas related to the theme. Figure 2-1 will show you what we mean. This is the initial phase. Notice that the webbing is quite simple and unsophisticated. Now look at Figure 2-2. This will give you some idea of how the early brainstorming has progressed on the basis of a second round. Both teachers and students should be involved in this stage of the project. The early phases are crucial because they give those involved a sense of efficacy and ownership in the problem. Also, by involving a large number of people in the planning, you get a wonderful return on the investment of widespread creativity.

Not everything that is placed on the webbing becomes an object of study. In some cases, ideas are offered merely in the spirit of brainstorming. They may have little potential or they may create little real interest.

FIGURE 2-1

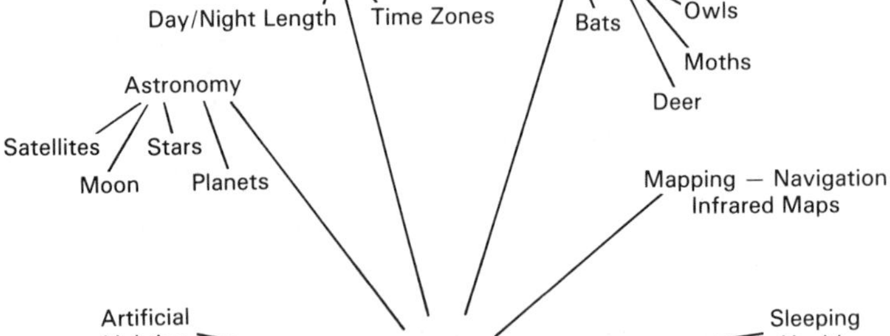

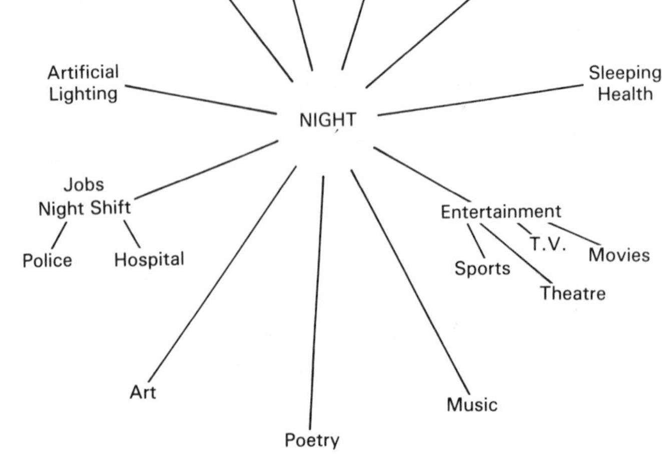

The point is to be open at the outset and to consider everything. Also, ideas will emerge along the way and can be added to the course of study. Not every child will study every topic listed on the webbing. Special interest will prevail. But a common focus has been established, and each student's activities (whether group or individual) will be related to the theme. It is crucial that the class be kept "together" in that all the activities are related and interdependent. Themes are most successful when they include a great deal of group work, sharing among students, and cooperative learning. In fact, we recommend that you attempt, at some point, a school-wide theme. An effort mounted at this scale involves everyone: principal, custodian, librarian, clerks, students, teachers, parents, etc. An elementary school that takes on a school-wide theme is an exciting place to be.

In the following pages you will find an interdisciplinary unit titled, "Inventions." It is meant as a point of departure and not as a finished product. The idea is for you to add and/or subtract from the unit what you

FIGURE 2-2 A webbing for the theme, "Inventions."

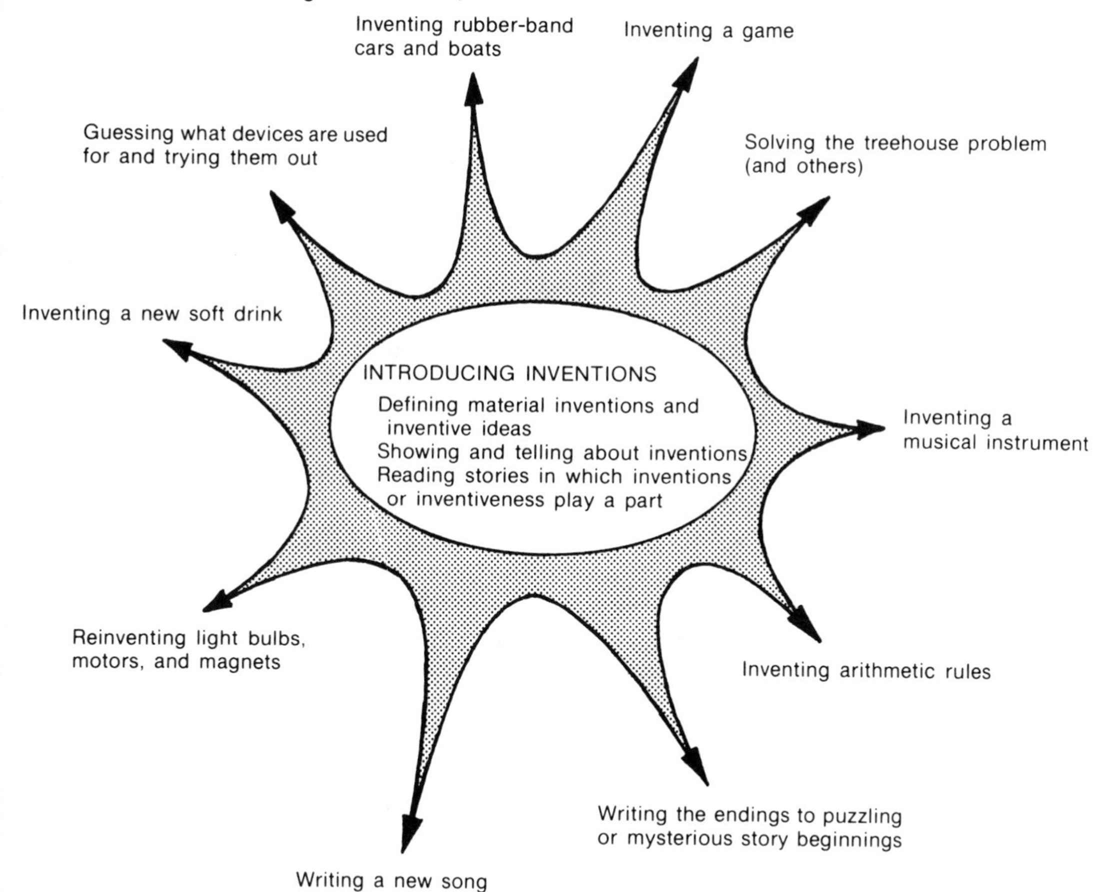

will, depending on the age and interests of the children you work with. Interdisciplinary units are best approached from an open, fluid perspective, and it would be indeed remarkable if any two individuals ever taught a given unit in exactly the same way.

Inventions

INTRODUCTION

Children at play discover many things. They find that wagons will coast downhill but must be pushed up. They find that a yo-yo will come back if it is spinning, but will not return if it is motionless. They find that water poured onto sand at the beach soaks in rapidly, but water poured on the sidewalk forms puddles or runs off.

This unit suggests several ways of helping children learn to pose and solve problems through invention. More specifically, the unit explores some of the hows and whys of fabrications, fictions, devices, and substances, and then presents a variety of problem situations in which children are challenged to complete a story, devise an explanation, or create something that is needed.

As teachers, we know that it is difficult to structure learning situations for children in which creativity and inventiveness occur. Since it is very difficult to create or invent on order, we are tempted to build learning situations in which each child succeeds at a simple task. That is part of the intent of this unit. For that reason, its structure is somewhat looser than that of previous units. Through this more open-ended organization, we hope to free you to allow your students' interests and creativity to determine the time given to each activity of the unit, and the number of activities pursued and completed.

On the pages that follow you will find first three general activities to begin to get your class involved in this unit. These are followed by twelve invention and discovery areas that small groups can explore or follow. Undoubtedly, your students' investigations will turn up other equally workable areas of exploration and should be encouraged. Please remember that all of the units in this book are intended as starting points, and not completed plans. All unit planning should be based largely on the characteristics and interests of your students, time, and resources abailable, as well as on your own areas of expertise.

Unit Objectives:

The students will:

1. find out about many of the inventions and creations we enjoy and use.
2. discover that objects can have many functions.

3. understand what "to invent" means in the broad context.
4. have the freedom to create ideas, stories, poems, new objects, and new things from existing objects.

Appropriate Grade Levels:

Three to Six

ACTIVITY ONE: PRETEST AND UNIT INTRODUCTION

Objective: to measure general inventiveness before beginning the unit, and to introduce the unit theme (Note: this is essentially a teacher's objective.)

Materials: paper, pencils, and crayons if desired.

Procedure: To begin the inventions unit, give your students the following directions:

> Pretend that your neighbors cleaned out their garage and piled up things for the garbage man to haul away. In the pile were a pair of old roller skates, a tire, some boards, several cardboard boxes, a plastic bucket, a box of mixed nails, screws, and tacks, a broken tricycle, a leaky hose, and a coil of rope. You can have any of the things in the pile. Write a paragraph describing an item you could make using several of the throwaways. Then draw a picture of it.

Next, select one or two simple inventions (a board for carding wool, a spinning wheel, a butter churn, a rolling pin) and present them to your class explaining that these items were used when the related tasks were done by hand. Mention some tasks that are still done by hand (folding letters to go into envelopes, tying shoe laces, peeling oranges) and ask if there is an invention or device that might do these tasks.

However, be sure to explain to children that inventions aren't just limited to devices that perform particular tasks. Inventions in a broad context include verbal fabrications, fiction, new art forms, new solutions to problems, and new songs as well as new devices and substances. To conclude this unit introduction, you may wish to present stories without endings or puzzles for students to complete or solve as a beginning to being inventive.

Evaluation: completion of written and drawn assignments, participation in group activities and discussions.

ACTIVITY TWO: BEGINNING RESEARCH

Objective: to find and use resource materials related to inventing.

Materials: a variety of resource materials in your school library.

Procedure: As further preparation for the unit, send your class to the school resource center. Ask the librarian or media specialist to set up a cart of books, games, puzzles, etc. that could be kept in your classroom for a few days. You might also want to have the librarian give your students directions that will help them locate appropriate resource materials for themselves.

Upon returning to your classroom, put the webbing diagram from the opening page of this unit on the board or have your students create a web of their own. From this, allow students time during which they can explore their resources and begin to identify possible projects.

Evaluation: successful location and perusal of library materials related to inventions

ACTIVITY THREE: PROJECT PLANNING

Objective: to begin planning group projects and to collect related materials.

Materials: variable, depending on projects identified.

Procedure: At this point, all of your students should have had time to seek out and look through a variety of resource materials. They now need to divide into small groups, each of which can identify an invention or category of inventions on which they, as a group, wish to work. The best way to divide the class is to have students contribute project ideas to a class list, and then have the children organize according to their project choice. Another method would be to set up groups first and then allow time for each group to choose one project to be completed.

Once groups have identified the "invention" on which they wish to work, your task will be to help children with suggestions, ideas, sources of information, and materials needed for construction. However, be sure to encourage groups to plan their investigations before you make suggestions. When help is sought from you, suggestions in the form of questions can help direct thoughts and encourage alternative approaches so that the students are ultimately finding their own answers and solutions.

Once each group of students has selected a project idea or area, suggest that they consider several related investigations. For example, if the children in one group choose "Inventing a Soft Drink," one of the general areas listed for exploration in subsequent pages of this unit, they could find out about two or more of these:

1. soft drink flavors
2. carbonation and CO2
3. history of the soft drink industry
4. natural and artificial flavors
5. bottles, cans, and recycling
6. trademarks
7. inventing a new flavor

Help each group to first choose a few themes of high interest for study and then develop daily plans for the following two or three days. Discuss with them the nature of the final report on the invention or discovery that you will expect from each group. You will find it helpful to have each group submit a set of plans and a description of their proposed report in advance. Such plans will not only help you keep track of progress made, but will also be useful guides for the students themselves. In addition, these written plans would be useful evaluation guides for both you and your students.

You may also want to make some related assignments, such as the development of a report or minibook describing their experiences or discussing other inventions which fit into the same category as the item they have developed. For example, a group making rubber-band cars could make a collage of auto pictures and describe a variety of cars and their histories.

Finally, if possible, the children's completed inventions should be displayed in a central location in the school so their ideas and creations can be shared with other students.

Evaluation: project plan submitted by each group

ACTIVITY FOUR AND BEYOND: TWELVE INVENTION AND DISCOVERY AREAS

The following pages contain activity suggestions in a variety of general areas of invention and discovery. As explained in the unit introduction, this list is certainly not complete or all-inclusive of possible fields of exploration. Rather, it is intended to be used by you as a set of examples of how students can branch out within a general area of interest and study.

The general planning and implementation procedures for these twelve activities have been outlined within Activity Three. The areas for investigation included here are:

1. cars
2. games
3. music
4. numbers
5. stories
6. songs
7. light bulbs and motors
8. soft drinks
9. inventions needed
10. fortresses, castles, and hideaways
11. steam engines
12. airplanes

In each area, the objective of the activities will be the completion of the identified projects, and materials will be dependent upon the project undertaken. Evaluation would then be based on completion of the project, and perhaps on the planning that precedes it.

ACTIVITY FOUR: AUTOMOBILES

1. Set up a toy auto display showing the make and year of several cars.
2. Make posters or drawings of automobiles, dream cars, racing cars, modified cars, dune buggies, and others.
3. Find out what makes automobiles go, including information on gasoline, diesel, and battery powered cars.
4. Research what percent of a newspaper is devoted to autos by measuring the space and used by articles, feature advertisements, classified advertisements, and parts ads.
5. Write and/or read stories about autos.
6. Write and/or sing songs about autos.
7. Do research on foreign automobiles, their makes and history.
8. Find out about automobile racing and stunt driving.
9. Build scale model autos from kits.
10. Construct rubber-band-driven autos or create vehicles using Tinkertoys. Solve problems related to connecting rubber bands, wheel friction, axle construction, and so on.
11. Hold auto races and measure the speed of travel of the cars used. One way to do this is to lay out a marked track on the floor. Using a clock, watch, or one-second pendulum, the speed of cars be measured.

$$\text{speed} = \frac{\text{distance travelled}}{\text{time}}$$

EXAMPLE:

$$\text{speed} = \frac{6 \text{ meters}}{4 \text{ seconds}} = 1.5 \text{ meters per second}$$

ACTIVITY FIVE: GAMES

1. Find as many kinds of puzzles and games as possible. Find out what the difference is between a game and a puzzle.
2. Research a wide variety of games, finding out kinds and rules of:

card games
board games
playground games

3. Look into a variety of puzzles, including interlocking and number combinations such as magic squares and many others.

4. Create and play games and puzzles intended for one or two players or for teams.

5. Compare games of strategy (checkers, Chinese checkers, chess) and games of chance (using spinners, card turning, or dice).

6. Learn about the psychology of games. For example, try to answer the questions, "Can you play a game better if you practice?" and "Can you flip a coin or roll a die better with practice?" Plan a study to find out if practice improves one's ability in both chance and skill games.

7. Study the mathematics of chance. In particular, dice offer some interesting investigations. Some examples follow:

a. roll a single die (six sides numbered one through six.) Keep a record of the number of times each face is up in ten, fifty, and seventy-five rolls. Predict the number of times each face will be up in 100 rolls.
b. Roll two dice. Keep a record of the number of times twos, threes, fours, through twelves are rolled. Make a histogram of 100 rolls.
c. Devise a chance table for two dice showing how many times each sum (two-twelve) can be expected to appear in seventy-two rolls.

8. Invent a game. First, complete a description table indicating the game's use, chance or skill, number of players, card, board, or other, what other game it is like, how many minutes it takes to play, and what you will learn by playing the game.

9. Invent a puzzle involving a maze or pieces. Find out what skills are needed (i.e., fitting parts) and what puzzle it is like.

ACTIVITY SIX: MAKING A MUSICAL INSTRUMENT

1. Make a list of as many musical instruments as you know. Divide the instruments according to how they make sounds. Find out what is needed to play each group.

2. Find out how sirens work. Make one using a piece of cardboard, a hole punch, and a straw. Use a Tinkertoy support. Find out what makes the siren loud or soft, and high or low in pitch.

3. Make three lists of instruments. First, list instruments that make mostly low sounds. Second, group those making mostly high-pitched sounds. Third, find instruments that produce both low and high sounds.

4. Make a bottle xylophone. Tune bottles by partly filling them with water, each to a different level. Try creating a variety of tones by tapping the bottles with a wooden mallet and a metal spoon, or blowing over the tops of the bottles.

5. Make a one-string guitar, using a board, two eye screws, and a piece of fine wire stretched between the screws. The wire can be tightened by twisting one of the eye screws. Cut strips of wood for frets and set them in place so you can shorten the string and play different notes.

6. Make a tub bass, using a large metal can, an old bucket, or an old washtub. You will need a strong piece of cord, two pieces of wood, and a nail. Fasten the cord to the center of the tub using a short stick. The cord can be tightened by pressing down on the stick.

7. Make a bazooka from a piece of one-inch plastic pipe and two round pieces of wood.

8. Invent a new instrument that will play several notes.

ACTIVITY SEVEN: INVENTING NUMBER PATTERNS AND ARITHMETIC RULES

1. Design magic squares. Here is an example. In this square, the numbers in each row and the numbers in each column add to twelve. But the diagonal numbers add to seven and seventeen. Can you substitute numbers so the diagonals, too, will add to twelve? Can you now use the numbers 1, 2, 3, 4, 5, 6, 7, 8, and 9 in each of the cells so that the rows, columns, and diagonals will all add to fifteen? Try the numbers 10, 11, 12, 13, 14, 15, 16, 17, 18. How about 11 through 19? Invent a new magic square with a five by five matrix. When you are an expert, try a four by four magic square using the numbers 1-16. Warning: this can be very difficult!

2	4	6
3	4	5
7	4	1

2. Make discoveries using a hand-held calculator. Construct a matrix to generate fractions to decimals and write the answers in the matrix. Can you see any patterns? Before the matrix is complete, can you predict some of the decimals? Try several other matrices using different numerators and denominators.

3. Make some more hand-held calculator discoveries. Once you think you see a pattern, guess the answer before you press the = button.

1 × 11 = ______	4 × 11 = ______	11 × 11 = ______
2 × 11 = ______	5 × 11 = ______	100 × 11 = ______
3 × 11 = ______	10 × 11 = ______	101 × 11 = ______

NUMERATOR \ DENOMINATOR	6	7	8	9
6	6/6 1	6/7 .8571	6/8 .75	6/9 .6666
5	5/6 .8333	5/7 .7412	5/8 .625	5/9
4	4/6 .6666	4/7 .5714	4/8 .5	4/9
3	3/6 .5	3/7 .4286	3/8	3/9
2	2/6 .3333	2/7 .2857	2/8	2/9
1	1/6 .16666	1/7	1/8	1/9

Without using your calculator, predict the decimal equivalents of:

	Guess	Press
5/11	______	______
6/11	______	______
7/11	______	______
8/11	______	______
9/11	______	______
10/11	______	______

4. Complete calculator sevenths. Use your calculator to find decimal equivalence to six places for these fractions:

1/7 = ______ 4/7 = ______

2/7 = ______ 5/7 = ______

3/7 = ______ 6/7 = ______

Can you find a sequence of digits and a pattern that would help you write the decimal for any seventh? Can you find a rule that will help you predict the equivalents for:

8/7 = ______ How about: 15/7 = ______

9/7 = ______ 16/7 = ______

10/7 = ______ 17/7 = ______

11/7 = ______ 18/7 = ______

5. Complete more calculator fraction patterns. Work these problems with your calculator. Write the first six digits of each answer in the corresponding row in the Table:

	FIRST	SECOND	THIRD	FOURTH	FIFTH	SIXTH
1 ÷ 13						
2 ÷ 13						
3 ÷ 13						
4 ÷ 13						
5 ÷ 13						
6 ÷ 13						

Look at the first and fourth columns. What pattern do you see? Compare the second and fifth columns. What do you notice? Compare the third and sixth columns. Can you guess what numbers would be in the seventh column? Check your guesses using your calculator. What is the sum of the numbers in the first row? The last row? What about the other rows?

Expand the table to include 7 ÷ 13, 8 ÷ 13, etc. Are the patterns the same? Can you predict the decimal equivalent for 12 ÷ 13, and so on?

6. Collect at least six discs. Jar lids, plates, can tops, and wheels can be used. Measure the distance across each and the distance around each in centimeters. Chart this data:

Distance around						
Distance across						
Distance around ÷ distance across						

7. Count out 100 toothpicks. Draw parallel lines on a large sheet of paper. The lines should be exactly one toothpick length. apart. Hold the toothpicks about one meter above the paper and drop them one at a time. Keep a record of the number of toothpicks that touch one of the parallel lines. How many touched a line? How many did you drop? What number

do you get when you divide the number that touched a line into the number dropped. Try again and see if you get about the same number. Can you tell why you get this number each time?

ACTIVITY EIGHT: WRITING ENDINGS TO STORIES

1. Collect comic strips from several newspapers. Cut and past white paper over the word boxes. Then, reorder the pictures and write new dialogue. They can be used for announcements, bulletin boards, funny or sad stories.

2. Collect magazine pictures and mount them on one side of a page. Arrange them so they tell a story. Across from each picture, write one or two paragraphs of the story.

3. Cut full-page advertisements from magazines. Cut and paste white paper over the captions and writing. Write new captions and descriptions. Some can be funny, some mysterious, some ridiculous.

4. Collect several old "throw away" readers. Carefully cut out the pages and separate the short story. Rewrite parts of the story or the end of the story. Cut out paragraphs that are changed or not needed. Staple the new story together with a construction-paper cover.

5. Work with add-on stories. Have each person in a group write the first paragraph of a story. Then exchange papers and have each person read his or her paper and write a second paragraph. Continue until each story is complete. Hang up the stories so everyone can read them.

6. Have your teacher select an interesting story and read about half of it to you. Then, in a group, plan the remainder of the story and have each one in your group select a paragraph of the second half to write. When finished, the story can be read aloud or placed conveniently so everyone can read it.

7. Select one of the short super 8 mm film cartridges provided by your teacher and watch it on a projector. Then write a narrative and devise sound effects for appropriate parts of the film. When ready, use a tape recorder and make the sound track for the film. Share your final production with the entire class.

ACTIVITY NINE: SONGS

1. Work with a partner. Write out the words to a simple song you both know, one line at a time. Then sing the song and underline each word or part of a word that corresponds with a beat of the music. Now, using the same beat pattern, write a new verse to the melody.

2. This time, start with an unknown verse. Now, underline the beats in the verse and try several melodies until one is discovered that matches the beat. If you can, record it on a cassette and teach it during music class.

3. Write your own music and match it with a poem. Or write both the words and music for a new song. Teach it to a friend.

ACTIVITY TEN: INVENTING A NEW SOFT DRINK

1. How often have you wished for a new soft drink flavor? Create a new flavor by mixing two or more soft drinks together, keeping careful records of proportions used. You may choose from orange, strawberry, grape, lemon-lime, and cola. You will need several paper cups and a measuring cup. Once you have invented several new drink flavors, have other students taste and record preferences. You might also like to create names for your new beverages and draw posters to advertise them.

2. What makes the "fizz" in soft drinks? Learn about carbonation and CO2.

3. Find out about and compare artificial and natural flavors and sweeteners.

4. Conduct a survey of soft drink flavor preferences, comparing choices according to age and sex.

5. Study the history and development of the soft drink industry. Find out how long people have been drinking soft drinks, where they were first manufactured, and so on.

6. Find out about soft drink packaging and recycling of bottle and cans. Plan and carry out a recycling program in your class, school, home, or neighborhood.

ACTIVITY ELEVEN: SURVEYING FOR NEEDED INVENTIONS

Categorize the things you do during the day and write these on a recording sheet. Ask other children and adults what item, thing, or device that they do not have or that needs to be improved, they would find helpful in each category. Some category headings you may wish to used include:

clothing
toys and sports equipment
transportation
food
beverages
cooking equipment
home items
containers

Now reduce the list to those items that were mentioned several times. Select one suggested or needed item and design such an item. Your design should include a drawing and a description.

ACTIVITY TWELVE: FORTRESSES, CASTLES AND HIDEAWAYS

Cardboard boxes are thrown away daily. Yet they can be cut apart, fastened together, stacked, and in general used for building projects. A good fastening agent is liquid contact cement (water base). To use it, brush the cement on the surfaces to be joined and allow it to dry until the gloss disappears. Then press the surfaces together. The bond is instantaneous.

You can build such things as puppet stages, reading hideaways, towers, tunnels, rockets, and geodomes. Cardboard is easy to cut with a pair of stout scissors or light tin snips. The finished product can have holes cut for window and can be painted with leftover interior wall plant.

Before you start, you will need to do some planning. First, create a satisfactory design. Next, assemble all needed materials and equipment. While building, be sure to cut safely and follow the gluing directions carefully. Finally, check over your finished product for any modifications needed or desired.

ADDITIONAL ACTIVITIES

1. Have your students explore the lives of famous inventors. Written or oral reports or pictorial displays can be created from their findings. Later in the unit, have them create a similar item by interviewing their fellow classroom inventors about what they invented and why.

2. Ask students to make lists of the most important inventions ever created. Have each student choose one of these inventions and explore its effect on mankind. Direct them to predict how civilization might have developed differently had that item not been invented.

3. An exploration of science fiction literature can turn up a wide array of imagined inventions. Your students might search older science fiction books to find devices that have now been built, or predict which of those from current literature, may, in the future, become actual objects. Finally, encourage them to create, in drawings, writings, or three-dimensional representations, possible future inventions.

4. Many inventive projects can be found in Steven Caney's *Play Book* (New York: Workman Publishing Co., 1975). These can be followed by your students as directed or used as inspirations for original creations.

SUMMARY

Language arts is a curriculum of possibilities. Anything can be logically related to this core subject. By approaching a language arts experience from an interdisciplinary point of view, teachers and students are free to explore topics on the basis of individual and groups interests and abilities. The thematic nature of interdisciplinary teaching and learning ensures a central focus to a unit while allowing students the freedom of choice of topics within a conceptual framework. Not all teaching lends itself to the interdisciplinary approach. There are times when each subject should be taught in its own context. But all too often we miss the golden opportunities to synthesize and integrate learning. Children come to us thinking holistically. We need to capitalize on their view of the world.

The idea of bringing the curricular subjects together is, however, only half of the equation which comprises interdisciplinary teaching and learning. This is also the time to bring people together. The social interaction which occurs so naturally in this context makes it possible to bring teachers together to share their strengths and interests and with students of different grade or age levels. As we mentioned earlier, the best interdisicplinary units occur school-wide, involving everyone in the school as well as interested people from the community.

SUGGESTED ACTIVITIES

1. Select a theme (e.g., "water," "kites," "Fall") and develop a webbing for that theme. Try doing it alone, and with a group of three or four other people. Compare your results.
2. What are your perceptions of some possible strengths and weaknesses to the interdisciplinary approach to language arts instruction?
3. The school curriculum is found in textbooks which are devoted to separate subjects such as "science," and "math." Why do you think that this is so?
4. It was suggested in this chapter that perhaps an entire school should study an interdisciplinary theme. How might such a school-wide experience change the social structure of the school?

SUGGESTED READINGS

Benson, Cal, and Doane, M. (1982, September). Project basic: Building art systems into the curriculum. *Art Education*, pp. 40.42.

Comber, Barbara. (1987, February). Celebrating and Analyzing Successful Teaching. *Language Arts*, pp. 182-194.

Goodlad, John. (1984). *A place called school.* New York: McGraw-Hill.

Humphreys, Alan, Post, Tom and Ellis, Arthur. (1981). *Interdisciplinary methods: A thematic approach.* Santa Monica: Goodyear Publishing Company.

Johnson, D. W. et al. (1986). *Circles of learning: Cooperation in the classroom.* Edina, MN: Interaction Book Company.

Tonkin, H., and Edwards, J. (1987). "A world of interconnections." in G. Hass, (Ed.), *Curriculum Planning.* Boston: Allyn and Bacon, Inc.

Ellis, Arthur, Mackey, James, and Glenn, Allen. (1988). *The school curriculum.* Boston: Allyn and Bacon, Inc.

Dewey, John. (1910). *How we think.* New York: D. C. Heath.

Kilpatrick, William H. (1918). "The project method." *Teachers College Record, 19,* (4).

3

PLANNING INSTRUCTION IN LANGUAGE ARTS

The following chapters will give you the scope of the language arts curriculum. Your task as a classroom teacher is to determine how *best* to provide language literacy for your students. To accomplish that formidable task, you will need to think through your (1) instructional objectives; (2) teaching strategies; (3) methods of evaluation. All three of these considerations require careful planning.

Instructional objectives, teaching strategies, and evaluation measures all need to fit under the umbrella of your goal structure for language arts literacy. Let's look at a goal structure for the major areas of concern within the language arts: literature, reading, writing, speaking, listening, and, as a part of all these areas, thinking.

Let us look now at a set of goal statements for the teaching of language arts. These goal statements were derived by the National Council of Teachers of English and published in a position statement. *Essentials of English 1982*.

LITERATURE

Literature is the verbal expression of the human imagination and one of the primary means by which a culture transmits itself. The reading and study of literature adds a special dimension to students' lives by broadening their insights, allowing them to experience vicariously places, people, and events otherwise unavailable to them, and adding delight and wonder to their daily lives.

Through their study and enjoyment of literature, students should:

- realize the importance of literature as a mirror of human experience, reflecting human motives, conflicts, and values.
- be able to identify with fictional characters in human situations as a means of relating to others; gain insights from involvement with literature.
- become aware of important writers representing diverse backgrounds and traditions in literature.
- become familiar with masterpieces of literature, both past and present.
- develop effective ways of talking and writing about varied forms of literature.
- experience literature as a way to appreciate the rhythms and beauty of the language.
- develop habits of reading that carry over into adult life.

COMMUNICATION SKILLS

Communication is language in action, by which individuals participate in the affairs of society through reading, writing, speaking, listening, and using electronic media. The study of English develops fundamental communication skills that prepare students to engage in fluent and responsible communication and to analyze information that comes to them.

Reading

Students should:

- recognize that reading functions in their lives as a pleasurable activity as well as a means of acquiring knowledge.
- learn from the very beginning to approach reading as a search for meaning.
- develop the necessary reading skills to comprehend material appearing in a variety of forms.
- learn to read accurately and make valid inferences.
- learn to judge literature critically on the basis of personal response and literary quality.

Writing

Students should:

- learn to write clearly and honestly.
- recognize that writing is a way to learn and develop personally as well as a way to communicate with others.
- learn ways to generate ideas for writing, to select and arrange them, and to evaluate and revise what they have written.
- learn to adapt expression to various audiences.
- learn the techniques of writing for appealing to others and persuading them.
- develop their talents for creative and imaginative expression.
- recognize that precision in punctuation, capitalization, spelling, and other elements of manuscript form is a part of the total effectiveness of writing.

Speaking

Students should learn:

- to speak clearly and expressively about their ideas and concerns.
- to adapt words and strategies according to varying situations and audiences, from one-to-one conversations to formal, large-group settings.
- to participate productively and harmoniously in both small and large groups.
- to present arguments in orderly and convincing ways.
- to interpret and assess various kinds of communication, including intonation, pause gesture, and body language that accompany speaking.

Listening

Students should:

- learn that listening with understanding depends on determining a speaker's purpose.

- learn to attend to detail and relate it to the overall purpose of the communication.
- learn to evaluate the messages and effects of mass communication.

Using Media

Students should:

- become aware of the impact of technology on communication and recognize that electronic modes such as recording, film, television, videotape, and computers require special skills to understand their way of presenting information and experience.
- realize that new modes of communication demand a new kind of literacy.

THINKING SKILLS

Because thinking and language are closely linked, teachers of English have always held that one of their main duties is to teach students how to think. Thinking skills, involved in the study of all disciplines, are inherent in the reading, writing, speaking, listening, and observing involved in the study of English. The ability to analyze, classify, compare, formulate hypotheses, make inferences, and draw conclusions is essential to the reasoning processes of all adults. The capacity to solve problems, both rationally and intuitively, is a way to help students cope successfully with the experience of learning within the school setting and outside. These skills may be grouped in three major categories.

Creative Thinking

Students should learn

- that originality derives from the uniqueness of the individual's perception, not necessarily from an innate talent.
- that inventiveness involves seeing new relationships
- that creative thinking derives from their ability not only to look, but to see; not only to hear, but to listen; not only to imitate, but to innovate; not only to observe, but to experience the excitement of fresh perception.

Logical Thinking

Students should learn:

- to create hypotheses and predict outcomes.
- to test the validity of an assertion by examining the evidence.
- to understand logical relationships

- to construct logical sequences and understand the conclusions to which they lead.
- to detect fallacies in reasoning.
- to recognize that "how to think" is different from "what to think."

Critical Thinking

Students should learn:

- to ask questions in order to discover meaning.
- to differentiate between subjective and objective viewpoints; to discriminate between opinion and fact.
- to evaluate the intentions and messages of speakers and writers, especially attempts to manipulate the language in order to deceive.
- to make judgments based on criteria that can be supported and explained.

THE RESPONSIBILITY OF TEACHERS OF ENGLISH

The study of English offers varied opportunities for the individual to mature intellectually and emotionally. We believe in basic competency in English as a means by which the individual can acquire self-sufficiency and work independently in all disciplines. We believe further in challenges to both the analytical and creative capabilities of our students.

Toward accomplishing these aims, we as teachers of English hold ourselves responsible for:

- helping all students become literate and capable of functioning in an increasingly complex society.
- directing them to read and view materials appropriate to their abilities and interests.
- encouraging them to exchange ideas, listen perceptively, and discuss vigorously.
- urging them to write honestly in the spirit of open inquiry.
- helping them expand their interests and reach their fullest potential through language.

By contributing in these ways, we hope to expand the capacities of the human intellect and to preserve the tradition of free thought in a democratic society.

Scope and Sequence of Elementary Language Arts

Regardless of the level which you teach, you need to be aware of the scope and sequence of the entire language arts curriculum. This is crucial to the developmental introduction, maintenance, and extension of basic skills.

TABLE 3-1 Language Basics Plus

Word And Sentence Building		1	2	2CE	3	4	5	6
WORD BUILDING	Using Prefixes		95	85	174	174	235	235
	Using Suffixes		97	87	176	176	238	238
	Using Combining Forms						241	241
	Compound Words	40	99	89	76	72	96	97
	Contractions	96	69	61	72	76	103	100
	Blend Words, Clipped Words, & Acronyms							103
WORD STUDY	Homographs				T141	142	192	192
	Homophones		T39	T34	140	140	192	192
	Opposites		38	33	144	144	189	189
	Synonyms		38	33	142	144	189	189
	Easily Confused Words			See USAGE				
SENTENCE BUILDING	Simple Sentences							
	compound subjects				208	254	281	257
	compound predicates				210	256	281	257
	prepositional phrases						251	251
	participle phrases						T287	287
	Compound Sentences				212	258	297	297
	Complex Sentences							
	subordinate clauses						284	281
	relative clauses						287	284

Harper and Row, 1980, p. 25.

You must keep in mind that the effective teaching of English is a long-term effort in which you are a critical link. Factors of readiness, direct instruction, and enrichment depend upon timing, reinforcement, and proper sequencing if they are to be meaningful realities and not merely more educational terminology.

Scope refers to the actual material to be covered whether within one lesson, a unit, a year's instruction, or throughout the entire language arts curriculum. Thus in language arts, scope refers to such topics as grammar, vocabulary, usage, composition, and literary form. Sequence refers to the order in which things are taught.

Tables 3-1 and 3-2 illustrate selected portions of the scope and sequence protocols from an elementary language arts series.

Long-Range Planning

Perhaps one of the most persistent problems in teaching language arts, or any other subject for that matter, is the failure on the part of teachers to develop long range instructional plans. This is understandable because teaching children has about it a sense of immediacy. The demands placed on teachers by students are many and there is little time for reflection in the typical day. While we can readily concede these realities, we can also observe that long range planning is crucial to the pursuit of excellence whether in teaching automobile production, or operating a home.

The failure to develop long range plans often leads to needless repetition, gaps in content coverage, inability to finish the prescribed course of study in a year's time, and lack of meaningful attention to individual differences.

The obvious time to develop your long range instructional plan is prior to the beginning of the school year. You might want to begin by talking with fellow teachers who teach at the grade levels preceding and following yours in order to find out what kinds of things they emphasize. Thus if you teach third grade and you are told by the second grade teach-

TABLE 3-2 Language for Daily Use

Skill/Concept	K	1	2	3	4	5	6	7	8
LITERATURE									
FICTION									
Picture Stories		T	M	M					
Short Stories		T	M	M	M	M	M	M	M
Fables, Tales, Myths, Legends			T	M	M	M	M	M	M
Novels								T	M
NONFICTION									
Biography and Autobiography			R	T	M	M	M	M	M
Newspaper and Magazine Articles			R	T	M	M	M	M	M
Letters							T	M	M
Essays							T	M	M
POETRY									
Lyric Poetry (sonnet, haiku)		R	R	R	R	T	M	M	M
Narrative Poetry (ballad, epic)							T	M	M
DRAMA AND SPEECH									
Plays		T	M	M	M	M	M	M	M
Speeches								T	M
LITERARY DEVICES		R	T	M	M	M	M	M	M
Characterization, Plot, Setting									
Sound Techniques (rhyme, rhythm meter, alliteration)	R	T	M	M	M	M	M	M	M
Figurative Language (simile, metaphor, personification)		R	R	R	T	M	M	M	M
Point of View, Tone, and Style						T	M	M	M

R = Readiness T = Teach M = Maintain

Harcourt, Brace, Jovanovich, 1983, p. 59.

TABLE 3-3 Vocabulary Skills*

	2nd grade	3rd grade	4th grade
Synonyms	I	T	M
Antonyms	I	T	M
Compounds	T	M	M
Homophones	N	I	M
Prefixes	T	M	M
Suffixes	T	M	M
Root Words	N	I	T
Word Choice	I	T	T
Word Usage	N	I	T

*N = Not taught I = Introduce T = Teach M = Maintain

ers that they *introduce* the topic of research reports and the fourth grade teachers tell you that they emphasize certain "advanced" research skills, then you know that you will definitely need to emphasize basic research report skills with your third graders throughout the year. The same idea would apply to other topics such as paragraph construction, dictionary skills, critical thinking, and so on.

If you develop an outline of major topics which you will be teaching during the year, then you have a discussion list to take to the teachers who teach the levels above and below you. They can tell you, for example, if they (1) do not teach a given topic, (2) introduce the topic, (3) teach the topic at something deeper than an introductory level, (4) expect the topic to have been learned in most cases. Your list for Vocabulary Skills might look something like that shown in Table 3-3.

This simple two step process of (1) outlining the language arts topics which you intend to cover during the year and (2) talking with the teachers who work with the students who precede and follow your level will go a long way toward articulating a long range goal structure for the systematic teaching of language.

Unit Instruction

After you have thought through the scope and sequence of your language arts program for the entire year, you are ready to break down that very large block of time into several smaller blocks of time called units. A unit is a teaching sequence of several weeks duration in which instruction is based on a central or organizing theme. While your unit titles and subtitles may correspond to the chapter titles and subtitles of your language arts textbook, you may wish to make certain modifications which reflect your own personal strengths or interests or which are more suited to your community. For example, one teacher who is an amateur history buff taught her Research Report Writing unit around the theme of "Backyard Histories." By doing this, she not only (1) accommodated her own interests (a very important dimension in teaching since teacher enthusiasm is a key variable in achievement), but she also was able to (2) work within the context of the local community and (3) integrate her language and social studies teaching.

A VISUAL FRAME FOR PLANNING

Mind-mapping (see chapters 2 and 7) is an effective tool for planning and organizing language arts activities around a particular theme.

The mind-map (or web) shown in Figure 3-1 (p. 38) was developed from a story in a reading textbook. This kind of a map, developed around any single concept or content theme, forces you to see possibilities for integrating language arts skills into all curricular areas. From a map like this you can choose areas of emphasis and develop daily lesson plans.

A Unit Outline

In some instances, your units will be developed from the units prescribed by your language arts textbook. The text can be a very helpful source of organization, materials and ideas. They are best used flexibly, however, to fit your needs and the needs of your students and not in a page one to page three hundred progression.

At this point let us turn our attention to an outline format for unit development. We can begin by listing the unit topics that we will be teaching. Here is an example from a unit on *Listening and Speaking.*

Major Topics for Listening and Speaking Unit

Listening	Speaking
for sequence	giving directions
to directions	discussion
to rules	formal/informal speech
to fact & opinion	describing
to detail	storytelling
for main idea	oral reading
for appreciation	to groups
courtesy	reporting
interviews	interviews

Once you have listed the key topics which will be covered in your unit, you need to develop a *unit overview,* which provides (10 a rationale for your instruction, (20 a central theme or generalization, (3) a list of key concepts and skills, (4) a set of block plans, (5) a list of unit activities, and (6) a list of unit resources. A sample of each follows.

Cap O' Rushes — *Cap O' Rushes* p. 268 of Level q, Ginn 360

Literary Awareness

Plot and Style
- How is a folk tale different from a fable?
- How is this folk tale like others?
- Did you notice anything that reminds you of other stories?
- Can you make a comparison to Cinderella or other stories?

Language
- Note differences in the way story was told from the way we would say it

Characterization
- Discuss whether you know Cap O' Rushes well as person from story.
- Discuss which is more important in the story — plot or character development.

Observation Skills

1. Bring in some swamp grass or reeds or rushes. Have students examine them carefully — texture, smell, flexibility.
2. Find 2 records, one that has swamp and bog noises portrayed, scarily and another portrays them naturally. Compare and discuss.
3. Tell students to look around, notice three things not seen before. Discuss.

Reading Comprehension

Questions from end of story.
Workbook p. 102-103.
Literal Comprehension — WSAW p. 70, additional exercises, Teacher's Manual p. 327
Inferential Comprehension — selecting an adjective that expresses the main idea of a paragraph WSAW p. 69.

Decoding Skills

Suffix *pre*
Workbook p. 104
Manual p. 326

Related Literature

Folk tales
Joseph Jacob's *Favorite Tales Told in England,* retold by Virginia Haviland.
Amabel Williams - Ellis, *Fairy Tales for the British Isles*
Read aloud other English tales to students.

Dramatization

1. Dramatize story. Useful in doing this, Manual p. 326. Reread story and discuss sequence of action in story.
2. Puppet show of story. Divide students into groups. Have each group plan and construct puppets and scenery for part of story.
3. Imagine being in a bog. Discuss how it would feel, smell, what see. Dramatize doing a variety of things in a bog.

Personal Response

What is your reaction to the story? Did you like it?
How would you feel if you were told to leave home?
What would you do? Where would you go?

Reading Study Skills

Organizing information and choosing relevant details to plan dramatization. Teacher's Manual p. 326.
Bring title to attention students. Apostrophe what means. Where used?

Creative Writing

1. Rewrite the story introducing an element of magic to the story.
2. Rewrite story as if it were happening now.
3. If Cap O' Rushes had kept a diary, what might she have written after she left home, met the master's son or married, and was reunited with her father.
4. Provide a lead-in sentence for a folk tale and some questions useful as guidelines and request students to write a folk tale.
5. After reading story up to a point, have students write what they think will happen next and how the story will end.

Reading Vocabulary

Words for attention

gruel	sly
pretended	wove
bog	clothes
feast	daughters
hood	servants
scrape	rushes

1. Encourage students to decode words on their own.
2. Discuss meanings of various words, if not sure meaning look up in glossary or dictionary.
3. An exercise employing context cues. Sentences taken directly from the text containing the vocabulary words. Blanks replace words. Fill in.

Artistic Expression

1. Draw comic strips of the story, with conversation bubbles. Each student could do a section of the story individually or divide into small groups and each do a section of the story. Also, children could make comic strip of their own stories.
2. Draw or paint a mural of the story on a big sheet of paper.
3. Construct a Cap O' Rushes out of reeds or swamp grass.
4. Illustrations to accompany their folk tales.
5. Draw a bog and the things in it.
6. Illustrate favorite scene from story.

FIGURE 3-1

LISTENING AND SPEAKING: UNIT OUTLINE*

Overview

This unit focuses on the process of communication with particular emphasis on listening and speaking. In the Language section of the unit, the students learn some practical techniques for listening in class, conducting a formal meeting, making introductions, conducting interviews, and presenting oral reports. The Study Skills section enhances communication as the students study synonyms and antonyms as well as how to use a thesaurus. In the Composition section, the students write friendly and business letters. Letters to E.B. White from a group of sixth graders comprise the literature selection.

Central Theme

Listening and speaking skills are useful and necessary to the conduct of our everyday lives. They are the basic skills that all students must acquire.

Block Plans

LISTENING AND SPEAKING UNIT

Monday	Tuesday	Wednesday	Thursday	Friday
1 Sharing ideas	2 Listening in class	3 Listening in class	4 Speaking in a small group	5 Speaking in a small group
6 Speaking in class	7 Speaking in class	8 Conducting a meeting	9 Resource speaker	10 Review session
11 Making introduction	12 Interview people	13 Oral history	14 Oral history	15 Preparing a report
16 Preparing a report	17 Reporting to class	18 Reporting to class	19 Presenting to other classes	20 Review session
21 Review session	22 Unit test			

*Adapted from Level 6, *Languages for Daily Use*, Harcourt, Brace, Jovanovich, 1983, pp. T312-313.

Key Concepts

Language. Instructions, directions, main idea, details, parliamentary procedure, chairperson, secretary, minutes, treasurer, recognize, motion, second, introduction, interview, oral report.

Study skills. Opposite, similar, antonym, synonym, thesaurus.

Literature. Letters, theme, main idea.

Unit Activities

Language Listening and Speaking.

1. Critical listening is an important listening skill. Write these words on the board.

most	believe	no one
everyone	should	never
worst	ought to	best
think	always	must

   Have the students use each word in a sentence. First to express a fact and then to express an opinion. Determine whether or not some words can be used only to express opinions.
2. Ask the students to listen to the tone (word choice not voice pitch) of a report delivered by several different speakers. Discuss how the tone of two people describing the same event may differ. For example, how would a newscaster, a firefighter, and a resident tell about a house fire? Sample paragraphs may be written to illustrate this variety in tone.
3. If your class has class officers, encourage the students to apply the rules of parliamentary procedure in their class meetings.

Study Skills: Effective Words.

1. Ask the students to compile lists of synonyms and antonyms from vocabulary in various subject areas such as reading, spelling, and social studies. Provide a space in the classroom where the students can post their lists.
2. Post a "word of the week" from lists of words that will be new to your students. Encourage them to use the dictionary and thesaurus to define the word and to list its synonyms and antonyms. You might ask the students to contribute new words to the list.

Compositions: Letters.

1. Pen pals have always been a source of friendship as well as information about distant places. Your students might start a Pen Pal Club in class, circulating a list of the names of interested students among others in another state or country.

2. Using the Bulletin Board Suggestion, encourage the students to write a friendly letter to a famous person. Challenge the class to write things about themselves that would be of interest to that particular person.

Literature: Reading Letters

1. Have your students go to the library to locate letters that were written in the past. They might be from historical figures such as Abigail Adams, or they might be more like the entries Anne Frank made in her diary (which she wrote in letter form). Ask the students to copy a passage that interests them and then to tell to whom the letter was written and why the particular passage proved interesting. These excerpts can be shared with the rest of the class.
2. Using the Bulletin Board Suggestion, discuss with the class possible topics that each famous person might discuss in a letter and to whom each letter might be addressed.

Bulletin Board Suggestion.

Collect pictures of famous people from magazines, posters, newspaper articles, and the like. Number each picture and initiate a contest to see who can identify the most people. Have your students submit their lists at the end of a certain time period. Then use the pictures throughout the unit as suggested in the Unit Activities.

Lesson Plans

Now that you have a framework for unit instruction, the next step is to articulate the daily lessons themselves. Thoughtfully developed lesson plans are crucial to the enterprise of excellence in language arts instruction. There is a widespread belief that writing lesson plans is merely an exercise for the undergraduate, something she must do in order to pass a course in educational methods. Nothing could be farther from the truth. Oustanding teachers invariably write lesson plans for their instruction. The fact that mediocre teachers do not write lesson plans (they don't do a number of things that would obviously raise achievement standards) ought not to be considered a useful argument against their development. Perhaps the most persistent problems that arise from the failure to write articulated, sequential plans is the tendency for a teacher to fall prey to doing random activities rather than achieving instructional objectives in an ordered, systematic way.

Lesson Plan Theory and Practice. Madeline Hunter has developed a useful procedure for thinking about and acting on the variables in the instructional process. Essentially, she identifies two aspects of teaching: (1) what will be taught and (2) how the students will behave. She writes

> While the first decision of teaching is based on content, the *what* of teaching, the second decision is directed to the *student behavior* that makes learning possible, the student's *how* of learning. There are two aspects of a student's

FIGURE 3-2 Madeline Hunter's White Sauce Recipe or Eight Steps for Effective Instruction

1. *Anticipatory Set*: Set the stage. Focus student attention on the topic. This is the teacher behavior that causes the student to attend. It can build on previous learning.
2. *Behavioral Objective*: A description of a pattern of behavior (performance) you want the learner to be able to demonstrate.
3. *Purpose*: Why are you doing this? Why did you establish this objective?
4. *Input*: Introduce the material. Use visual and auditory modes of learning. Spend time here if you want the children to work independently.
5. *Modeling*: Should be used with *every* lesson. Demonstrate what is expected of the students. Show them.
6. *Check for Understanding*: Students tell *you* what is expected. Don't ask, "Does everyone understand?" Ask something like, "Can you tell me what we will do, Jim?"
7. *Guided Practice*: Students are guided by you as they work through one or two problems and/or the students begin working while the teacher circulates, assisting those who need help.
8. *Independent Practice*: Student completes task alone. Spend time and effort on steps 5, 6, and 7 to make this a successful task. If a child practices incorrectly, you will have to *undo* it and reteach.

FIGURE 3-3 Instructional Events Related to Quality Instruction. (D.A. Squires et al. *Effective Schools and Classrooms: A Research-Based Perspective,* Washington, D.C.: ASCD, 1983, p. 20.)

PRESENTATION
- Overview
  - Review
  - What
  - Why
- Explanation
- Students Demonstrate Understanding

PRACTICE
- Guided/Controlled
- Independent

PERFORMANCE
- Daily Work
- Unit Tests
- Periodic Review

FEEDBACK

learning behavior. One aspect is focused on the input modalities the student will use to acquire knowledge or skill. Will she read, discuss, listen, observe, do? *There is no one best way to learn,* and use of a combination of these input behaviors usually is more effective that relying on one.*

Hunter's instructional model, which she calls a "White Sauce Recipe," or "Eight Steps to Effective Instruction," provides a clear summary of a stylized lesson. Her model is shown in Figure 3-2. An example of a language arts lesson which utilizes Hunter's eight step progression is shown in Figure 3-3.

LESSON PLAN

NAME *Alice McGee* SCHOOL *Jefferson Elem.* DATE *Apr. 12*
SUBJECT *Language Arts* GRADE *6* NO. STUDENTS *28*

Lesson Generalization: The predicate of a sentence may consist of a transitive verb, which requires a direct object, or an intransitive verb, which does not.

Lesson Behaviors: Given a list of sentences, students will be able to identify those which contain transitive verbs and those which contain intransitive verbs.

Lesson Component	Procedure	Specific Time Resources
Anticipatory Set	Ask students to try an experiment. Write the following on the board: swam, hiked, borrowed, slept, built, threw. Students use their own names in front of each of the words (for example, Tim swam) to see which could be complete sentences. Ask why some of the words complete a sentence and some do not.	5 min
Input	Show transparency which contains List A (transitive verbs) and List B (intransitive verbs). Ask how the lists are different. Introduce terms:	5 min
	transitive, intransitive, direct object. Define them and show examples from sentences in a story on a transparency.	10 min
Modeling	Return to original list on board and write sentences using teacher's name. Explain how transitive verbs require direct objects and intransitive verbs do not.	10 min

*Hunter, Madeline, *Mastery Teaching*, el Segundo, CA: TIP Publications, 1982, p. 5.

Lesson Component	Procedure	Specific Time	Resources
Check for Understanding	Ask for definitions: transitive verb, direct object, intransitive verb. Ask for volunteers to complete the following orally: Teresa ______ (ran saw spilled sold)	5 min	
Guided Practice	Give students a worksheet which calls for identification of type of predicate. Work the first three examples together.	3 min	
Independent Practice*	Students complete worksheet.	12 min	

Vocabulary words: transitive verb, intransitive verb, direct object.
Additional resources: transparencies
Enrichment level: find examples of types of predicates in science and social studies books.

*Slow learners work with teacher.

Lesson Plan Models

There is, of course, no one right format for writing lesson plans. They can be written in a variety of ways. The important thing to bear in mind is that they should be useful and practical. Typically, however, they are written to include an objective, a procedure for the teacher and students to follow, and a practice session which may be guided or independent, sometimes in the form of homework.

Instructional Objectives

More than two decades ago, Robert Mager wrote a book titled, *Preparing Instructional Objectives* (Fearson Publishing Co., 1962). Using ideas from behavioral psychology, Mager stressed that, in order for teaching objectives to be clear and meaningful, they would have to address the following three questions: (1) What should the learner be able to do? (2) Under what conditions do you want the learner to be able to do it? and (3) How well must it be done?

Mager thus established explicitly the criteria for instructional objectives. They are:

1. *Performance.* An objective always says what a learner is expected to be able to do.
2. *Conditions.* An objective always describes the important conditions (if any) under which the performance is to occur.
3. *Criterion.* Wherever possible, an objective describes the criterion of acceptable

performance by describing how well the learner must perform in order to be considered acceptable.

Take a moment to consider the following two language arts objectives. Determine whether they meet the three criteria for instructional objectives.

1. Students will develop a clear understanding of topic sentences in paragraphs and will be able to recognize them.
2. Using a worksheet containing six brief paragraphs, students will underline the topic sentence in at least five of the six paragraphs.

Objective number one is not clear about what students are to *do*, does not specify the conditions under which they will perform, and does not establish the criterion for success. Objective number two tells us what students will do (underline topic sentences, how they will do it (on a worksheet) and the measure of successful performance (five out of six correct). *A note of caution.* Behavioral objectives are helpful because they specify what students will do with their time and to what extent they must perform to be judged successful. While this ensures accountability of instruction, it cannot, of course, guarantee the quality and ultimate purposefulness of instruction. It is well to remember that teaching is as much art as it is science, and that not everything you teach your students needs to be accounted for in strict behavioral terms. This is not a way of saying that accountability and precision in teaching/learning are trivial matters. Rather, we are saying that good teaching, which is a very complex enterprise, is the outcome of a variety of approaches.

Clear Versus Unclear Verbs for Writing Objectives

Unclear Verbs	Clear Verbs
enjoy	list
value	identify
know	classify
appreciate	select
realize	construct
become aware of	compare/contrast
understand	demonstrate
	describe
	write
	define
	measure

MANAGING THE LANGUAGE ARTS

The teaching and learning of the language arts is too important to be left to random, unstructured encounters with language. Language arts must be taught in a systematic, sequential, and structured manner if we are to produce students with deeper, more abiding levels of literacy. For instructional purposes, this means that there must be formal time allotments for grammar, spelling, handwriting, listening, speaking, literature, and writing. This statement means simply that more time is to be given language arts during the school day than is given to any other content or skills area.

While it may seem that such areas of the language arts as creative writing and literary appreciation lend themselves to unstructured inspiration, that in fact is not the case. Research findings tend to support the use of direct instruction with high academic learning time, teacher-strong classrooms, an orderly, well-disciplined learning climate, and monitored assignments, including homework. Let us look in turn at each of these variables.

Direct instruction refers to time spent by the teacher with the whole class during which time the teacher performs such functions as explaining, checking for pupil understanding, giving instructions, and conducting discussions. A high degree of correlation exists between the amount of time the teacher keeps the students on task (academic Learning time) and the levels of academic achievement which those pupils attain in various language arts skills.

In a direct instruction environment, the teacher generally instructs the whole class rather than using groups. The instruction is systematic, that is, the teacher (1) introduces the lesson to the class by explaining what will be taught, follows the introduction by (2) illustrating the skills which the students are expected to learn, (3) elicits questions from the students in order to determine their level of understanding, and (4) assigns seatwork in order to give the students guided practice as they work on the skills which have been taught. During seatwork, the teacher circulates around the room monitoring the students and doing any additional tutoring which seems to be necessary.

Teacher-centered classrooms are characterized by a high teacher profile. The teacher in such rooms does little sitting at the desk. Rather he or she moves about the room while students are at work in their seats and during discussions or explanations, plays the dominant role in their direction. This is not to say that small group discussion and organized nondirected approaches to teaching and learning are not useful, but such time usage must be carefully used for clear instructional purposes. It is, after all, to be assumed that you know the skills of the language arts and that you will teach them directly and systematically to your students.

Order and discipline are crucial to improved achievement in language arts. Your classroom should have a firm, friendly, businesslike atmosphere. There should be no doubt as to who is in charge (you are) and it should be clear in everyone's minds that the classroom is a workplace. Only those who wish purposely to create an oversimplified dichotomy between a grim, overbearing prison-like workplace and a noisy, cheerful, fun-loving atmosphere, where the joys of childhood are celebrated daily ought to argue this point. As a teacher, you were hired because you have the ability to teach children to read, write, speak, and listen.

You must monitor students' progress through frequent evaluation and feedback about the results of their efforts. Everyone wants to know if they're doing the work right. Providing students knowledge about their progress provides further incentives for their continued improvement.

Not all formal language arts learning takes place during the time alloted in the curriculum. Studies of effective teachers and effective schools support the idea of systematic homework assignments in the basic skills areas from about third grade on. Whether younger children should be given homework in language arts lies outside the range of demonstrated research evidence, but it is our opinion that they should be introduced to the responsibilities and carry-over values of homework.

Homework assignments in language arts are most useful when a few simple guidelines are followed. First of all, homework is not a type of punishment, but rather a matter-of-fact logical extension of the school day. In most cases, homework should provide reinforcement of skills and concepts previously introduced during the day. Keep in mind that it is unfair to both students and parents (who may be trying to help them) to introduce a new concept or skill which has not been explained in class through a homework assignment.

Another point is that of time expectation. At the intermediate grade levels (grades four through six), where most elementary homework is assigned, an hour is probably the maximum expectation. Remember, you may be giving homework in other curriculum areas, too, so you need to coordinate assignments in order to stay within the one hour time frame. For primary children, the homework that you do assign should be brief, perhaps fifteen minutes to a half an hour.

Homework assignments should be meaningful and not merely a series of worksheets and busy work assignments. Remember, if the homework was worth assigning, then it is also worth correcting and returning to those who completed it.

ACTIVITIES FOR TEACHER EDUCATION CLASSES

1. At your grade level, outline a long range language arts plan for a school year.
   What criteria would you use to determine the content to be covered in each area?

2. Select a broad theme such as friendship, weather, or the study of the Incas. Develop an activity mind map around this theme as the basis of a unit plan for the exploration of that theme in a language arts class. Write two or three behavioral objectives related to sub topics on your mind map.
3. Write one lesson plan for your chosen theme based on a section of your mind map. Use the lesson plan form described in this chapter on p. 43.

REFERENCES

Essentials of english: a document for reflection and dialogue. (1982). Champaign-Urbana: NCTE.

HUNTER, MADELINE. (1962). *Mastery teaching*. El Segundo, CA: TIP Publications. 5.

MAGER, ROBERT. (1982). *Preparing instructional objectives*. Fearon Publishing Co.

SQUIRES, D.A. et al., (1983). *Effective schools and classrooms: a research based perspective*. Washington D.C.: ASCD. 20.

GENERAL BIBLIOGRAPHY

BELL, MARION V., AND SWIDAN, ELEANOR A. (1982) *Reference Books: A brief guide* (8th ed.) Enoch Pratt Free Library.

CALKINS, LUCY MCCORMICK. (1986) *The art of teaching writing*. Portsmouth, Heinemann.

GOODMAN, KEN. (1986) *What's whole in whole language?* Portsmouth: Heinemann.

GRAVES, DONALD. (1983) *Writing: teachers and children at work*. Portsmouth: Heinemann.

HENNINGS, DOROTHY G. (1978) *Communication in action: Dynamic teaching of the language arts*. Rand McNally.

HENNINGS, DOROTHY G. (1974). *Smiles, Nods, and pauses: Activities to enrich children's communicative skills*. School Book Service/Citation Press.

NEWMAN, JUDITH. (1985). *Whole language theory and use*. Portsmouth: Heinemann.

ROUTMAN, REGIE. (1988) *Transition: literature and literacy*. Portsmouth: Heinmann.

UNIT RESOURCES FOR THE STUDENT

Books

DEINDORFER, SCOTT (compiler). (1978). *Dear Scott*. Workman Publishing Company.

TUSAN, STAN. (1971) *Girls and boys write-a-letter book*. Grossett and Dunlap.

WEBSTER, JEAN. (1940). *Daddy long-legs*. Meridith Press.

Audiovisual Materials

Letter writing basics (1980). (filmstrips and cassettes). Eye Gate Media.

Synonyms and antonyms (1975). From *Developing english skills* (filmstrip and cassette). Educational Activities, Inc.

Synonyms, antonyms, and homonyms (1977). (filmstrip and cassette). Eye Gate Media.

Using language effectively (1965). (filmstrips and cassettes). Eye Gate Media.

Words Have Histories (1980). (filmstrip and cassette). Harcourt, Brace, and Jovanovich.

4

CHILDREN'S LITERATURE

Children's literature is often thought of as a subset of reading. Consequently, few teachers have a planned literature program. In this chapter we focus on the innate values of literature and on developing a planned literature program.

This chapter is intentionally paced toward the beginning of the book to emphasize the importance of literature in all of the language arts. Subsequent chapters will discuss literature's impact on the development of oral and written communication.

THE CONTRIBUTIONS OF LITERATURE

Charlotte Huck (1979) has distinguished between the intrinsic and extrinsic values of literature in children's lives. The intrinsic values "are the reward of a lifetime of wide reading recognizable in the truly literate person" (Huck, 1979). Among these are reading for enjoyment, personal growth, and increased understanding of others. The contribution of these values alone make literature an essential part of children's education. The extrinsic values, by definition, facilitate the development of language skills and knowledge.

Intrinsic Values

Enjoyment. Enjoyment is at the heart of the literary experience. Children delight in the rhythm of Mother Goose verses, laugh at the ridiculousness of the Emperor without his clothes, and tremble as Manolo faces his first bull in *Shadow of a Bull.* It is the skilled teacher who uses the entertainment value of literature to intensify and enhance children's enjoyment of prose and poetry. By reading regularly, reading aloud, reading independently, and discussing literature in the classroom, a teacher exposes children to many types of literature. As they find pleasure in one book, they will conclude that there are others they would like to read. Pleasure strengthens a child's personal commitment to reading and ultimately this commitment will extend through his or her lifetime.

Personal Growth.

> When I read a biography, I feel like I'm the person in it. When they are hurt, it is as if I am too . . . *Blubber* is the kind of book I really like the most because it gives me the feeling that I'm a character in the book. [Smith, 1982]

These sixth graders have taken on the identity of these literary characters. Identification occurs as the reader enters the imaginary situation and emotionally matches himself or herself with the problems, adventures, and feelings of the literary characters. While all readers are not always able to "lose themselves" in this manner, when they do they gain insight from the experience. The reader learns that others share similar problems, questions, and feelings. This helps to ease the pain of growing up. Literature becomes a source of reassurance.

Identification also prepares children for situations outside the realm of their immediate life. For example, the child who is able to identify with the Austins in the death of their uncle, in *Meet the Austins*, will be better prepared to encounter death in her own family.

Understanding Others and the World. Literature provides children with a window on the world. Through it they may observe people and their behavior. As characters react to other characters and situations, the reader learns motivations for and the results of the characters' behavior. For example, in *Mistress Masham's Repose,* Maria is unhappy because of her dominating governess. Then Maria discovers a colony of Lilliputians and they become the delight of her life. This relationship, however, begins to break down when Maria assumes a domineering role. Older children familiar with use and misuse of authority will see the impact that dominance can have on a relationship.

Literature helps children to form new perspectives on societal problems. By reading *Door in the Wall* one may gain more compassion for the handicapped. *M. C. Hiffins, the Great* presents the cultural viewpoint of a minority group.

Through reading children vicariously experience humor, disorder, pleasure, security, and so on. In *Charlotte's Web* there is humor in Wilbur's naivete and Templeton's sarcasm, but the underlying theme of friendship provides reassurance and security. Marshall's *George and Martha* shows us that relationships can be worked out. When motivated by the pleasure of reading and given the opportunity for wide literary experiences, children will use literature to make sense of their world.

Extrinsic Values

Developing Language Skills. Literature immerses children in language. Animated words, descriptive phrases, dialogue, metaphors, the formal language of informational writing are all part of the literary experience. Research (Chomsky, Cohn, Cullen) has shown that children who read and/or hear the rich and varied language of literature are more likely to use broader vocabularies, more complex sentences, and more diversified language styles. The results of these studies also indicate that children's language gains are greater when language related activities follow a literary experience. These findings underscore the importance of response to literature. As children respond to books, through oral and written activities, they use and internalize the vocabulary and language styles of literature.

Developing Knowledge. Literature also serves to impart factual knowledge. This begins in kindergarten as children build and extend concepts. Young children learning social studies and science concepts require both first hand experiences and literature which will enrich their experiences. For example, children who have observed the activities in an ant farm will appreciate and understand *The Story of Ants.*

Literature in the primary, intermediate, and upper levels is a key element in an integrated elementary curriculum. Informational books, poetry, and fiction reinforce and extend children's knowledge, as well as provide primary sources of information.

THE PLANNED LITERATURE PROGRAM

With the rigorous demands of teachers' daily schedules and the current emphasis on teaching skills, the literature program too often becomes incidental or a subset of the reading program. In order for the potential values of literature to be realized, it is necessary to plan a separate literature program. The main objective of the planned program is to cultivate enjoyment of reading that will lead to a lifetime appreciation of literature. This is accomplished by:

1. Surrounding children with books
2. Guiding their book selection
3. Scheduling daily silent reading
4. Reading aloud to children each day
5. Encouraging them through instructional activities
6. Integrating literature with other content areas

The following is a framework around which to plan your literature program:

The Classroom Library

If children are to become independent readers, they must have the opportunity to look at and read books on their own. A portion of the classroom set aside as a library corner provides such an opportunity. The room library should contain poetry, fiction, and informational books at different reading levels. A special section may comprise printed materials on a topic of current study. Additional sections might include books which have been read aloud, books by the same author, or books relating to a particular interest. The collection should be changed frequently so that it will always provide a new reading adventure.

Children will want to spend time in the library corner if the area is attractive and comfortable. Books on display are inviting. An area rug with bean bag chairs encourages children to sprawl out and be alone with a story. A bulletin board of colorful book jackets, announcements about new books, or pictures and writings by children about literature creates interest in books and reading.

Time for Literature

The time allocated for literature is an important aspect in encouraging children to read. Children need time to browse and explore a variety of genres. In helping children scan and select books the teacher can learn more about an individual's interests and encourage reading in additional areas and at higher reading levels.

Daily time needs to be set aside for silent reading. Uninterrupted Sustained Silent Reading (USSR) is a popular organizational plan that provides time. Under this plan everyone, including the teacher, reads something of his or her choice. This may be a book, a newspaper, a magazine, or a comic book. The time spent in USSR may vary from classroom to classroom (kindergarten may spend 5 to 10 minutes and fifth grade may spend 20 to 30 minutes) but within a classroom the specified time is constant and at the same time each day. In scheduling time to browse in the library and for daily silent reading, adults are communicating that they value literature.

Knowing Children's Literature

A knowledge of children's literature is essential for teachers who want to inspire a love for reading. Teachers need to be familiar with the literature that has been enjoyed for generations, literature which is entering the marketplace today, and criteria for selection and evaluation. Taking a children's literature course and reading texts such as Huck's *Children's Literature in the Elementary School* or Arbuthnot's *Anthology of Literature* will introduce them to a multitude of established excellent children's prose and poetry. Annotated bibliographies (see appendix B) and periodicals which review current publications, such as *The Horn Book* or *Language Arts*, help teachers to keep up with what is currently available. But the way to become best informed is to examine books yourself, to read, browse through, scan, and come to know a number of author's and illustrator's works. All teachers should spend time in their school and/or public library familiarizing themselves with the literature for their particular grade level (see Huck pp 31-36 "Books by Ages & Stages") and listing books which would be good to read aloud and which pertain to specific interests and topics of study. It is a good idea to repeat this process on a regular basis in order to stay abreast of new additions and to find books that fit the needs of individual children.

Introducing Literature to Children

It is the teacher's responsibility to systematically introduce children to different kinds of literature. Generally this is accomplished through a "genre approach" or an "issues approach." Appendix A provides an example of the genre organization. It is an annotated bibliography of fine literature arranged according to the different literary categories of children's books. These include traditional literature, modern fantasy, historical fiction, contemporary realistic fiction, biography, poetry, and informational books, listed under the headings of social studies, sciences, and fine arts. The genre approach has the advantage of providing the student with a basic knowledge of the various literary forms and an organized way of categorizing and reacting to books.

The issues approach introduces children to a book or books which deal with a particular issue. Most often these are social issues such as family relations (divorce, sibling rivalry), gender roles, death, or coping with a handicap. For example, Viorst's *I'll Fix Anthony*, Klein's *Naomi in the Middle*, and Cleary's *Mitch and Amy* show how sibling rivalry is handled in children's literature. This approach allows children to explore and confront an issue through a protected vicarious situation.

We think that a combination of both approaches is necessary to accomplish the objectives (see Chapter 1) of the literature program. The genre approach ensures exposure to the various literary forms. This is important, since children's experiences are limited and a planned exposure to a wide variety of writings broadens and deepens their experiential and language backgrounds. This thesis is supported by Dr. Northrop Frye, a renowned scholar of literature in the elementary and high school. Frye believes that literature is cumulative; what we read today enables us to get more out of what we read tomorrow. He views literature as a unified whole constituting the story of humanity. According to Frye some aspect of the story of humankind is the theme of most literature and our reading of one work helps to interpret other works. He states

> . . . you recreate the meaning of everything you read. You translate everything you read into your own orbit of interests and your own particular background of knowledge. . . . Literature . . . must continually be recreated in that fashion. (Dillon p. 201).

When you appreciate the cumulative quality of reading you recognize that by introducing children to the genre of literature you are contributing to their literary, language, and experiential knowledge.

Because children relate literature to their own lives, the issues approach may also be effectively used. When the class, a child, or a small group of children have a concern literature may offer them insight into the situation.

The potential value in making a match—putting the right book in the hands of the right child at the right time—emphasizes the need for the teacher to know each child. Observing how children confront problems, how they interact with others during play and work, and how they work alone offers insights into the individual. Listening to children during classroom discussions and informal conversations and observing the type of books they select when several are available provides you with information about their interests, concerns, and knowledge. Observing and listening to children as they read, and analyzing their comprehension, tells you about their reading abilities. Keep a file on each child, record his interests, the titles of books he has read, and information about his reading ability. This takes time, but after a while you will be able to say "Brook enjoyed Marshall's humor in *George and Martha.* I think that she would enjoy Allard Marshall's *Miss Nelson is Missing.* Kipp is really into dinsosaurs; I wonder if he has read *Patrick's Dinosaurs* by Carrick. Jessica is having problems learning to read but because of her new baby brother she might like to try *Peter's Chair.*" Matching children and books requires a thorough knowledge of both.

Reading Aloud

Reading aloud is the primary method in the elementary school of bringing children and books together. It is frequently used during the primary years but infrequently during the middle and upper years. This is unfortunate for older elementary students, because a planned read-aloud program introduces children to fine literature in the different genres, assures a cumulative effect, is pleasurable, stimulates interest in literature and reading, and enables children to realize the intrinsic and extrinsic values of literature.

Reading aloud gives students and teachers, the opportunity to enjoy a book together. When you share poems and stories that you like you are stimulating an interest in literature and reading. Your enthusiasm is contagious. As students see their teacher and peers enjoying a book they become infected with a desire to read.

Reading aloud is a good way to extend interests, challenge reading abilities, and explore new ideas. When children particularly enjoy a selection they are motivated to read other books by the same author or on the same theme. Make these books available by placing them in the classroom library. In some instances you may want to share an exceptional book that is within your students' interest realm but beyond most of their reading abilities. This enables everyone to hear a good literary work and it challenges some to stretch their reading abilities by rereading it on their own.

As you read in a variety of moods and genres you are offering students the opportunity for thought and discussion about varying customs, values, and attitudes, and helping them develop concepts and background knowledge.

The following are points to remember when reading literature aloud to children:

1. Select a book that you like.
2. Select one that is well written so children have the opportunity to hear new vocabulary, a distinctive language style, a well developed plot, vivid characterization, and interesting dialogue.
3. Consider length in relation to the attention span of the children.
4. Effective oral reading requires that you preread, not only to evaluate the plot but to think about the theme, learn the author's style, the character's personality traits, and the general tone.
5. Practice reading parts or all of the story. Dialogue requires particular attention. Consider the personality of the character. Use the pitch, tone, and pace of your voice to communicate fear, anger, happiness, uncertainty, or whatever the character is communicating.
6. Selections with dialect, such as the Uncle Remus stories, require diligent practice.
7. Poetry is made to read aloud. The cadence contributes to the action, mood, and/or meaning of a poem. Practice a poem to interpret it and to communicate it more effectively.
8. When reading a selection to young children make certain that they have time to examine the illustrations. In a picture book both the text and the illustrations sustain children's interest, carry the story line and portray subtle changes in expression and mood. After reading a story make the book available for the children to look at, remember, and "read" again.
9. When reading a chapter a day to older children, let them, not you, review what has happened before continuing with the next chapter.
10. Watch for facial expressions that reflect emotional and intellectual involvement with the selection being read. Accept and encourage overt responses.
11. Read to children daily.

Responding to Literature

If children are going to appreciate literature, extend its meaning and relate its content to their lives, they need to express their thoughts, feelings, and questions about what they have read. They need the opportunity to respond to literature.

Before discussing how to encourage response we will talk about types of response. Sutherland and Arbuthnot (1986)have divided children's literary responses into four reactions, emotional, interpretive, critical, and evaluative.

Emotional. An emotional reaction is a personal reaction. When a child says she has felt as lost and frightened as Mafatu in Sperry's *Call It Courage*, or when children exclaim that they, like Peter in *The Snowy Day*, like to make angels-in-the-snow, they are reacting in a personal way. An emotional response indicates that the reader is interacting with the story. This is important for "without emotional interaction young people are not likely to go on to develop a broad range of responses" (p. 552).

Interpretive. Interpretive responses made by elementary school children usually pertain to the meaning they have derived from a character's behavior, a specific event, an author's use of imagery, or the theme. One child after reading *The Lion, the Witch, and the Wardrobe* concluded that C. S. Lewis was symbolically telling the Christian story. Reacting to a character's behavior, another child said that he thought Templeton, in *Charlotte's Web,* was funny but he wouldn't want him for a friend. Interpretive response may go beyond textual interpretation and children may relate literature to their lives. After reading *Deenie,* a child may write about her friendship with a girl whose handicap confines her to a wheelchair. Interpretive response is firmly rooted in personal involvement. When a child cares enough about a character, an underlying idea, or a particular event he will try to interpret it. Therefore it is up to us to provide children with exciting, compelling literature for response.

Critical and Evaluative. A critical or evaluative reaction is judgmental reaction. In writing about critical reactions Sutherland and Arbuthnot cite children's judgments about literary elements. A child who says the descriptions in *Wind in the Willows* "make everything really real" is making a judgment about Grahame's writing style. In writing about evaluative response they also cite children's judgments about the worth of a literary work. "A reader who likes a mystery because the plot is different from most is evaluating the author's method of writing as well as evaluating the selection as a good example of its genre" (p. 556). Critical and evaluative responses are intimately linked with the reader's personal involvement in the book.

The studies Rapport mentions in her 1983 review of response to literature reveal a developmental pattern. Until ages 6 or 7 most responses were retellings of the story. Children ages 7 to 11 shifted from literal retellings to summarizing a narrative. They were able to categorize and describe works, respond to them emotionally, evaluate whether they were good or bad, and interpret them. But the children were not able to explain their interpretations. Responses of children ages 12 and above contained more interpretations and discussions of characters and their motives.

It is important to listen for and recognize the different types of response that children are capable of making so that you can acknowledge and encourage children to expand on them. If a reader finds *Frog and Toad* funny it would be interesting to ask why. What is it about them that is amusing? By helping children explore a response you may also elicit a reaction about a literary element. In the case of *Frog and Toad*, talk about how humor comes from the situations they get into and Lobel's use of understatements. It is important to remember that "At the elementary level, however, we are not as interested in instruction as we are in releasing response in children" (Sutherland & Arbuthnot p. 556).

In the elementary school "releasing response" is usually accomplished through oral discussion. Most typically discussions are organized around a selection that has been read aloud by the teacher or read silently by individuals. Discussion may be with the entire class, a small group of five or six, or in a teacher-child conference.

While a discussion may begin with a review of the characters and sequence of events, this literal reiteration of "what happened" is only the basis for eliciting emotional, interpretive, critical, and evaluative responses. If a discussion is to be productive, a teacher needs to prepare and ask a sequence of open questions. Open questions do not require a single correct answer, but they evoke a variety of possible responses. For example:

- If _______ continues to act the way she does what do you think will happen?
- We do not know everything about _______. What would you guess about him that the author has not told us?
- Did _______ do anything you would do? Did she do anything you wouldn't?
- Do you know anyone like _______ and _______? Describe them.
- Did any of the characters change as the story went on? How? What caused them to change?
- How did you learn what the characters were like? Was it what they said or did? Was it what the narration said about them? Was it what other characters said about them? Was it the way other characters behaved toward them?
- Is there a major event in the story? What circumstances led up to this event?
- Did anything happen in the story that you would like to have happen to you?
- Did the setting of the story affect it in any way?
- What do you think the author is trying to tell us? How did the author make you feel?
- How would you describe the story to a friend? What would you say if someone asked you if you liked it?
- What does _______ (a symbol or figurative language) mean?

Open questions cause children to think about the theme, what motivated a character's behavior, the meaning of events, and how the author's ideas relate to their own lives and the lives of other people they know.

Time is necessary for children to develop these understandings. One experience is not enough to evaluate or make inferences about language style, theme, or characterization. To feel comfortable and develop a broad range of responses children need to be involved in many book discussions.

Chapter five will provide you with further information about organizing and conducting discussion groups. Creative Drama and choral speaking are additional ways of encouraging oral response to literature. These are also discussed in Chapter five.

Writing is another means of responding to literature. However, the traditional book report is not the best way to encourage response. The purposes of the book report have been to help the student crystallize his experience, to generate enthusiasm for books, and to evaluate the child's writing. While the intentions are good the methods have not always proved effective. Competent readers have tended to emphasize quantity over quality and raced through "easy" books just to get stickers. Slower readers become discouraged and give up. Another problem is that too often book reports all sound the same, with each child telling the title, author, and why they liked the book. The monotony of such weekly reports stifles the interest of the reader and the audience. Consider the following alternatives which allow the reader to get into the story, identify with characters, and interpret events.

1. Children may write a letter to one of the characters telling them how they felt about an event in the story, what they wished the character had done or said, how they felt about the actions of a different character, and so on. Or a student may write to an author and express her reaction to the book.
2. Describe the setting and its importance (or lack of it) in communicating the plot and theme. A student may wish to illustrate a particular scene to more accurately express his response.
3. A student might write a poem which communicates how he feels about a particular book or character.
4. A student might write a report through the eyes of one of the characters. This could be in the form of a summary or as a portion of a diary that a character may have kept.
5. Have each student keep a journal record of the books that he or she reads throughout the year. The writings need not be lengthy but they ought to be reactions. Review the journal, with the writer, at regular intervals. This is an opportunity to reinforce and guide reading selections and response styles.

As children write about literature they are also learning about writing. They gain insight into characterization as they summarize a story from one character's point of view. They employ the vocabulary and language patterns of the text as they describe the setting. These experiences carry over into and enhance children's creative writing endeavors. Chapter 9 elaborates on literature's impact on children's writing. Literature breathes life into all areas of the curriculum, not just the language arts.

A Literature Web

A single book may be the impetus for an art project, the writing of a story or poem, a discussion, and so on. Webbing or mind mapping is the process of planning strategies that naturally evolve from a book. See the map in Chapter 3 as an example of this kind of webbing. A teacher should not use all of the ideas on a web because that would over-expose the book and students would lose interest. Rather teachers should select ideas based on curricular goals, past experiences, and students' interests and knowledge. Webbing is an excellent technique to help the teacher visualize the potential in a book.

POETRY

Teachers tend to share poems with children which they read themselves as children. Because of this, children do not have much experience with poetry beyond traditional narrative poems and humorous rhymes and limericks. They grow into adults who are illiterate in the reading and understanding of contemporary poetry. Yet in recent years modern poetry is being represented in attractive collections for children. Professionals in the language arts and children's literature fields recommend that we expose children to more contemporary poems. How do we find and select these poets? What are the criteria for our choices? What kind of poetry do children like? What do they need to know about poetry in order to enjoy it? How can we encourage children's responses to poetry and help them give their responses form? The following section will discuss these questions.

Criteria for selecting poetry for children are the same as in all literature for all audiences. They are based upon the needs of the child and the literary qualities of the poem. We'll start with the poem.

What Makes a Poem a Poem?

Imagery. A poem written for a child, if it is a strong poem, springs from the same source as all good poetry. It also travels the same winding path from the writer's initial response to a sensory experience through all the associative hills and connective music of sensory memory, through the symbolizing processees of the mind, and finally out onto the page. Image making is basic to the process of creating a poem. What is it? Where do images come from?

Objects, things natural and manufactured, are the wellspring of our images. As experience gives birth to images, the images invest experience with new and intense meaning. It is through image making that we participate in a feeling relationship with the world around us. For the poet, it is a journey, an exploration, that moves outward from an initial response to an experience. It involves the mind's ability to leap, to associate quickly in response to a stimulus and to express those associations. Metaphor provides the possibility of communicating what cannot be literally expressed. The two-year-old who says, "When I say timber, nothing falls" is expressing a feeling of helplessness that he would not be able to express in literal language. Likewise, it would probably be impossible to express literally the feelings expressed by Michael Dennis Browne in the "Child's Elm Song," Even in a poem as short as this one, enough detail is given to help the reader build a literal meaning as ground for the metaphor in which the child "becomes the tree."

Child's Elm Song

If there were no trees
I would take my turn
and stand in the street in spring
with arms wide open
in case there were birds
who needed a place to sing

Michael Dennis Browne (1985)

One of the genuine pleasures of poetry is the resonance or simultaneity of language which depends upon loyalty to the literal as well as to the metaphorical reality. In a strong poem, both levels are experienced simultaneously. In the short poem "Family Reunion" all the words, including the title, build the literal image of uncles at a party so that the simile, when it happens, is surprising and at the same time rings true.

Family Reunion, 1950

When you whisper
they don't stoop
down.

Uncles are more like trees.
You cross the grass,
climb up.

Nouta Dittberner-Tax (1984)

Both of these short poems conjure up the scene literally, and at the same time elicit an emotional response through the power of the metaphor at work. While children will enjoy experiencing images and metaphors found in strong poems, it is also important to remember that the inclusion of the literal level of meaning is especially important in poetry for children. Child readers or listeners must be fully grounded in the details of a scene before they can be expected to make an imaginative metaphorical leap with the poet.

Rhythm. Imagery does not in itself make the poem, but brings with it its own music. Poetry is image put to music. It is sound and takes place aloud, not necessarily in speaking but in the voice of the mind. It is the "hum" inside all of us. Poets "mutter" when they first begin to write a poem. The poet is like the inchworm lifting itself up, becoming prostrate, then inching its body up again. Poetry is born in a series of rhythmic surges or movements. Robert Frost has said that baseball and poetry are akin. This observation may spring from the fact that athletes experience the body as giving forth a series of rhythmic movements.

We are familiar with the rhythm and rhymes children love which often follow the typical iambic line of traditional English poetry. In such verse, a series of surges runs through a line of about ten syllables and produces four (or sometimes three or five) beats. Illustrative of this well know form are these lines from "Humpty Dumpty's Recitation" by Lewis Carroll:

In winter when the fields are white
I sing this song for your delight—

In spring, when woods are getting green
I'll try and tell you what I mean.

Rhythm and rhyme help to create the musical qualities of the Carroll poem, the "singingness of words" to which children harken. Yet the poem does not convey the "singsongingness" of doggerel, because it is coupled with strong images. But when a poem lacks imagery and depends on forced rhyme, the poem succumbs to doggerel. Therefore, children need to be freed from the notions that all poetry must rhyme and that all rhymes are poetry. This freedom will encourage journey-taking via images, allow for imaginative leaps, and stimulate personalized responses.

Twentieth-century poets such as William Carlos Williams cut the sing-song line into three-beat lines and other variations. Sharon Chmielarz, in her poem "Cat and Mouse Fugue," broke the pattern into two-beat lines and controlled the rhythm surges with her line endings.

The Rain and the Cat

The rain and the cat
came to the door
at the same time.

Both wanted in.
The cat from the rain and
the rain from the wind.

The door opened
a crack

and the cat

squeez-
        ed
            through. That left

a puddle on the floor,
a shadow of the wind
in the corner and tracks

to the cat who sat
whisker to rainstroke at the window.
"Let us in!" cried rain and wind.

When cat woke, night
looked in, his long, black
cloaktail pulled right

up to his chin.
Only one white tooth
showed in his grin.

Sharon Chmielarz, *Cricket,* May 1986 vol. 13, number 9

The music still surges through the familiar iambic structure, even though the lines are cut up into two-beat lines.

The changes in contemporary American poetry have provided the image with more ways of determining the music of a poem. Walt Whitman removed the dependence upon a ten-syllable line. He also returned to the use of parallel structure. Parallel structure reflects the influence of biblical writing, medieval writing, and primitive poetry.

The music of modern poetry seeks out the beauty of this speech pattern of the past; a strong example of this is "Lamb" written by poet Michael Dennis Browne (1980).

Lamb

Saw a lamb being born.
Saw the shepherd chase and grab a big ewe
and dump her on her side.
Saw him rub some stuff from a bottle on his hands.
Saw him bend and reach in.
Heard two cries from the ewe.
Two sharp quick cries. Like high grunts.
Saw him pull out a slack white package.
Saw him lay it out on the ground.
Saw him kneel and take his teeth to the cord.
Saw him slap the package around.
Saw it not move.
Saw him bend and put his mouth to it and blow.

Doing this calmly, half kneeling.
Saw him slap it around some more.
Saw my mother watching this. Saw Angela. Saw Peter.
Saw Mimi, with a baby in her belly.
Saw them standing in a row
by the dry stone wall, in the wind.
Saw the package move.
Saw it was stained with red and yellow.
Saw the shepherd wipe red hands on the ewe's wool.
Heard the other sheep in the meadow calling out.
Saw the package shaking its head.
Saw it try to stand. Saw it nearly succeed.
Saw it have to sit and think about it a bit.
Saw a new creature's first moments of thinking.
Felt the chill blowing through me.
Heard the shepherd say:
"Good day for lambing. Wind dries them out."
Saw the package start to stand. Get half-way. Kneeling.
Saw it push upward. Stagger, push. And make it.
Stand, standing.
Saw it surely was a lamb, a lamb, a lamb.
Saw a lamb being born!

The repeated questions in "What Is It Like to Be Indira Gandhi?" give this poem its music, shape and wholeness.

What Is It Like to Be Indira Gandhi?

What would it be like to be Indira Gandhi?
Do you mean
what would it be like for me
to be Indira Gandhi?
If I am being her, where does she go?
What would happen to the vacuum in my body?
Or do we trade places? Would two souls collapse
into one? And go back and forth?
No, no, what I mean is
what is it like for Indira Gandhi to be Indira Gandhi?
You might as well ask what is it like
to speak in Hindi? To walk barefoot in the garden?
What is it like to be Indira Gandhi
for the millions of native Hindi speakers
who have no idea what it is like to be a head of state—
much less what is is like for Indira Gandhi to be Indira Gandhi . . .
What is it like to be a head of state?
What is it like to rest in state,
to hear the crowds shouting "immortal, immortal"?
What is it like to lie on a bed of sandalwood

dressed in a robe of flowers?
What is it like to watch
your son touch your third eye with fire?
What is it like
to watch your soul rise with the smoke,
your bones scattered
across 13 sacred rivers?
What is it like to be Indira Gandhi?

What is it like to be Indira Gandhi?

Roseann Lloyd (1984)

The music of modern poetry is also based on all the rhythmic noises of the world that have haunting effects on us. The baby's babbling and trilling, the crooning between parent and child follow an open Whitmanesque line.

These natural rhythms surge through the images of "Sunrise on Lombard" by Norita Dittberner-Jax (1988).

Sunrise on Lombard

Oakie you're old, doggie.
The world is running out of bones for you.
Even so, you're hopeful,
you limp through fences
over the stonewall
leading with your nose, wet
as the morning grass.

Coming down Lombard
I see you cross to Mrs. Rumble's house.
She has surely saved you the neck
from last night's stew.

At the horizon
the sun stands like God
witnessing every particular.
It lifts you in its rays
as if you were a saint.

In much of modern American poetry, speech patterns determine the line, as in this example from Patricia Barone (1987).

August: Seeds Grow Heavy and Fall

The purple/black eggplant
swells, a singleflow
fall to the ground
all summer,

more—
hidden
eggs in the rain
barrel, haybale, corn crib,

Bantum Buff Orpington hen,
Dusty Orange Cornish, Favarolle,
Silver Pencil rooster,
Rhode Island Red: sown for color in
an evening garden.

Yolks revolve in albumin,
small suns thicken the air
and fall,
each spoke cools
to bone and rises feather.

Eggs layer
inside to outside,
fall
oval
slow:
limestone
water
drops.
Guinea hens scratch and glow.

Line breaks are one of the most important choices of writers of free verse as they put their poems to music. Poets whose songs resonate with today's children make many other choices also. In examining image making which involves sound symbolism per se, we can see how the poet evokes concrete auditory associations. In the poem "An Old Melody on Skye" the writer makes sound visible. Not only do we hear the sound of the bagpipes, but we see it as well.

An Old Melody on Skye

Highland man steps slow
round the stone circle by
the Loch
slow and quiet
dark so near
the song he plays
lifting ones hair
uncanny
it rises and rises
over the bare hills
tearing at my heart
the piper marching there

with the tune leaping up
the moor and echoing
it belongs to times
we have no knowing
only a memory
of monastery bells
buried beneath the sea
o ringing down the valleys
cry of one man
o mountain
cry of one woman
o wild rocky shore
cries of those in small rooms
o heat singing in the radiators
and the rain filled clouds
roll slowly in

Mary Kay Rummel

Sound. Three types of sound symbolism create images in poetry. One we recognize as onomotopoeia, the use of speech sounds which imitate real world sounds in order to evoke feelings or images. These "echoic words" tend to be inexact approximations suggestive of natural sounds. They may produce a mental effect we recognize as similar to that produced by the sound source. The word *bang*, for example, is not the sound of a gun firing, in reality. Yet, the initial speech sound *b* gives an impression of a sudden violent noise with impact, followed by a resonance produced by the vowel *a* plus *n*. The word *clang* produces a similar effect. Sharon Chmielarz has tunefully created the sound of the rain and the wind trying to get in the house.

Cat and Mouse Fugue

Did J. S. Bach
have a cat like mine?
Did he write her a song
with a mouse inked in?

curled up in a staff,
nibbling on a note,
a cheese with a dot
a mouse could bite off?

Cat smells mouse
in the music's house
and the chase begins—
up and down the

scale, from the

attic to the bottom
chord in the cellar.
and pounce!

Cat leaps. Bach's pen
stops the song.
Cat sits down.
Mouse is gone.

Sharon Chmielarz, *Children's Magic Window* January/February 1987

Using a second technique, the sound imagist may arrange speech sounds so that they are easy or difficult to articulate in a poem. Specifically, the poet may convey difficult or violent movements or harsh effects through using clusters of consonants which require difficult or labored production. In contrast, the poetic music maker may conjure images of smooth movement, flow, or tranquility by words that move easily in utterance. Herb Julich chooses his words aptly to contrast the soft melody of the moon and the nightingale with the harshness of the sun and the dawn.

I Love the Moon

The silver sliver moon
Who's so in love with shining
That she soars above
The morning mists
With wistful smile
Ignoring all the while
The brash imperious sun.

Only the nightingale
Who revels all night long
And then, still
Drunk with song,

Sings on,
Understands the moon,
And the indifferent dawn.

A third and related technique uses phonetic intensives, speech sounds which themselves suggest meaniongs. For example, long vowels which are naturally uttered slowly are suggestive of movement. The slow dreamy state of the moon is reproduced in this poem.

Use of phonetic intensives at the beginning of words is called alliteration. The speech sounds of /sl/sh/st/ seem to give a sense of thinness or narrowness in slightly, shaved, stacked. Become aware of your visual image as you read these stanzas from "A clear Cold Light" by Mary May Rummel.

This morning
the full moon slightly shaved
sails above the valley

over mountains stacked
across the sky
like bone china plates

touched with light
like the moon like myself
centered and singing.

After considering these imagistic techniques, one realizes that, unfortunately, much of what passes as poetry for children is just verse frequently and not poetry at all. Witness Shel Silverstein's popular verse or this stanza from Vachel Lindsay's "The Little Turtle."

There was a little turtle.	He swam in a puddle.
He lived in a box.	He climbed on the rocks.

It is fun, it is play with language, but it is thin and lacking in nourishment for the imagination. This verse tends to be unidimensional, based on a single aspect, such as word play or rhyme, or on observation only. It lacks the quality of imagination which would make it transcend mere verse. The insightful critic recognizes that it is not the ability to see or experience things that makes the poet, but rather the ability to respond to those things imagistically, to see them in fresh associations, implications, and significances unthought of by the casual observer. Observation or experience is a necessary basis for poetry. It is the "caterpillar on the leaf of reality," says Nina Walter. But "imagination is necessary to transmute it into the butterfly. Without imagination, a poem never takes wings" (1962, pp. 28-29).

The beginning of this paper described the poem-making process as a journey outward through the associations of the poet onto the paper. However, the journey of the poem does not stop on the paper. In order to fulfill its meaning as a poem, it must follow a new pathway. This part of the journey moves inward through the individual associations, the special music of each reader. This response is necessary to complete the poem, but even then its journey continues. The poem resonates in continually new forms through the responses of its readers.

Trends in Contemporary Poetry for Children

For Young Children. A current trend in children's book publishing is that of presenting single longer poems in book form. Many of these are picture books for young children, full of rhythm, color and sound such as *Truck Song* by Barton Byron (1984). Kirra Ginsberg's *The Sun's Asleep Behind the Hill* (1982) is the retelling of an Armenian lullaby. Young children also love the rhymes of Jack Prelutsky. These poems are strong in imagery as well as rhythm.

Outstanding recent poetry collections for children deal with topics that call forth strong feelings in children. One of these is *Secrets of a Small Brother* by Richard Margolis. When choosing poems that help children recognize and give form to their feelings, you must be sure that the poems really do relate to children's real lives. They should also be characterized by specific language and imagery. Any child will be able to relate to the experience and feelings described in Carol Master's (1981) poem, *Late.*

Late

The first time you're late for school
the air stops,
the unmoving sunlight
presses hard on the street
suddenly all angles
as in a city with no trees.

Voices drained out of the playground
while you dawdled
stirring a puddle
to watch the mud from the bottom
come up in smoky circles.

Singing begins
behind the doors.
You don't belong anywhere.

The silence is
what you hear when you wake
during dream music
waiting for the next measure,

the smile of a stone angel,
her lips plump and curved
like white worms.

Many poems that are written from and about nature will appeal to children. In the best of these poems you will find powerful examples of imagery as in this poem by Sharon Chmielarz.

A Hazy Morning

Last night the devil
set fire to the clouds—

fire spread quickly
up rose walls

and in the rooms
blazed so hot

the copper clock
turned red.

Then night lowered
the blanket and
smothered every flame.

This morning
over my house
haze remains.

Sharon Chmielarz, *Children's Magic Window,* March/April 1987

Guiding Children's Responses to Poetry

How can we best help children express their responses to poetry? Since poetry depends upon the visual (images) and aural (sound) senses, art and music are natural avenues of response. Let children draw what they "see" in a poem. Let them clap out and dance to the rhythm and, of course, since reading leads to writing, teach children to write in response to poetry. After hearing "Shadows" by Siv Cedering Fox, children will regale you with descriptions of their own night visions. This is a perfect moment for writing. So let them write.

Sharing Poetry with Children

Poetry is meant to be heard and (except for poems from the oral tradition) read. It is first a sound experience and you need to practice reading a poem before you read it to children. Contemporary poetry, with its irregular line breaks, is meant to be read with a stop at the end of each line. Notice how stopping at the end of each line creates energy in this poem by Roseann Lloyd (1986). Read it out loud.

Lessons from Space

Astronaut is a foreigner in a silver suit
walking on the moon but *Teacher*
is our familiar—only one step
away from *Mother*, the first step out the door.
Teacher, we say, and we can see her hands again
covered with the chalky dust
of our own first grade. We can hear
her voice, insistent, explaining
why and *how to* as we print
with our fat red pencils—
lower-case s's
fill all the spaces between the sky-blue
dotted lines.

Now we are paying attention
to the front of the room where Ginny Lindstrom
is holding up an orange, representing earth,
and Walter Locke is holding up a lemon,
representing moon. Stephanie Jones gets to hold
the flashlight, representing light.
Teacher, we say, *we don't get it.*
Just try, she always answers, *everything*
will be O.K. if you will only try.

Now she is mixing bright blue Tempra
which we will apply—*not too thickly*—to our maps
of the seven seals which swirl
around our wobbly pears
of continents, whose names we must also
memorize. *You must learn*
all about the universe. Teacher is moving
about the room, her sleeve is smudged and dusty
like everything else in here, even the solitary
plant that shoots its flat spikes up
in front of the blackboard, which is
also swirling dusty white, like the Milky Way.

After lunch, we put our heads on our desks.
Teacher is reading. She explains the hard parts,
how it is possible in the story
for Harriet Tubman to be underground
and following the stars at the same time.
This is inconceivable as death or the idea of space
having no end.

We turn away from knowledge
and admire our snowflakes, falling across
the glass. We folded white paper and cut them out
yesterday. Teacher says every snowflake
is unique, which means, unlike any other. Teacher
says each of us is a unique individual, special
unto ourselves. It is snowing now, for real.
We can't see the stars at the end of sky.

If Teacher goes away, who will teach us *how to*
and *why?* How to cut out free-hand
hearts. How to find
the drinking gourd on a starless night.
What is burning in those smudge
pots in the orange groves? What happens
to machines when it's freezing cold?
Why does the t.v. say
blow-up, melt-down, O-rings
out of round? Why
are they looking for freedom up there
in the swirling clouds, in the sky-
blue sky?

Children also need to see copies of poems, usually during a second reading, in order to understand the shape of the poem.

Poetry should be included as part of every unit theme.

REFERENCES

BARONE, PATRICIA. (1983) *Germination.* 7, 2.

BARONE, PATRICIA. (1987) *Germination.* 11, 1.

BROWNE, MICHAEL D. (1980) *News of the universe: poems of twofold consciousness.* Robert Bly, ed. San Francisco: Sierra Club Books.

BROWNE, MICHAEL D. (1985) *Smoke from the fires.* New York: Carnegie Mellon.

CHMIELARZ, SHARON. (1986, May) *Cricket.* 13, 9. May.

CHMIELARZ, SHARON. (1987, January) *Children's magic window.* 1987.

CHMIELARZ, SHARON. (1987, March) *Children's magic window.*

CHOMSKY, CAROL. (1972) Stages in language development and reading exposure. *Harvard Educational Review.* 42.

COHEN, DOROTHY H. (1968, February) The effect of literature on vocabulary and reading achievement. *Elementary English.* 45, 209-13, 17.

CULLINAN, B. E., A. JAGGER, AND D. STRICKLAND. (1974, January) Language expansion for black children in the primary grades: a research report. *Young Children.* 29, 98-112.

DILLON, DAVID A. (1980, February) Perspectives: literature, language, and learning—northrop frye. *Language Arts.* 57, 2, 199-206.

DITTBERNER-JAX, NORITA. (1988) *Lake street review.* St. Paul: New Rivers Press.

DITTBERNER-JAX, NORITA. (1984) *Border crossings: a Minnesota voices project reader.* St. Paul: New Rivers Press.

HUCK, CHARLOTTE S. (1976) *Children's literature in the elementary school* (3rd ed). New York: Holt, Rinehart and Winston.

HUCK, CHARLOTTE S. (1979, April) Commentary literature for all reasons. *Language Arts.* 56, 4, 354-355.

LLOYD, ROSANNE. (1986) *Tap dancing for big mom.* St. Paul: New Rivers Press.

LLOYD, ROSANNE. (1986) *Minnesota monthly.* 1986. St. Paul: New Rivers Press.

MASTERS, CAROL. (1987) *Outside the museum: contemporary writings. 1.*

MCCRACKEN, ROBERT A. (1971, May) Initiating sustained silent reading. *Journal of Reading* 14, 521-4, 582.

MONSON, DIANNE L., ED. (1985) *Adventuring with books: a booklist for pre-k-grade 6.* Urbana, Ill.: National Council of Teachers of English.

RAPPORT, REBECCA T. (1983) Reader initiated responses to self-selected literature compared with teacher initiated responses to teacher selected literature. Doctoral dissertation. Minneapolis, Mn: University of Minnesota.

RUDMAN, MARSHA K. (1984) *Childrens literature: an issues approach* (2nd edition) New York: Longman, Inc.

SMITH, LEWIS B. (1982, April) Sixth graders write about reading literature. *Language Arts.* 59, 357-363.

SUTHERLAND, ZENA AND MARY HILL ARBUTHNOT. (1986) *Children and books* (7th ed) Glenview, Ill.: Scott Foresman and Co.

TERRY, A. (1974) *Children's poetry preferences: a national survey of upper elementary grades.* Urbana, Ill.: National Council of Teachers of English.

TOM, C. LOW. (1973, January) Paul Revere rides ahead: poems teachers read to pupils in the middle grades, *The Library Quarterly* 43, 27-38.

Appendix 4-A: Annotated Bibliography

This annotated bibliography was taken from *Adventuring With Books*, a booklist for prekindergarten through the sixth grade, published by National Council of Teachers of English. Books were selected primarily for their "literary and artistic quality" with additional attention " . . . given to characteristics of books that might influence their appeal for children."The annotated selections were published after 1981. "Quality books from the past" are also included. The bibliography is arranged by genre. It is further divided into subcategories to facilitate the selection of books for instructional purposes. We chose to reproduce a portion of this text due to the quality of the selections, their currency, and organization. The following is a selection from the "Contemporary Realistic Section."

BATES, BETTY. *Picking Up the Pieces.* Holiday House, 1981. 12 and up. When Nell's romantic relationship with Dexter is nipped in the bud by beautiful Lacey and her fast crowd, Nell is hurt and bewildered. It takes an automobile accident in which Dexter is seriously injured to make Nell realize just how strong her feelings for him are. Nell is a likable, well-drawn character, but Dexter's defection to the fast crowd remains a bit of a puzzle.

CARRICK, CAROL. *Ben and the Porcupine.* Illus. by Donald Carrick. Clarion Books, 1981. 6-9. Using two colors with black, the artist skillfully brings out many warm tones in his double-page spreads. Ben the dog is given importance as the main character as he is placed in the scenes of an appealing countryside. The depth in the shadows of the woods and the rolling hillsides brings the reader into the scenes. The drawing of the family pulling the porcupine quills out of Ben would be more convincing if there were a sign of struggle. (Picture book)

CLEARY, BEVERLY. *Dear Mr. Henshaw.* Illus. by Paul O. Zelinsky. William Morrow, 1983. 9-12. Leigh Botts reveals his loneliness and yearning for his father to return through his letters to Mr. Henshaw, a writer whose books he loves. Later, the letters are largely replaced by diary entries, but the continuing influence of Mr. Henshaw on Leigh's thinking and on his writing is clear. A sensitive treatment of a child's feelings when parents divorce. Newbery Medal Book.

CLEAVER, VERA, AND BILL CLEAVER. *The Kissimmee Kid.* Lothrop, Lee & Shepard Books, 1981. 10-12. Twelve-year-old Evelyn and her nine-year-old brother, Buell, arrive in the cattle country of central Florida's Kissmmee Prairie expecting a vacation with their ranch-hand brother-in-law, Cam, and sister, Reba. Instead of peace and relaxation, they stumble upon a cattle-rustling scheme that forces a choice between family loyalty and moral values. The fast-paced adventure with well-developed main characters and a clear theme presents a good starting point for discussion.

CLYMER, ELEANOR. *My Mother Is the Smartest Woman in the World.* Illus. by Nancy Kincade. Atheneum, 1982. 8-12. A painless way for young readers to learn about politics at the grass-roots level as fourteen-year-old Kathleen campaigns for her mother, who is running for mayor. The light, fast-paced style will keep the reader involved. Black-and-white ink drawings.

GATES, DORIS. *A Filly for Melinda.* Viking Press, 1984. 8-12. Melinda and her filly, Little Missy, will appeal to horse fans. Told in the first person, the story moves smoothly. Horse lovers will enjoy descriptions of training and showing a young horse. Even nonhorse fans will appreciate Melinda's place within her family and the decision she must make. A sequel to *A Morgan for Melinda.*

GREENE, BETTE. *Get On out of Here, Philip Hall.* Dial Books for Young Readers. 1981. 10-14. In this sequel to *Philip Hall Likes Me, I Reckon Maybe,* Beth Lamberg finds her self-confidence challenged and her pride destroyed. Beth's growth is painful, but she accomplishes it surrounded by a number of very human characters who love her. Individualized characters, realistic dialogue, and plenty of humor.

HAMILTON, VIRGINIA. *A Little Love.* Philomel Books, 1984. 13 and up. A sensitively told story of a girl's search for love and for self-identity and acceptance; it will immediately involve the reader in the girl's yearning and emotional problems. Black English may prove difficult for some readers initially, but the dialogue makes the characters come alive. The language is eloquently descriptive, and there is a satisfying, realistic ending.

HOUSTON, JAMES. *Black Diamonds: A Search for Arctic Treasure.* Margaret K. McElderry Books. 1982. 9-12. This well-constructed adventure makes the reader not want to miss a clue but, at the same time, want to move along to the resolution. The drama of searching for gold, black gold, in the Arctic is carried out by two adolescent main characters who are supported effectively by adults. The story follows the characters from *Frozen Fire*, but it can stand alone. It reads well orally.

LINDGREN, ASTRID. *The Runaway Sleigh Ride.* Illus. by Ilon Wikland. Viking Press, 1984. 4-10. A complex story with unusual touches of realism in a book for small children. A resourceful girl who hitches a ride on a drunkard's sleigh is abandoned in a forest. Her rescue makes exciting reading. Bright paintings depict the Swedish village and forest.

O'DELL, SCOTT. *The Spanish Smile.* Houghton Mifflin, 1982. 11-14. For those who crave melodrama, here is a well-written story of a sixteen-year-old daughter held prisoner by her wealthy, insane father on an island off the California Coast. Too many bizarre elements, such as crystal coffins guarded by a poisonous snake and an experimenting doctor who was formerly a Nazi, make this tale unconvincing.

Appendix 4-B: Contemporary Poetry For Children A Selected Bibliography*

POETRY FOR YOUNG CHILDREN

BARTON, BYRON. *Truck Song.* Illus. Diane Siebert. Crowell, 1984. 2-8.

GINSBURG, MIRRA. *The Sun's Asleep Behind the Hill.* Illus. Paul Zelinsky. Greenwillow, 1982. 2-6.

KUSKIN, KARLA. *Night Again.* Little, Brown & Co., 1981. 2-6.

LALICKI, BARBARA, COMPILER. *If There Were Dreams to Sell.* Illus. Margot Tomes. Lothrop, Lee & Shephard, 1984. 2-8.

PRELUTSKY, JACK. *It's Snowing! It's Snowing!* Illus. Jeanne Titherington. Greenwillow, 1984. 2-8.

PRELUTSKY, JACK. *Ride a Purple Pelican.* Greenwillow, 1986.

RUSSO, SUSAN, COMPILER AND ILLUS. *The Ice Crean Ocean.* Lothrop, Lee & Shepard, 1984. 2-8.

WHITESIDE, KAREN. *Lullaby of the Wind.* Illus. Kazue Mizumura. Harper & Row, 1984.

*Adapted from work by Mary Kay Rummel and Rebecca Rapport, 1985-1986.

CHILDREN'S FEELINGS

ADOFF, ARNOLD. *Outside, Inside Poems.* Illus. John Steptoe. Lothrop, Lee & Shepard, 1981. 8-12.

ADOFF, ARNOLD. *Today We Are Brother and Sister.* Illus. Glo Coalson, Lothrop, Lee & Shepard, 1981. 8-12.

FOX, SIV CEDERING. *The Blue Horse and Other Night Poems.* Seabury, 1979.

MARGOLIS, RICHARD. *Secrets of a Small Brother.* Illus. Donald Carrick. MacMillan, 1984. 5-12.

MEMOIR

JANECZKO, PAUL B., Compiler & Illus. *Strings: A Gathering of Family Poems.* Bradbury Press, 1984. 12-Adult.

RYLANT, CYNTHIA. *Waiting to Waltz.* Illus. Stephen Gammell. Bradbury Press, 1984. 10-Adult.

STRECH, CORRINE. Compiler. *Grandparents' Houses.* Illus. Lillian Hoban. Greenwillow, 1984. 8-Adult.

GENERAL

JANECZKO, PAUL B. Compiler. *Don't Forget to Fly.* Bradbury Press, 1981. 10-Adult.

MERRIAM, EVE. *A Word or Two With You.* Illus. John Nez. Atheneum, 1981. 6-12.

MOORE, LILLIAN. *Something New Begins.* Illus. Mary Jane Dunton. Atheneum, 1982. 6-12.

NATURE

AMON, ALINE. Compiler and Illus., *The Earth is Sore:* native Americans on nature. Atheneum, 1981. 10-15.

BAYLOR, BYRD. *Desert Voices.* Illus. Peter Parnall. Scribner's, 1981. 2-12.

BAYLOR, BYRD. *A God on Every Mountaintop.* Illus. Carol Brown. Scribner's, 1981. 8-12.

ESBENSEN, BARBARA. *Cold Stars and Fireflies.* Illus. Susan Bonners. Crowell, 1984. 6-12.

ESBENSEN, BARBARA. *Words With Wrinkled Knees.* Crowell, 1986.

HOPKINS, LEE BENNETT. Compiler. *The Sky is Full of Song.* Illus. Dirk Zimmer. Harper & Row, 1983. 4-10.

HUGHES, TED. *Under the North Star.* Illus. Leonard Baskin. Viking Press, 1981. 8-Adult.

LAWRENCE, D. H. *Birds, Beasts and the Third Thing.* Poems by D. H. Lawrence. Selected and Illustrated by Alice and Martin Provensen. Viking Press, 1982. 8-adult.

HUMOROUS

ADOFF, ARNOLD. *Eats.* Lothrop, Lee and Shepard, 1979.

ADOFF, ARNOLD. *Sports Pages.* Lippincott, 1986.

KENNEDY, X.J. *Brats.* Atheneum, 1986.

VIORST, JUDITH. *If I Were In Charge of the World.* Atheneum, 1982.

5

LANGUAGE DEVELOPMENT

The ability to speak is generally acquired at an early age. Two-year-olds put sentences together. Five-year-olds exhibit a basic mastery of spoken language which needs only fine tuning. Of life's basic skills, language is one of the earliest to develop. It rivals the ability to walk. The vocabularies and grammatical constructions of the young are deficient by adult standards, but the basic power of oral communication is there. This ability, acquired so early in life, is a wonder when one considers the young child's inability to comprehend cause and effect relationships, ideas of size and space, distance, time, and other factors of reason and logic possessed by adults.

The study of language development has resulted in three competing theories about language acquisition. They are the behaviorist, nativist, and cognitive theories.

Behaviorist Theory. Very briefly, the behaviorist theory holds that since all normal children learn the language spoken around them, the acquisition of the elements of language—sounds, words, and phrases—must be a result of interaction with the environment. Furthermore, the form that interaction takes is in the classic behaviorist mode of conditioning, imitation, and reinforcement.

These elements surely play a part in language acquisition, but, alone, they are insufficient to explain the phenomenon. For example, children produce sentences and sentence structures such as "all-gone milk" which they've never heard (imitation), and for which they are not rewarded. The behaviorist theory falls short on many other technical aspects that need not be gone into here.

Nativist Theory. The nativist theory, which is almost diametrically opposed to the behaviorist theory, holds that humans are biologically endowed with a capacity for language. That potential is fulfilled by exposure to spoken language which enables the child to formulate the rules governing his/her language. The nativists point to a number of linguistic universals such as the presence of nouns, verbs, and adjectives in all languages and the fact that any human can learn any language in the world as evidence of some innate (or native) capacity within human beings.

The nativist position is stengthened by the same evidence which weakens the behaviorist position. The "all-gone milk" example represents, according to the nativist position, the child's early and imperfect attempt at formulating rules.

Cognitive Theory. The cognitive theory represents an attempt to stake out a middle ground. Cognitive theorists are interested in how children learn in general. They see language as only part of the information a child must process. And, while conceding an innate capacity for language, they tend to concern themselves with the broader question of the relationship between thought and language. Vygotsky (1962) for example studied the progression from talking (outer speech) to reasoning (inner speech).

These three major theories of language acquisition contribute further to our understanding not only of language acquisition but also to our understanding of language in general. As more evidence is gathered, analyzed, and discussed, our understanding grows.

There are three elements of language: phonology, the sounds of the language; syntax, the way words are ordered in sentences; and semantics, the meanings that are attached to words.

PHONOLOGICAL DEVELOPMENT

Phonological development is, broadly stated, the elimination of all speech sounds *not* used in the native language. Babies are capable of babbling in virtually all the sounds of languages throughout the world. But as early as six months of age, a baby begins to babble in her own language. That is, she has eliminated from her repertoire of sounds most, if not all, of the sounds not used in her language. If you are monolingual, you have control of the sounds in your language. If after years of being monolingual, you studied another language, you probably found it difficult to make certain sounds of that language. The reason is that you were making, or attempting to make, a sound not in your first language's phonological system. The same explanation holds for people who speak with an "accent." Though they may have been English speakers for years, the phonological system of the language they first spoke impinges on their English, producing what we commonly refer to as an "accent." It is usually only by careful work with a speech teacher that such accents are eliminated. Where an accent is not so "heavy" or "thick" that it interferes with normal communication, there is probably no need for speech training. Besides, many of us find accents charming.

For native speakers, the phonological system is, with some notable exceptions, complete by the time a child enters school. Some children may experience trouble producing "l" and "r" sounds, for example, or may suffer speech impediments which require the ministrations of a speech therapist. But, for the most part, the phonological system is fully and firmly in place for children entering school.

In American English, there is no single phonological system. Each speaker learns the phonology of the dialect of English that is spoken around him/her. It is that phonological system that is complete, not some mythical "best" sound of American English.

MORPHEME DEVELOPMENT

The subtleties of sounds come slowly to a child. Sounds begin to translate to recognizable speech for most children between the ages of 12 and 18 months. In time, phonemes are combined by the child into *morphemes,* the smallest units of meaning. The earliest morphemes a child learns are almost always those for mother and father. Words of things and other people in the child's environment follow. By the age of 18 months, the average child has developed a spoken vocabulary of perhaps 50 words. By two years of age, simple sentences appear to articulate a vocabulary of 300 to 600 words. The child's syntax is telegram-like, omitting articles. Thus, we have "all gone," "go bye-bye," and "see mommy."

As English-speaking children develop their speaking skills, they tend to over-regularize the language. We have all heard young children use "goed" for "went," "runned" for "ran," and "taked" for "took." Psychologist Roger Brown has stated, "The important thing about these errors is that they are good errors." Good, in the sense that each one is perfectly intelligible, a quite reasonable overextension of certain regularities that do exist in English and apply in most cases.

As the child's language develops, he begins to use articles, "a," "an," and "the," as well as appropriate pronouns "her," "me," and "it." In his ability to use English or any other language, the child now enters a linguistic thicket. Languages evolve over time and their proper use tends to be rather complex. Chomsky's theory of deep structure or intended meaning speculates that human beings have an innate ability to perceive the intent of a speaker. If Chomsky's idea is correct, then a "universal grammar" exists, and that means there is a common scheme for organizing ideas that transcends language differences. The debate over Chomsky's language theories will continue for some time—as researchers continue their attempts to understand the marvel of language acquisition.

Parents facilitate children's language growth by encouraging semantic expansion in the child. They ask questions which cause the child to add to meaning rather than merely to repeat a corrected grammatical statement. When the child says, "Me want milk," the parent should respond with, "Why do you want milk?" instead of the grammatical correction, "Say, I want milk."

SYNTACTIC SYSTEM

The syntactic system is, very simply put, the way in which the words of a language are ordered. In English, we say "red house." In Spanish, it's "casa rojo" or house red. The most frequently occurring sentence pattern in English is subject, verb, object (S-V-O). "The man ate the fish." However, the same thought can be expressed in other orderings. "The fish was eaten by the man," or even "By the man was the fish eaten." (Sounds a little strange, but it's an allowable sequence in English.)

The importance of word ordering is easily demonstrated by switching about the words of the sentences written above. A quite opposite meaning is conveyed by "The fish ate the man" or "The man was eaten by the fish" or "By the fish was the man eaten." And the string "By eaten fish man the the was" is meaningless because it conforms to no English syntactic pattern.

For native speakers, the syntactic system is very nearly mastered by about age six. There are some constructions that aren't mastered by that age, but for most purposes it's safe to say the system is fully functioning at a surprisingly early age.

SYNTACTIC COMPLEXITY

As they mature children begin to transform the basic patterns of English sentences in order to express more complex levels of thinking.

The basic transformations which they make are described here:

1. Rearrangement
   The versions of "The man ate the fish" given above are examples of rearrangement, as is:
   The tree is tall.
   Is the tree tall?
2. Sentence Combining Transformations
   The tree is tall.
   The tree is straight.
   a. Conjoining
      The tree is tall and straight.
      The tree is tall since it is straight.
   b. Embedding
      The tall tree is straight.
      The straight tree is tall.
      The tree, which is tall, is straight.
      The tree, which is straight, is tall.

Walter Loban (1963) studied the language development of children over a twelve-year period and found that they showed an increase in complexity of sentence patterns throughout the years. Some of his findings are summarized here.

1. Children aged five and six use complex sentences with clauses beginning with why, because, and if.
2. Children aged six and seven use complex sentences, especially ones with an if clause and an adjective clause.

3. Children aged seven and eight use relative pronouns in adjective clauses. "I have a cat which. . ." and use subordinate clauses beginning with if and when more frequently. The average number of words per T-unit is approximately 8.0.
4. Children aged eight, nine, and ten use connectors to relate particulars to general concepts such as meanwhile, unless, even if, and although. The average number of words per T-unit is approximately 8.5.
5. Children aged ten, eleven, and twelve use all complex patterns and compound predicates such as, "We ate and finished up the candy." The average number of words per T-unit is 9.0.

Read through a paragraph of your own writing. Pick out the clauses which you have used. Do you use a recurring pattern in your syntactic structure? You can see how language development is closely related to the development of thought patterns.

Kellogg Hunt (1970) measured children's written language at grades 4, 6, 8, 10, and 12. In his analysis of children's sentences he used a communication unit called a T-unit (minimal terminal unit) rather than the sentence. Hunt defined a T-unit as "one noun clause with all the subordinate clauses attached to it" (1970, p. 20). He showed the T-unit to be a more reliable measure of language maturity than sentence length because children use run-on sentences. These sentences demonstrate the function of a T-unit.

1. The day was nice.
   The day was sunny.
   The day was warm.
   (3 sentences, 3 T-units, 12 words)
2. The day was nice, and it was sunny, and it was warm.
   (1 sentence, 3 T-units, 12 words)
3. The day was nice and sunny and warm.
   (1 sentence, 1 T-unit, 8 words)
   The day was nice, since it was sunny and warm.
   (1 sentence, 1 T-unit, 10 words)

Children use longer T-units as they develop in language ability and progress through elementary school. Although a variety of combinations are used by children in their writing at all grade levels, it is first done through coordination, then through subordination and embedding. Run-on sentences are typical in early elementary grades, but these should decrease as the child matures.

The three pieces in Figure 5-1 were written by the same child at grades 3, 4, and 5. Notice the changes in sentence patterns. How is the narrative written in fifth grade different from the narrative written in third grade?

Bryan Abrahamson Sept 7, 1979

My Autobiography (3rd grade)

My hole name is Bryan Miles Abrahamson. I'm 9 years old.
I'm a Diabetic.
I half to watch what I'm eating.

Theres 4 in my famly.
and we have 4 pets too.
My famlys name are Britt Grace and Sivaly. I was born Jan 10, 1970.

The best Things i like in school is Math, Gym Art and lunch.
and i like most of my theachers to Miss Bech and that's nice teachers

The only club i blong to is a basball club
I would play sortstop third–base or outfield

My favorte pets are my hermet crabs.

Bryan

The Skeleton (5th grade)

You are a very very old skeleton in the museum Life had been pretty dull for you until they moved you into the room with the giant staffed animals. Now you don't dare sleep for even a second. You know the awful truth about one of the gorillas in the room! The gorilla at night would open his eyes and he looked terrified and grunted loudly.
The skeleton said, "I'm scared to my bones if I had any bones left."
The next day came and parts of the skeleton's body was in the stuffed tigers and the lions mouth. The guards chatered, "If theres any disturbance phone security system. They closed up for the night. The two guards switched Shifts at night. The guards never found out about the mystery. The people who came never found out. They're still wondering today.

Bryan Abrahamson
Horrible Halloween

It was night and Me and Jeff walked into a old storage house. The shutters wer broken and it looked creepy.

We went upstairs and looked in the closet. It scared us. A skeleton was in the closit. The looked under the broke can bed. There was cob webs and a black cat. and some bats.

We looked in the cabinet. There wer 4 bottles in the cabinet. There names were Poison P. Bats and rats and old alley cats, buzzerd tails and old dried up snails. Poison C.

We went down the stairs slowly. I triped and fell down stairs. I said to Jeff. its all right come on. The cost is clere. We found an old clock. It looked like a pumpkin. It was a pumpkin. It was 15 feet wide 9 fut tall

FIGURE 5-1

SEMANTIC DEVELOPMENT

In the broadest sense, semantic development is a lifelong process. We continue to acquire new words and to refine our understanding of old words. This is not terribly surprising since new words enter the language frequently. For example, the words "cybernetics" and "bionic" have relatively short histories. In addition, words and phrases change meaning. The phrase "space invaders" a few short years ago meant just that, invaders from space. Now, however, most people know it as an electronic game.

Vocabulary also grows because there is a vocabulary to virtually every job a person might do. For example, a "choker" to a person who knows about jewelry is a kind of necklace. To a logger, a "choker" is a person who sets the cable by which a log is dragged to where it can be loaded onto a truck. To a homicide detective. . . . That is an example of fairly common words which take on a specific meaning depending on the context in which they are used. Let's consider some other such words. Line—to a mathematician, to a dancer, to a gambler. Pitch—to a musician, to a lumberman, to a salesperson, to a soccer player. These are examples of polysemous (multi-meaning) words. In addition to common words that have context-specific meanings, there are words which are unique to various vocations and avocations. "Polysemous" is unlikely to turn up anywhere but in discussions of language. "Zygotic" is unlikely to turn up anywhere but in biology. In fact, in the broadest sense, when we say someone is an educator, biologist, mathematician, model train hobbyist, we mean, at least in part, that she knows the vocabulary of that vocation or avocation.

Thus, from the newborn child who signals her needs by crying, to the toddler who can not only make her needs known but can talk about the events of the day and how she feels about things, the developmental sequence takes less than three years. The acquisition of language is our most impressive intellectual achievement as humans. And virtually everyone who is physiologically intact accomplishes this amazing feat.

DEVELOPMENT OF COMMUNICATIVE COMPETENCE

Communicative competence is a term that describes the person's ability to decenter in his communication or, in other words, to be aware of an audience. Development of this awareness follows this broad pattern:

1. Awareness of another point of view. The five-year old who is playing with a rubber worm and suddenly says, "This rock must look like a mountain to this worm," is exhibiting the beginning of this awareness.
2. Awareness of the usefulness of analyzing the other point of view. The young child learns to analyze her mother's moods very early.

3. Methods for analyzing point of view.
4. Ability to retain this awareness.
5. Ability to use this awareness.

These last three levels are an important area for development in elementary language arts curriculum.

GENERAL LANGUAGE ABILITIES TO WATCH FOR IN CHILDREN 5-12

Drawing up a valid age chart of sequence and stages is hazardous; at any one age, children vary tremendously in language ability. While there are no absolutes, there are some general predictions we can make. A composite picture and checklist was constructed from the research efforts of Loban (1963), Hunt (1970), and Cazden (1972).

Five Years

Receptive Skills

_______ interest in the meaning of words

_______ readily seeks information

_______ enjoys being read to

_______ difficulty distinguishing between fantasy and reality

_______ figures things out for himself. Makes own generalization after even one occurrence of an event.

Expressive Skills

_______ likes to talk and will generally talk to anyone

_______ interest in using new and large words

_______ innumerable questions

_______ grammar reasonably accurate

_______ uses language conformingly: "Is this the way to do it?"

_______ evaluates tasks: "that's hard" or "that's easy"

_______ can define simple words

Six Years

Receptive Skills

_______ increased ability to differentiate fantasy and reality

Expressive Skills

_______ uses language aggressively (slang)

_______ asks many questions

_______ very talkative

_______ uses telephone

_______ usually good pronunciation and fairly accurate grammatical form; can detect own errors and may accept correction

Seven Years

Receptive Skills

_______ interested in meaning and spelling of words

_______ reading

_______ listening to radio

_______ silent verbal planning

Expressive Skills

_______ uses language complainingly

_______ special telephoning to friends

_______ use of slang and clichés

_______ variable pitch of voice; voice generally loud, but may speak softly or mutter complaints

_______ estimates own ability: "I've never done that" or "I guessed it"

_______ criticizes own performance "What's the matter with me?"

_______ interest in endings "I've got it all up to here"

_______ can give similarities between two simple objects

_______ now relates thinking to head or mind "You have to think it up in your head"

Eight Years

Receptive Skills

_______ reading, audio record or tape, TV, and radio interests strong

_______ differentiations between fantasy and reality established

_______ distinguishes between original and acquired movement

_______ begins to understand cause and effect relationships

Expressive Skills

_______ talks a great deal

_______ exaggerates, boasts, tells tall tales

_______ uses language fluently, almost as adult does

_______ social use of telephone

_______ good pronunciation and good grammar as a rule

_______ beginning to use code language

_______ can give similarities and differences between simple objects

_______ can verbalize ideas and problems

Nine Years

Receptive Skills

_______ reading interests increase

_______ media interests increase

_______ emergence of independent critical thinking

_______ increasingly realistic conception of the world

Expressive Skills

_______ language used more as a tool and less for its own sake

_______ may return to many incorrect grammatical uses

_______ writes out lists and plans

_______ uses language to express subtle and refined emotions—disgust, self criticism

_______ extended use of code language

Ten, Eleven, and Twelve Years

Receptive Skills

_______ broad reading and media interests

_______ understand subtle meanings in humor

_______ increasing ability to judge linguistic messages critically

Expressive Skills

_______ uses language to frame hypotheses and envision consequences

_______ has difficulty distinguishing between uses of past, past perfect, and present perfect tenses of verb

_______ uses different styles of language for different purposes

_______ uses language creatively

_______ uses language critically

_______ grows in ability to analyze audience before communicating

LANGUAGE DEVELOPMENT AND SCHOOLING

Schools both augment and take advantage of the language capabilities of children. For example, beginning reading instruction relies on the language the child brings to school. It, for the most part, is concerned with teaching the child to recognize in print words she already speaks and understands from the speech of others. Except in the cases of those needing the help of a speech therapist, a fully formed phonological system is assumed. The same is true of the syntactic system.

What, then, is the school's role in language development, and in particular, what role is played by Language Arts instruction? The answer, in two words, is refinement and expansion.

Language Arts instruction refines and expands the uses to which language can be put. That is what this book is about—the ways in which language is refined and expanded through schooling.

A RICH ENVIRONMENT FOR LANGUAGE

There must be a language rich environment in the classroom in order to expand children's language and encourage further development. Some of the characteristics of a language rich environment are described here:

1. There is social interaction and peer collaboration. A major part of the curriculum involves talk between class members and among groups. The teacher structures the talk by giving purposes for talking and understand that oral language is the basic of all language development.
2. The teacher is the source of mature communication and new vocabulary. She does not "talk down" to students.
3. The teacher provides many role taking experiences in literature and drama in order to develop communicative competence.
4. One of the most important goals of the elementary teacher is to help children develop their written sentence complexity from "The dog is big" pattern. A child's linguistic maturity can be measured by the amount of detail that can be included about the dog in a given T-unit.
5. There is more emphasis on solving thinking and communication problems and less emphasis on content so children are involved in diverse and intellectually engaging learning activities.
6. There is a positive attitude toward error. The teacher understands that all language learning follows a developmental model and children move through succeeding stages learning through trial and error.
7. Questioning follows a "semantic expansion" model. Children are encouraged to specify and clarify their ideas.
   Through all of this linguistic experience, children gain the confidence they need to move through the stages of development easily and to say with great pride, "I can read. I can write."

VOCABULARY DEVELOPMENT

You have learned from the sketch of language development that vocabulary (semantic) development is a lifelong process. The part the school plays in that development is what the remainder of this book is about. In the school setting, vocabulary development and concept attainment and development are considered to be the same process. A thought is actually a set of mental pictures, sensations, emotions, and linguistic information. A concept label is a word used to describe those images, sensations, and so on. For example, "cat" is the word used to describe our pictures and sensations about a certain type of animal. When you learn that the label (word) cat is a certain type of four-legged animal, you have attained the concept. When you learn that there are many kinds of "cats" you are refining or developing your concept of "cat." When you say you know something, what you actually mean is that for a certain word you associate certain visual images, sensations, and so on. Your knowledge of the concept "cat" does not include a formal definition of the word "cat." You could probably make up a definition but it is not the way you know the concept.

We have four types of vocabularies: listening vocabulary, speaking vocabulary, reading vocabulary, and writing vocabulary. Listening vocabulary is concept knowledge. Your speaking vocabulary is those words or labels used in speech. Both reading and writing involve recognizing the orthographic or letter code for the word or label. All of these types of vocabulary add to the nature of a thought. Marzano and Arrendondo (1986) present these steps for teaching a concept or word to children:

1. Provide a direct or indirect experiential base for the new concept with a field trip, classroom activity, discussion describing the concept, or some personal examples of your experiences of the concept.
2. Have students describe the new concept (word) in terms of their experiences.
3. Using the information generated in step 1, have students form a strong mental image of the new concept.
4. Have students say the word to themselves so they can hear it in their mind's ear.
5. Have students see the word in their mind's eye.
6. Have students systematically review the newly learned concept, adding and deleting information (pp. 36-37).

It will be necessary within a school year to teach a few concepts in a more formal presentation. This is done through concept development. Most primary vocabulary will involve a concept attainment approach. Concept devlopment will lead to a formal definition and is used with older children in content area teaching. When you want to develop the understanding of a concept with children follow this procedure:

1. Identify the category to which the concept belongs.
2. Identify examples.
3. Eliminate irrelevant information.
4. Exaggerate important information.
5. Plan activities or questions which cause the students to discriminate between concepts which are similar and dissimilar to what you are trying to teach.
6. Have students define the concepts in their own words and make up their own examples.
7. Set up a new situation in which children can apply the concept.

Although much vocabulary is developed incidentally, vocabulary development must be a planned program. For example, a child brought a pet snake to class one morning. The teacher gathered the children around to look at and talk about the snake. They discussed shape, size, color, texture, and diet. They composed a story about the snake. These students had developed several concepts through this experience and the words associated with it. This is concept attainment. If she desired, the teacher could choose any one of these concepts to develop further if there is good reason to do so (for example, if it is a key concept for a whole area of curriculum such as a study of reptiles).

SUMMARY

A study of language development in children has important implications for the teaching of language arts. Language learning is a developmental, active process. Children must hear language being used and have opportunities to use it themselves in order to grow linguistically. The classroom must provide a language rich environment.

It is possible to trace a child's phonological, morphemic, syntactic, and semantic development and to recognize recurring stages common to all children. The elementary teacher works with children's syntactic development as children learn to transform the patterns of the English sentence and, most important, the teacher works with semantic development or vocabulary instruction. This needs to be a planned program which relates to all areas of the curriculum. In school some concepts are learned incidentally, but important concepts need to be taught through a concept attainment model. In the upper grades, a few important concepts need to be developed into formal definitions.

ACTIVITIES

For Teacher Education Classes

The Language Sample in the appendix to this chapter was taped and transcribed. The subject is a seven-year-old boy and the stimulus for discussion is *The Snowy Day* by Ezra Jack Keats. Read the sample and analysis by the researcher before doing the following assignments.

1. Using the check list on pp. 95-98 observe a child from a primary grade and a child from an intermediate grade. Notice developmental differences.
2. Collect short writing samples from children at three grade levels and analyze them for mean length of T-unit. Compare them with your own writing.
3. Choose one concept that you would teach to children at a particular grade level (round, continent, photosynthesis) and describe a plan that would lead to attainment of that concept. Then describe how you would develop that concept in a more formal manner.
4. Ask children of different grade levels to combine two simple sentences such as: The dog is big. The dog is fast. Look for the variety of ways they can do the transformations and the differences in ease with which they can do them.

For the Elementary Classroom

1. Have students keep a notebook of all concepts learned using the concept attainment process. For each concept, have them record the following information:
   a. Their description of the concept.
   b. The mental picture they associate with the concept (students can describe the picture, draw it, or symbolize it.)
   c. The physical sensations they have about the concept.
   d. Their emotions about the concept.

   Periodically have students go back and revise the information in their notebooks as their knowledge of the concept matures (Marzano and Arredondo, 1986, p. 39).
2. Select a book to read aloud based on its vocabulary and language value as well as its general appeal to children. Read the book to a group of students and afterwards discuss some of the special or unfamiliar words in the story. Choose one of the words to present using the concept attainment method.

THE LANGUAGE SAMPLE
"N" IS NORMA; "J" IS JONATHAN

N: OK, what do you think is happening in this first picture?
1. J: The boy's in the bed.
N: Anything else?
2. J: 'N he's looking outside. And he's sittin' down on his bed.
N: What could he be thinking about?
3. J: I don't know. 'Bout snow?
N: Maybe. What about the snow? Well, let's see what happens next. What do you think he's going to do?
4. J: Climb up snow.
N: What could you do on a day like this?
5. J: I don't know.
N: If you walked out of your house and you saw big piles of snow, what would you do?
6. J: Climb on it.
N: And what else?
7. J: Jump. Is this boy gonna do it? He didn't.
N: How did those tracks get there?
8. J: He was walkin' on it. (He counted the number of footprints.) Thirty-two.
N: Thirty-two! How did he make them look like this?
9. J: It was like this. (He stood up and showed me.)
N: They look different sometimes.
10. J: See (what he did).
N: How do you think those tracks got there?
11. J: By slide . . . sliding . . . ice-skating.
N: Do you think an animal made them?
12. J: Let's see.
N: No, you guess. We're just going to guess first.
13. J: Yes. No.

N: No? What do you think?
14. J: Boy.
N: You think what?
15. J: The boy done it. Check.
N: Wait, I have one more question. Why are there two here, and three starting there?
16. J: Because boy done it.
N: What did he do, do you think? How did he make that?
17. J: I don't know.
N: How would you guess?
18. J: By slide.
N: What do you mean?
19. J: By fingers.
N: You mean you think he . . .
20. J: He went like this. Then he went like this.
N: OK, let's see.
21. J: He had a stick!
N: He had a stick. Right!
22. J: (reading) "It was a sock."
N: What did you say it was?
23. J: Sock. Sick.
N: Stick. M-hm. Like you said.
24. J: (reading) "It was a stick."
N: Can you tell what is happening in these two pages?
25. J: No.
N: Look.
26. J: He's 'onna climb up here. He's 'onna put this stick up and he's climbin' up 'n climbin' up.
N: Why do you think this happened?
27. J: It'll fall . . . it'll take the snow off.
N: He's taking the snow off?
28. J: We'll see.
N: How could he do that?
29. J: By the stick.
N: And what would he have to do with it?
30. J: Climb up there.
N: He's not climbing up in the tree, so how could he get the snow off?
31. J: He can hold it like swish, swish.
N: Well, OK. What might happen to the boy if he keeps doing that?
32. J: Snow'll fall off.
N: And what will happen to the boy, do you think? What could happen to the boy?
33. J: Fall down?
N: He would fall down?
34. J: No, the chair fall down.
N: You think the tree would fall down? And then what?
35. J: Nuttin'. I don't know.
N: Where would it fall?
36. J: On his head.

N: Well, let's see. How did the snow get on his cap?

37. J: I don't know. By he takin' the snow off. Is this on (referring to the tape recorder)?
N: Taking the snow off of where?

38. J: Off of the branch.
N: Now this is an interesting picture. What do you think is going to happen next?

39. J: He's goin' home.
N: OK, let's see if he's going home.

40. J: Am I right?
N: What does it look like?

41. J: Boy . . . other boy 'n girls throwin' snowballs.
N: What would you like to tell the little boy in red?

42. J: Nuttin'.
N: If you were there, what would you say to him?

43. J: I don't know.
N: Look what's happening to him. Can you tell from the picture?

44. J: Threwin' snowballs.
N: Is he throwing one?

45. J: They are.
N: They are. What's happening to the boy in red?

46. J: Just sittin' there.
N: He's just sitting there and what happens when he just sits there?

47. J: He gets snowed all over.
N: Yeh. He's too small to throw snowballs and so the big boys throw snowballs at him. What would you do if you were the little boy in red?

48. J: I don't know.
N: Would you just stay and sit there?

49. J: No.
N: What would you do?

50. J: Go away.
N: And what could you do if you went away? You could go home.

51. J: Go home . . . I would go home.
N: OK, let's see if he goes home.

52. J: No.
N: No, he's having fun. Does that snowman look different from ones you've made? How?

53. J: We make three snowballs.
N: You make three snowballs.

54. J: 'N together. (?)
N: What?

55. J: We have . . .
N: How do you do it? Yours doesn't look like that?

56. J: Huh-uh. We got one top of the bottom 'n one top of the . . . side.
N: What does your face look like?

57. J: A carrot.
N: What is the carrot?

58. J: For his nose. And somebody ate it.
N: And what?

59. J: Somebody ate it.
    N: Oh! What do you do for the rest of the face?
60. J: That's all.
    N: The man just has a nose?
61. J: And a mouth.
    N: How do you make that?
62. J: With a long stick.
    N: Where do you put it?
63 J: In his mouth.
    N: And how do you make eyes?
64. J: Just put a stick in 'em, and put stick out.
    N: How does the snowman look like he feels?
65. J: I don't know.
    N: Look at that on his face.
66. J: Happy.
    N: Now, how do you make these things that look like angels?
67. J: Got to have a hill.
    N: You've got to have a hill, and then what do you do?
68. J: Lay down on it and do that what he's doing. I have this book. I do.
    N: OK, so he's still not going to go home. Can you tell from these two pages what the boy in red really likes to do?
69. J: Slide down.
    N: How does he do it, can you tell?
70. J: He climbs up 'n he slides down; he climbs up, slide down.
    N: What do you think happens to his pants?
71. J: Get ripped.
    N: It what?
72. J: 'll get ripped.
    N: It'll get ripped? Maybe. He's been doing an awfully lot on that snowy day. He's probably getting a little cold. We'll see. Now, what do you think this picture is about?
73. J: Snow. I don't know.
    N: What's he doing?
74. J: Taking the snowball.
    N: And how could he get a snowball?
75. J: I don't know.
    N: How do you get a snowball?
76. J: Just pickin' it up.
    N: Do you go to the store and buy it?
77. J: A snowball?
    N: Yea.
78. J: I don't know. I never buy a snowball.
    N: Then where do you get a snowball?
79. J: From snow.
    N: Does it snow snowballs? Do you have great big snowballs dropping on your house when it snows?
80. J: No.
    N: Where do they come from?
81. J: The snow.

N: And how do you make them?

82. J: Just roll snow.
N: You roll snow. OK, I think that's what he's doing. What it says here, that you can't tell from the picture, is that he's going to put the snowball in his pocket. And then where does he go?

83. J: Inside.
N: Inside. What do you think they're talking about?

84. J: The snow.
N: What would he be telling her?

85. J: All the things what he did and what somebody else did to him.
N: What happened to him while he was outside that he would tell her?

86. J: Sombeody throwed snowball.
N: What else did he probably tell her that he did?

87. J: He snow . . . he put snow in his pockets.
N: Yes. If you had just come into the house after playing in the snow, what would you like to do most?

88. J: I don't know.
N: Shall we see what he did?

90. J: Take a bath.
N: He took a bath. Where did those circles come from?

91. J: The bubbles.
N: Why are there bubbles?

92. J: In the bubble . . . bathtub 'cause he put some in 'ere.
N: Now what happens?

93. J: He's taking the snowball?
N: Why do you think there's a dark spot on his coat?

94. J: 'Cause he put it there?
N: He put the dark spot there?

95. J: No, snow did.
N: Why would the snow make it dark?

96. J: Because it melts.
N: So, the snowball is gone. How do you think he feels in that picture?

97. J: Bad.
N: Yea, I think he feels bad. Do you think he knows what happened? Can you tell what's happening in that picture?

98. J: The snow is all drippin'.

LANGUAGE SAMPLE ANALYSIS

3.79 - average number of words/CU

3 - total number of dependent clauses

2.14 - average number of words/maze

NOUNS

Exhibited a good variety: "boy," "bad" (1); "snow" (3); "stick" (21); "head" (36); "branch" (38); "home" (39); "girl," "snowballs" (41); "nose" (58);	Concrete rather than abstract

"mouth" (63); "hill" (67); "book" (68); "pockets" (87); "bath" (90); and "bathtub" (92).

Plural markers are used infrequently but correctly: "snowballs" (41, 44, 53, 54); "things" (85). Given the context of our conversation, in 87, "pockets" should have been "pocket."

ADJECTIVES

Appear infrequently: "three" and "long."

ADVERBS

Only 6: "outside" (2); "down" (2); "up" (26); "there" (30, 46); "off" (32); and "down."

PRONOUNS

Employed a good variety: "he" (16 times); "it" (3 times as a subject, 8 as an object); "this" (once as a subject, twice as an object, twice as an adjective); "I" (7 times); "we" (twice); "that" (once as an object); "what" (subject twice, object once); "him" (once); "his" (only possessive—4 times).

Referent was always clear.

Reflexes never appear.

"He" should have been "him" in "by he takin' the snow off." (37)
"All the things *what* he did and what somebody else did to him" *"What"* should have been "that."

ARTICLES

"The" appears 14 times, "a" 7 times.
The article preceding the subject noun was left out of 16, 32, and 41.
The article preceding an object noun was omitted in 4, 64, and 86.

PREPOSITIONS

Appear 23 times and with great variety.

VERBS

45 verbs were used (action type, active voice.
Passive voice used in 47: "He gets snowed all over."

Early developing passive

Auxiliary verbs are often contracted to the subject (1, 2, 26, 27, 41, 68, 72, 93).
Concatenative "gonna" appears 3 times.

Early appearing form of the infinitive

VERB FORMS	
Most predominant form is the use of -ing (15 times). Difficulty with -ing in 11, "By slide . . .] sliding. For the most part subject/verb markers were employed correctly. (Exceptions: Plural "boy and girl" requires "are" instead of "is" in 41. In 46, he uses "slide" rather than "slides" to agree with "he."	For each of these errors he has exemplified correct usage at another time. This inconsistency reveals that he is capable of employing language successfully.
Incorrect usage of verb tense 1. "Done" is used for "did." 2. "Got is used for "have" in 56. 3. "Throwed" instead of "threw" in 86. Related: In 44, he says "threwin' snowballs." 4. He switched tenses within 26—future "is gonna" to present "is climbin'" 5. In 90, "take" should have been "took". in response to the previous question.	Possibly dialectical Trace of Over-regularization
6. "Would" was omitted in 34.	Perhaps he was imitating the form of the preceding question.
VERB PHRASES	
Mainly copula and -ing (2, 7, 8, 26, 39, 41, 68, 93). Auxiliary verbs "will" (27, 30) and "can" (31) used. Most verbs are intransitive.	
PREPOSITIONAL PHRASES	
Error: Number 56 should have been "We got one (on) top of the bottom 'n one (on) top of the side."	
SENTENCES	
Delcarative sentences lack variety. Subject + Verb + Prepositional phrase (1, 2, 8, 9, 20, 34) Subject + Verb + Object (15, 21, 41, 53, 58, 68, 86) Subject + Verb + Adverb (32, 39, 47, 51)	Uses fewer words than good communication requires.
Many incomplete sentences. Conjoins independent clauses (26, 64, 68, 70). "See what he did." (10) Only imperative sentence.	A combination of problems eliciting and economical speech
Questions appear in 7, 32, 40. Each of these are the yes/no type in which	Later state of question development

auxiliary verb (7) or copula (37, 40) are correctly inverted to a position preceding the subject noun phrase.	
Numbers 3, 33, 54, 77, 93, and 94 are questions because of voice intonation.	
Negation appears in his often repeated "I don't know."	Memorized unit—no intonation
In 26, 64, 68, 70—conjoins independent clauses.	

In Overview

Jonathan meets success when he is expressing concrete ideas.

- uses concrete nouns
- most verbs are of the action type
- adjectives and adverbs are specialized and refer to location
- most sentences are declarative
- many sentences are incomplete
- few compound sentences

Language errors occur when he attempts to express a somewhat abstract thought.

- Number 26 reveals inconsistent tense within one sentence.
- When trying to describe how to make a snowman he uses an incorrect verb, leaves out two prepositions, and chooses the word "side" when semantically he should have said "middle" or its equivalent.
- When attempting to describe how to put eyes on a snowman his description becomes very difficult to follow (64).

Recommended Approach

- Focus on expanding his experiential background so that the conceptual basis for his language is broader. For example, field trips provide many opportunities for describing pictures or manipulative materials (concrete objects). This will provide practice with adjectives, adverbs, varying tense forms, etc.

REFERENCES

Cazden, Courtney B. (1972). *Child language and education.* New York: Holt.

Cazden, Courtney B. Suggestions from studies of early language acquistion. (Dec. 1969). *Childhood Education.* 46.

Hunt, Kellogg. Syntactic maturity in school children and adults. (Feb, 1970). *Society for Research in Child Development.* 25, 1.

Loban, Walter. *The language of elementary school children.* (1963). Champaign-Urbana: NCTE.

Marzano, Robert and Arredondo, Daisy. (1986). *Tactics for thinking.* Aurora, CO: Mid-Continent Regional Educational Laboratory.

Tepaske, Norma. *Language Sample.* University of Minnesota, 1980.

Vygotsky, L. (1962). *Thought and language.* MA: MIT Press.

6

ORAL COMMUNICATION

Oral language is what enables individuals to participate in their culture. It is the means through which we can express ourselves, make our thoughts and feelings known to others, as well as review the thoughts and feelings of others. It is important to be able to speak effectively. Effective communication plays a significant role in all human interaction. Adults with extraordinary speaking abilities have a significant social and professional advantage. Effective oral expression is important in school as well. Students who are competent speakers receive more recognition from their peers and teachers, achieve high grades, and are generally successful. Thus, the ability to speak effectively in a variety of situations and for a variety of purposes is a fundamental goal of the elementary school.

DEVELOPING ORAL LANGUAGE

During preschool years children achieve basic language competency, however, the amount of verbal stimulation and number of opportunities to interact with others varies greatly among those entering school. Therefore, it is necessary to carefully observe each child's use of language and determine his language abilities and areas of instructional need. The following questions offer a framework for assessing individual language strengths and weaknesses.

What is the child's attitude toward participation in verbal tasks? Some children need the opportunity to develop self-confidence in using language.

Is the child able to express his or her ideas and thoughts? Oral language is the tool a speaker uses to convey these ideas and thoughts. Children need opportunities to discuss experiences and express their thoughts in order to learn how to better communicate using oral language.

Is the child's vocabulary effective?

Does the child use a variety of sentence patterns? One's syntactical maturity is revealed in his or her sentence patterns and the subordination therein.

How does the child use volume, stress, pauses, and tempo? Meaning is communicated through stress, pitch, and juncture.

How does the child organize his or her oral expression? Attention must be made to the talk as a whole - the central point, sequence of events, place, cause and effect, main ideas, and supporting details.

In order to become effective speakers children need the opportunity to develop and enhance these language skills in a variety of settings. The discussion that follows outlines activities that will help you meet the oral language needs of your students.

LANGUAGE LEARNING ATMOSPHERE

Just as children enter school with a wide range of language abilities, they also enter school with a wide range of language attitudes. At one end of the continuum are children who are willing to express themselves and at the other end are chldren who are uncomfortable and reluctant to speak. It is the teacher's responsibility to strengthen all children's verbal confidence, since verbal confidence is essential to learning oral language skills. This takes time because attitudes develop slowly and are influenced by factors both within and outside school environment. By creating an atmosphere that promotes talk teachers can, at the very least, generate positive attitudes about speaking in school. How do you establish a language learning atmosphere?

Most important in creating a language learning atmosphere, is understanding the importance of oral language in the learning process. As children discuss learning experiences (ie: a film they have seen or a chapter in a textbook that they have read), they refine concepts and ideas. Through talk students come to learn what they know and think about a particular topic. Once teachers understand the power of language in learning, they can encourage students to orally describe, classify, inform, plan, and compare. Students will then both learn about their topic and learn better use of language.

A teacher's response to child language will convey the value that the teacher places on language and learning. A teacher should list the major points made in a discussion, summarize the group's ideas, take notes on what students say, and evaluate the content learned through oral communication. Students will then realize that their words count and that oral work is important. When teachers respond to child language in the above manner, they build students' self-confidence and willingness to speak.

Unfortunately, teachers do not always respond to child language in a positive way. Too often when a child is speaking to the class, the teacher will correct her language, take over and expand upon the content, or complete a clerical task (see Chapter 5). These actions convey to the speaker and to the other children that what the speaker has said is unimportant or not worth hearing. There are times when evaluative comments are appropriate but, in general, children ought to be attentively listened to. Teachers may plan a conference to discuss correct usage or presentational style.

Finally, a teacher must provide opportunities for children to talk. If children are to develop their verbal skills they must practice speaking. The activities in this chapter provide opportunities to practice oral language. Informal conversation, when it does not deter others from learning, is also a legitimate form of practice. In addition to casual conversation there are classroom activities that require conversation. These include rehearsing a

play, planning and painting a mural, or preparing a group report. These opportunities to speak provide for practice and, over time, build self-confidence and oral effectiveness.

In his book, *Life in Classrooms* (1968), Philip Jackson writes that the atmosphere for learning is perhaps more important than the subject matter itself—that the attitudes students develop toward themselves and toward learning are as crucial as what they learn. (Ellis, p. 284)

DISCUSSION

Oral discussion ought to be an everyday occurence in the classroom. Discussions can be used to plan, inform, deal with problems, and develop verbal expression.

Small Group Discussion

Classroom discussions usually focus on a topic of study, are teacher dominated, and include all the children in the class. Traditionally the teacher asks questions, a child responds, and the teacher evaluates each response. This format, while it allows the teacher to focus student's attention on major points, has limitations. Classroom discussions usually last 20 to 30 minutes and this limits the number of people who have an opportunity to talk. In order to cover all the aspects of the topic that the teacher has planned, his questions are frequently structured to require a short answer. This limits student language and cognitive growth. Small group discussion, on the other hand, provides for significantly more oral language opportunities. Fox and Allen state that in small group discussion:

1. The size of the group (usually 3-6 children) encourages each person to talk. Participants are likely to feel comfortable about expressing themselves, even shy members are not likely to be intimidated.
2. Language is informal because of the intimacy of the group.
3. Ideas are expressed freely.
4. Participants are willing to take risks and express incomplete thoughts.
5. Participants play a variety of roles. They support others ideas, clarify points, oppose viewpoints, help reduce friction, ask questions, and summarize.

Small groups may be organized to discuss any topic. Moffet (1968, as cited in Fox and Allen) suggests three types of discussion topics: topics of enumeration, topics of chronology, and topics of comparison. Topics of enumeration are good for introducing young children to small group discussion. Here children list items in a given category, such as types of transportation, occupations, zoo animals, etc. All elementary age students have many opportunities to discuss chronological topics. Planning a field trip, organizing and carrying out a science experiment, discussing events that led to the Civil War all require an ordering of ideas. Topics of comparison may range from distinguishing similarities and differences among flowers to comparing points made in the Lincoln - Douglas debates.

Small groups may convene only once or they may require several meetings. Topics of enumeration would require only one meeting. Students who are reading a book together (see Figure 6-1) would meet many times. A discussion group organized to deal with a problem, such as building a model, requires several meetings to experiment, plan, work, and finally produce a product. The number of meetings required depends upon the purpose of the group - to plan, share information, or deal with a problem.

Guiding a Discussion

While children are familiar with the structure of conversation, they need many opportunities to acquire discussion skills and their initial discussion experiences require teacher guidance. Coody suggests the following guidelines for introducing children to discussion.

1. Students need to have knowledge about the discussion topic.
2. The teacher, or a student, introduces the topic by making an opening statement.
3. It is the teacher's or leader's, responsibility to keep discussion going by posing questions and encouraging participation.
4. At times the teacher may want a student to clarify or extend an idea. This can be done with a minimum amount of teacher intervention. He may merely say "Please explain. . . ." or "Please give us more information about. . . .".

Children who have read the same book may form book discussion groups. Such groups stimulate oral language, for children enjoy comparing their feelings and thoughts about a literary character or episode. The teacher may add structure to the group by suggesting discussion questions and books to read.

A variation is to focus discussion on a book that is being read aloud to the class. Using this format children will talk about points of interest as the book progresses and speculate about what will happen next. A second variation is to read a book together. A small group of children reads a book aloud, each taking a turn and passing it on when tired of reading or upon reaching a predetermined spot. Discussion focuses on the unfolding story.

FIGURE 6-1 Sharing Books

5. The teacher needs to draw out thinking and information on all sides of the problem through questioning. She must also maintain a neutral attitude. If the students sense that the teacher is biased they are less likely to give open, candid answers.
6. It is the teacher's role to maintain discussion on the topic.
7. Teachers must give students adequate time to respond. Students need time to think, analyze, and put information together before they speak. Research has demonstrated that greater "wait time" leads to responses indicating higher levels of thinking.
8. The teacher needs to encourage the participation of less verbal students.
9. Summarize the main points and conclusions. This ought to be done by the students, but initially it may be done by the teacher.

It is a good idea to start with only one group while the remainder of the class works independently. As the students gain more discussion experience they will need less guidance. Additionally, groups may then be started and the students can begin to lead their own discussions. The purpose of a discussion will also determine the amount of teacher guidance that is needed. Describing how a poem makes you feel requires less guidance than does comparing different books of the same genre.

Effective Questioning

It is evident that leading a discussion group requires skill in questioning. The types of questions that teachers ask determines the level of the students' response in terms of thinking and language. Ellis presents a concise version of Blooms Taxonomy of question types. The following is taken from Ellis, 1986 p 201-207.

1. Knowledge—can students recall information? Recalling information requires students to bring to mind facts, data, or specific items from material they have read, heard, or seen.

Example 1: Students have seen a film on a bakery. The teacher asks the students to name three jobs people have at a bakery.

Example 2: Students have read a textbook passage on the Bushmen of the Kalihari. The teacher asks the class what foods the Bushmen eat.

2. Comprehension—can students explain ideas? In order to explain ideas the students must understand what is being communicated. This is the lowest level of understanding. They can explain how something works or give reasons for things, but they do not have to relate this to other material or see it's fullest implications.

Example 1: The class has been studying Brazil. The teacher asks students to give reasons why Brazil is a major coffee producer.

Example 2: The class has been learning about various traffic safety rules. The teacher asks the class why we have traffic rules.

3. Application—can students use ideas? Application requires students to use general ideas, rules, or methods in a novel situation.

Example 1: The teacher asks students to graph some new data using the bar graph method which they studied the day before.

Example 2: The class has been comparing and contrasting experimental research and survey research. The teacher asks students to decide which research procedure would be more appropriate to determine students' preferences in the upcoming vote for new school colors.

4. Analysis—do students see relationships? Analysis requires students to break a communication down into its constituent parts so that the relative hierarchy of ideas is clear and the relations between ideas are expressed and made explicit. Analysis is intended to clarify communication, to see how the communication is organized, and how it conveys its effects. Analysis questions ask students to make comparisons, state contrasts, determine structures, and look for patterns.

Example 1: Ask students to cite similarities among three books that were written by the same author.

Example 2: Students have read a copy of a letter written by a colonist who witnessed the Battle of Lexington. In addition, they have read several historical summaries. The teacher asks the class to analyze the colonist's account of the battle.

5. Synthesis—can students combine ideas? This involves working with pieces, parts, ideas, etc. and arranging them and combining them to produce a structure or pattern that was not there before. This may require students to use multiple sources or arrive at novel solutions to problems or to create new systems.

Example 1: Discussion groups are asked to develop plans for the construction of a nature center on land adjacent to the school.

Example 2: Students have been studying the genre of fantasy. Ask them to hypothesize how the story of Henry Huggins would have been different if it were set in another country or on another planet.

6. Evaluation—can students make judgments? Evaluation requires students to make judgments about the value of material or methods in relation to criteria. The criteria may be their own or it may be given to them. During evaluative discussions there will not be unanimity of opinion and teachers and students need to be tolerant of views different from their own. Students should be encouraged to state their differing ideas and be expected to support and defend them.

Example 1: The class has just listened to the story "The Fisherman and His Wife". The teacher asks students how they feel about the wishes the wife made.

Example 2: Students have just listened to a debate about whether a nuclear power plant should be built at a particular site. They are then asked to make and support their own judgements.

Generally speaking, knowledge and comprehension level questions require students to recall information and explain ideas. Use them to clarify facts and establish a common base of knowledge. Higher level questions require students to think at more complex levels. Use them to extend the thinking and language of the students in the discussion group. It is the teachers responsibility to ask a balance of both question types.

Ask questions which encourage more than one student to answer. Penetrating and provocative higher level questions elicit answers from several students and thereby promote child-to-child language. One student may build upon a point made by the first person's answer; another may develop a parallel idea; another may oppose an answer; another may ask a question.

Reinforcing student questions also promotes child talk. If you praise students when they ask questions they will be encouraged to do it again.

Ask a minimal number of questions. Teachers should have a few preplanned questions to bring out specific information and to extend students' thinking. Too many questions, however, will result in more teacher talk than child talk.

Questions and questioning strategies are key components in guiding small group discussions. A judicious selection of questions and knowing when to ask a question, probe a student's comment, or pause, can raise the students' level of thinking and enhance their language growth.

Small group discussion is loosely structured. Panel discussions and roundtable discussions are more formal and build upon the skills learned in small group discussions.

Panel and Roundtable Discussions

Panel discussions are designed to present information to an audience. Panels are usually comprised of five to eight members and a moderator. It is the responsibility of each member to prepare and present a different aspect of the topic. The moderator is responsible for pre-presentational and presentational organization. He or she decides what aspects of the topic will be covered and monitors the discussion. This includes typing ideas together, posing question, and summarizing. At the conclusion of the presentation the audience is invited to ask questions of individual panelists or the panel as a whole. The moderator is responsible for maintaining a lively, yet controlled, discussion.

BUILD A
HIGHER THOUGHT

Some of the Verbs You Can Use . . .	Some of the Products You Can Get . . .	
Editorialize, Decide, Evaluate, Dispute, Rate, Discuss, Certify, Judge, Grade, Choose, Assess, Select	Judgment, Panel, Opinion, Verdict, Scale, Value, Recommendation, Conclusion, Evaluation, Report, Investigation, Survey, Editorial	EVALUATION
Hypothesize, Imagine, Compose, Combine, Invent, Create, Infer, Estimate, Produce, Forecast, Design, Predict	Formula, Invention, Film, Prediction, New Game, Story, Poem, Solution, Art Product, Project, Media Product, Machine, Advertisement	SYNTHESIS
Summarize, Abstract, Classify, Dissect, Compare, Contrast, Deduce, Order, Investigate, Differentiate, Categorize, Separate	Survey, Questionnaire, Report, Graph, Chart, Outline, Diagram, Conclusion, List, Plan, Summary, Category	ANALYSIS
Show, Apply, Make, Translate, Illustrate, Record, Teach, Construct, Demonstrate	Illustration, Diagram, Diorama, Collection, Map, Puzzle, Model, Diary, Report, Lesson, Photograph	APPLICATION
List, Identify, Locate, Memorize, Review, Match, Name, Read, Recall, Reproduce	Labels, Names, List, Definition, Fact, Test, Reproduction, Recitation	RECALL

Includes:
KNOWLEDGE and
COMPREHENSION

FIGURE 6-2 Thinking Skills

In contrast to small group discussions, panel discussions are more formal, more audience-orientated, and require more preplanning. Roundtable discussions share characteristics with both formats. They are audience-oriented, yet there is informal give-and-take among participants, and the audience may be invited to contribute to the discussion. Both roundtable and panel discussions are used successfully with the content areas.

REPORTING

In the elementary school, oral reports are preorganized talks or speeches that are presented before the entire class. Oral reporting is an important activity as it provides the opportunity to utilize a formal language style for a specific purose. The topic of the report determines the type of language needed. For example, the teacher may want to use reporting to enhance the child's abilities to:

1. *inform.* Topics tend to be in the content areas of social studies or science.
2. *describe.* Topics may include the description of a setting in a story or a trip to a nearby factory.
3. *convince.* Topics may include convincing the PTA that the school playground needs a tether ball, or defending a position on a current issue.
4. *explain.* Topics may include giving instructions to perform a magic trick or how to design and construct a relief map.

As reporting is clearly intended to address an audience, it requires preparation and attention to certain skills. First of all a topic needs to be selected. After the general topic has been chosen, it may be narrowed by generating questions, and selecting one or two areas to focus the presentation on.

Second, information should be gathered from a variety of sources and notes taken on the topic. Note taking may be developed through discussion. As the teacher and students discuss a story or film on a classroom experience, they should collectively decide and record the important points. In determining what the important points are, the cognitive skills of noting details, perceiving relationships, and making generalizations are being developed. As children attain some degree of competency in note taking, they can work in small groups and then individually. The same method may be utilized to guide students in making summary statements. When children use a direct quote it is important to instruct them to credit the author.

The third preparatory step is to organize one's notes. This involves dividing the information into topics and then sequencing these topical lists. Developing the skill of outlining may be begun in the primary grades. For example, as a class plans for a field trip or a party, they make lists of what needs to be done, then classify the items and order the topical lists according to importance.

Fourth, the presenter needs to practice giving his or her report, giving attention to an interesting beginning and ending, language style, and the amount of time the report requires.

Oral reports may sometimes be enhanced when visual aids are used. Charts, diagrams, drawings, or an outline depicting the main points can clarify the content and minimize the self consciousness of the speaker as the audience's attention is focused on the aid. A slide presentation offers another format that makes some children more at ease with oral reporting.

Oral reports ought to be followed by discussion. Through this verbal exchange major ideas can be emphasized and different points of view may be talked about. In addition, the teacher may want to make one or two evaluative comments. At this time you should point out what the presenter did well because in doing so you are also instructing the other children and creating an environment which encourages children to talk.

STORYTELLING

The art of storytelling is one which all teachers should cultivate. This oral tradition provides pleasure, aids in oral language development, and exposes children to a wide variety of literature which they may not otherwise encounter. Many children will become motivated to tell stories themselves. This, however, will only occur if they have had the opportunity to hear a variety of tales; therefore, teachers must model the art.

Teachers As Storytellers

In selecting a story to tell it is most important that you like it, that it is interesting and entertaining to you. It must also fit your personality, style, and talents. This is important because, as the teller, whatever pleasure you get from telling the story is conveyed to the children.

The selected story must also be appropriate for the listeners. Ask yourself the following questions. Is it appropriate for the age of the group? Will it appeal to the interests of this particular group? Is the length appropriate for this group of children?

Other criteria to consider when selecting a story include:

(1) a plot that has action, yet is uncomplicated and easy to follow, and, (2) setting, language, and characters which are authentic and consistent with the plot. Folk tales are especially well suited to storytelling. They are exciting, enjoyed by all ages, and offer simple plot development and characterization. *Chicken Little* and *The Three Billy Goats Gruff* are among the favorites of young children. Those in the intermediate grades enjoy the tall tales of American Folklore, such as *Pecos Bill*, myths, and legends.

Storytelling should be carefully prepared. Stewig (1983) suggests the following steps. First divide the story into units of action, that is, identify the major events of the plot. If you strip away the descriptive material, most stories easily divide into definable series of actions. The second step is to identify any recurring phrases or refrains that need to be memorized. For example, in the *Three Little Pigs*, the wolf consistently threatened to "Huff and puff and blow the house down." This needs to be told exactly as it appears in the story in order to retain the spirit of the tale.

The third step is the practice. Order the units of action and in easy conversational tones practice saying what happens in each unit and you will be learning the story. Stewig and other experienced storytellers caution against memorizing a story. It results in a stiff, artificial delivery, and the intimacy that is inherent in storytelling is lost.

Given the amount of time and effort storytelling requires, some teachers might question its merit. Assuredly, the values gained from storytelling make it well worth the time of teachers and children.

First, by exposing children to a wealth of literature, storytelling stimulates their interest in reading. This exposure also introduces them to cultures and values that may be different from their own. Storytellers provide the opportunity to hear rich, vivid language and language patterns, thereby facilitating vocabulary development and demonstrating ways of using language, both orally and in writing. Storytelling aids in the development of listening and comprehension skills. Finally, the teacher, as a storyteller, models the art itself and kindles the students' desire to tell stories themselves.

Children As Storytellers

Children's storytelling need not be based on a literary selection. Personal experience stories are a good way to begin. Stories related during "show and tell" provide practice and involve children in the storytelling process.

Chain stories also help children to develop storytelling skills and confidence. In small groups of four or five, one child begins a story and each child, in turn, adds to it. In a like manner, children in pairs may complete unfinished stories or change the plot of a familiar one.

Wordless picture books provide an excellent framework for the novice storyteller. The plot, characters, and sequence are depicted visually, thereby lending structure as the child reads the pictures. Children who wish to tell a story to the class need practice and feedback. They need to get used to the sounds of their voices and to experiment with vocabulary and language patterns. Initial practice should be private but when the student is ready he or she may tape record his or her storytelling. The student, with the teacher, may then listen and evaluate the telling. Through this discussion the teacher may review guidelines for storytelling. Evaluative questions might include: Did I relate all the events? Were they in proper order? Did I describe the characters? Did I speak slowly? Did I vary my language?

Children also need to develop a sense of audience. When the student is ready the teacher arranges time for storytelling. The audience may consist of the entire class or a small group of peers. For those who are tentative, one fifth grade teacher arranged for her class to share stories with children in the primary grades (Stewig, 1978, Farnsworth). It is a good idea to tape or transcribe childrens' stories as they tell them. These may then be placed in a learning center to be enjoyed again.

The values inherent in childrens' storytelling are many. It facilitates cognitive organization as children are required to properly sequence events and to select appropriate vocabulary, gestures, and pertinent details. As children practice stories, they experiment with phrasing, tempo, volume, and pitch. This helps them learn to express themselves creatively and effectively. Storytelling, over time, also provides the teacher with valuable insights into a child's language growth (Picket and Chase). Children's storytelling occupies a special spot in the language curriculum as it is one of the most pleasant and effective ways of developing competency in verbal expression.

CHORAL SPEAKING

Choral speaking, also termed choric speaking or choral reading, refers to a group of children reciting a piece of literature. Many of the benefits of choral speaking are the same as those of storytelling: more effective verbal expression, increased interest in literature, and enjoyment. In addition, choral speaking is an excellent technique for building verbal confidence. As children blend their voices with others, they readily become comfortable speaking literature aloud.

Although choral speaking is not restricted to poetry, it is most often used because the cadence makes it a natural for saying or reading aloud. Through oral presentation we get the full effect of the rhythm and are able to appreciate the poets work.

Choral speaking begins with listening to poetry. As children hear a variety of verses, they acquire familiar favorites. Invite the class to join you in the recitation of these. These first experiences should be spoken in unison as this allows children to get the feel of rhythm and timing. Selections such as "There Was a Crooked Man" and "Stopping by Woods on a Snowy Evening" and many Mother Goose rhymes lend themselves to unison speaking.

As the class repertoire of poetry increases the speaking arrangements may vary. Poems which consist of stanzas and a refrain call for a solo voice or choir to speak the body, and for all to join in on the refrain. Rachel

Lindsey's "The Mysterious Cat" is an example.

Antiphonal or two-part choral speaking is used to depict dualism in a poem. Question-and-answer poems contrasts of mood or plot, invite two part division. For example, in "Swift things are beautiful" Elizabeth Coatsworth contrasts "swift things" and "slow things." The make-up of the chorus - high versus low voices, boys versus girls - convey the intent.

The line-a-choir or a line-a-child arrangement calls for groups or individuals to speak different lines or stanzas of the poem in sequence. The following selection from *Mother Goose* (M. Johnson) lends itself to the line-a-child arrangement.

Gay go up and gay go down,
To ring the bells of London town.

Bull's eyes and targets,
Say the bells of St. Marg'rets.

Brickbats and tiles,
Say the bells of St. Giles.

Oranges and lemons,
Say the bells of St. Clement's.

Pancakes and fritter,
Say the bells of St. Peter's.

To sticks and an apple,
Say the bells at Whitechapel.

Old Father Baldpate,
Say the slow bells at Aldgate.

Maids in white aprons,
Say the bells at St. Catherine's.

Pokers and tongs,
Say the bells at St. John's.

Kettles and pans,
Say the bells at St. Anne's.

You owe me five farthings,
Say the bells of St. Martin's.

When will you pay me?
Say the bells at Old Bailey.

When I grow rich,
Say the bells at Shoreditch.

Pray when will that be?
Say the bells at Stepney.

I'm sure I don't know,
Say the bells at Bow.

Here comes a candle to light you to bed,
Here comes a chopper to chop off your head.

Each of these arrangements may be varied to best convey the interpretation of the speakers. The major value of choral speaking lies in the process of interpretation for it is here that children gain insight into the system of language. As you and the class decide where to pause, when to stress a word, whether to speak rapidly or slowly, the children are learning how these elements communicate meaning and emotion. They learn the importance of voice quality, enunciation, articulation, and voice modulation. As different ways of speaking are tried these should be discussed and the interpretation to be used decided upon by the teacher and the students. This process creates a spirit of cooperation as well as effective speakers.

Variations include adding a musical background to accompany the choral speaking or adding a sound that compliments the rhythm and the meaning of the poem. For example, with "Hickory, dickory, dock" one group simulates the sound of a clock all through the poem saying "tick, tock, tick, tock", while another group recites the verse:

Hickory, dickory, dock,
The mouse ran up the clock.
  The clock struck one
  And down he run,
Hickory, dickory, dock!

Presenting more than one interpretation of the same poem stimulates creative thinking and gives children an added sense of language. Suggest a poem which lends itself to many adaptations ("Pop Can Sing" by Nancy Byrd Turner), and then allow different groups of children to explore various ways of presenting it. After each has worked out a pattern for presentation, bring the groups together and have them share their ideas.

Remember, choral speaking is an effective part of the language curriculum when children find it pleasurable and when they are closely involved in the process and not merely the presentation.

CREATIVE DRAMA

Creative drama refers to informal drama which is created by and for the participants. The content is taken from literature or is an original plot improvised by the players. There is no script. Lines are not memorized or written down, rather dialogue and plot evolve spontaneously. Creative drama does, however, have form. There is planning, playing, evaluating, and replaying. With each replaying, the story becomes more detailed and better organized, yet remains extemporaneous. Creative drama "is done for the purpose of deepening understanding and strengthening the performers, rather than perfecting a product" (McCaslin p. 10).

Creative Drama as a Learning Medium

The process begins. A third grade class has been reading a series of stories about small animals in a large world. Their teacher wants to make the experience of being very small in a large world real to the children. She decides to use creative drama as a learning medium, as a way of using their own experience to understand the experiences of others. She takes them through these steps:

1. Warm-up: Find a space that is your own. Curl up as small as you can. You are a tiny seed. Now you grow slowly (with the sound of a tambourine) into a tree. You wave in the wind. Your seeds drop. Now you are a seed asleep in the ground again.

2. You are a tiny animal. You wake up into a large world. Look at everything around you. What do you see? What does it look like? What do you hear? What does it sound like? What do you touch and smell around you? Move slowly. You need to find food. What do you eat? How does it feel in this large world? What can happen to you?

3. Improvisation: The children are put into groups of four. They are to be families of small animals. They must decide what they look like, where they live, what they eat, etc. They are taken through a short period of time in the life of the family.

4. Now the teacher introduces a problem. The family must move. Bulldozers are coming close. Where will they go? How? What will they take with them? The children plan.

5. Now it is time to start on the journey. They begin. Each family is in a line and they move in silence. As they go they encounter problems. The teacher suggests some - a ditch, a river, etc. Then the children think of and react to their own problems. Finally they reach their new home. During the journey when she wants the children to concentrate and think about difficulties they might have, the teacher plays music. The end of the music signals the end of the journey.

6. Reflection: The children gather in a circle. One person from each group tells that groups' story. Then, as individuals, they go off and draw and write their individual stories.

In a forty-five minute period, these children have experienced communicating orally through group planning and storytelling, and in writing and drawing. They have used their imaginations to define sensory impressions and to empathize with individuals confronted with a new environment. They have refined responses to literature, used new vocabulary, and experienced social studies concepts on an active level. In 1967, James Moffett said that drama is central, not peripheral, to a language curriculum: "Drama is the matrix of all language activities" (p. 130). The purpose of informal drama when used in education is not to train actors or produce plays for an audience. Nor is it primarily the development of appreciation for an art. The purpose of informal drama is to help students become better learners and better people.

Creative dramatics cannot just happen. It demands careful guidance and organization. A sequential program of dramatic arts activities requiring a regular period of time each week must be planned. The material for drama can be taken from any subject area. Drama is best approached in an integrated way.

Beginning Children's Classes in Creative Drama

Because the aim of creative drama is to develop children, not drama, the program in creative drama must begin with the resources of the child. According to Brian Way (pp. 11-14) there must be:

1. Regular practice at concentration through the use of the sense
2. Regular practice at using the sense to stimulate the imagination
3. Regular use of the imagination to stimulate movement and speech
4. Regular use of movement to stimulate further awareness of and mastery of the body in space
5. Regular use of speech in order to communicate one's own ideas and feelings to others and to be able to listen to the communications of others
6. Regular practice at becoming aware of others in order to stimulate and develop sensitivity
7. Regular practice at using that sensitivity to control one's emotion
8. Regular practice at using oneself in order to discover more about others

All of these are ultimately embodied in improvisation which shows the outward development of each resource (209).

Planning for Creative Drama

A typical creative drama lesson would include a warm-up or limbering up activities which focus on: (1) concentration and sensory imagination; (2) individual role playing activities; (3) large or small group improvisation; (4) reflection. Some ideas for each of these are listed here.

Limbering Up Activities

Can you imagine yourself to be a:

- tire . . . . driven over a nail

- an ice cream cone . . . . left on the table
- a balloon . . . . let go
- an egg . . . . knocked off a table
- a power mower . . . . turned on
- a rubber band . . . . stretched out
- a watermelon . . . . dropped by someone
- a stick of match . . . . lit
- an electric mixer . . . . plugged in
- a stick of fireworks . . . . lit
- a marshmallow on a stick . . . . put over the fire
- a kernel of popcorn . . . . put on the heat
- an eraser . . . . rubbed on paper
- a mechanical toy . . . . turned on

The role of the teacher is most important in these early exercises. You should encourage children to talk about the characters they are portraying. "What does it feel like to be driving a truck?" "What did you think when you realized you were lost in the woods?" This helps to develop concentration and involvement. You also need to help children evaluate and refine their own pantomime: "What could you do to show the road suddenly becoming bumpy?" A general question may be more appropriate: "What did you like about what you did?" "What would you change?" These questions create stronger visual images and encourage careful observation. By observing people, children learn appropriate movement and gestures and are better able to portray believable characters.

Concentration Exercises

Children must be able to concentrate in order to make the creations of their imaginations vivid. Early exercises in concentration start with the use of the five senses. These exercises should be regular even while other activities are proceeding. Often they will be a part of other activities or used as a warm-up at the beginning of the sessions.

Listening

1. Listen to sounds outside of the building, outside of the room, and inside of the room.
2. Listen and identify the sounds.
3. Pay attention to just one sound. Try to imagine a person connected with the sound.
4. With the whole class or in pairs, discuss the sounds heard.
5. With your eyes closed, identify sounds made by the teacher.
6. Remember the order in which the sounds were made.
7. In pairs and later in groups have one partner make sounds while the other partner guesses the source of the sound.

8. Pass sounds around a circle.

Looking

1. Look at things that are very personal, such as the palm of a hand.
2. Look at things within the environment, then look at things outside the immediate environment.
3. With a partner examine and discuss, in detail, one object.
4. Observe arrangement of objects on a table. After changes have been made, identify them.
5. A member of a pair goes through a whole sequence of movement. The other repeats.
6. With the whole group play "Simon Says" in rhythm, using different parts of the body progressively.
7. One group arranges itself into a statue. The other group observes and repeats the same statue.

Use of Space

1. Fill as much space as you can (give motivation).
2. Stretch from side to side (give motivation).
3. Use your hands to keep the walls from closing in on you.
4. You are being sought after by the police. Make yourself small enough to hide in a small box.
5. The only way to get out of the house on fire is through a small narrow tunnel . . . see if you can get out of this house.

Use of Weight

1. You are trapped in a hold; the only way to get out is to lift the trap door which is very heavy.
2. You are trying to keep someone from pushing your door open.
3. You are a very light object. (Name some) The wind blows you all over. What happens?
4. There are a whole lot of different sizes of stones in your way . . . you'll have to carry them over to the other side so you can continue to drive your car. Show how heavy your stones are.

Activities to Stimulate the Imagination

Here are a list of activities which will stimulate imagination through sensory impressions:

Hearing:

- hear a sound early in the morning that rouses you to specific action
- be startled by an unexpected crash
- listen to a band in a circus parade
- hear a sound like a far-off voice while exploring a dark cave
- listen to a sea shell

- ring a bell . . . .Think about what it reminds you of
- respond to music

Touch:

- walk barefooted on cool sand, hot sand, wet sand
- walk into the ocean
- try to cross a stream . . . . step on a rock
- pull bubble gum and get some stuck on your face
- get cobwebs out of your hair, face
- pick up a baby kitten
- scour a pan
- try on shoes of different sizes

Taste:

- try a new dish
- drink ice cold lemonade on a hot day
- drink chocolate that is too hot
- lick a frosting bowl
- peel and eat an orange
- eat corn on the cob

Smell:

- walk into the house and smell your favorite cookies
- smell a skunk
- smell different kinds of foods
- walk around a garden

Exercises for Developing Imagination Through Story-Making

The following exercises also use sensory impressions to stimulate the imagination. In these exercises, the children make up stories in response to their sensory impressions.

Listening

1. Use rhythmic sounds to stimulate associations, for example, tambourine
2. Use short passages of recorded music for story-making.

Sight

1. Pass objects around a group. Compose a group story from the objects.
2. Make up a story an object at different periods of time or seasons.
3. Make up a story after beginning or ending is given.
4. Give students an object which they can imagine is anything they choose. They can create stories around it, for example, Magic Ring.

5. Use pictures to stimulate stories.
6. Make up stories from ink blot and paint blot pictures.

Touch

1. While students have eyes closed, pass around an object for them to touch, for example, a peeled grape. Have them make up stories.
2. Touch things in places such as a musty old attic. Respond to textures.

Smell

1. Have students create stories around a pleasant, mysterious, or terrifying smell.

IMPROVISATION

Improvisation is playmaking without a script. It moves from simple being and doing to the addition of conflict, attention to characterization, and response to conflict, atmosphere, mood, and emotion. The exercises used for speaking, defining the senses, developing the imagination, and beginning movement can also be used to start improvisations.

Ideas for Pantomimes and Characterization

1. Men moving a piano, large glass, etc.
2. Explorers setting up camp.
3. Witches putting ingredients into a cauldron.
4. Servants preparing a feast
5. Toys in a toy shop
6. Animals
7. Circus acts
8. House burning
9. Accidents
10. Telephone pole
11. Restaurants
12. Machines
13. Sports

Ideas for Improvisation

Any of the above with conflict added.

1. Astronauts assembling a space platform in outer space.
2. Miners working to reinforce a pit that is caving in.
3. Clumsy men getting a grand piano down a staircase.
4. Craftsmen putting work on display.
5. Divers clearing a wreck undersea.
6. Explorers loading their ship.

7. Refugees piling up possessions prior to leaving country.
8. King hunting in the forest.
9. Children in haunted house.

Story Dramatization of Literature

Improvisations may also be based on a story. After the story has been read or told, children plan how to organize it. Discussion should include descriptions of the characters and a review of the plot. For manageability and organization, divide the plot into scenes. For example, in "The Three Billy Goats Gruff", each goat's crossing would be a separate scene. When the teacher feels that the group has the details of a scene well in mind they may begin to play it.

Before you end a session it is important to critique the playing with the participants. Did you tell the story? Would the author be pleased with the characterizations? How would you improve it next time? What did you learn? With each replaying it is hoped that the participants will gain deeper insights, more freedom, and self-confidence.

Reflection

This is the most important part of the drama process. It is where learning on the enactive level is processed and organized. In describing the work of Dorothy Heathcotte, a leader in educational drama, Betty Jane Wagner says, "She knows what her own goal is and imagines beforehand what responses from the children are likely and how she can use these to work toward her end. Her aim is always to reflect on those facets of that experience that are part of the universal lot of humanity," (p. 21). This connection with the universal meaning of experience occurs during reflection. For example, the point of children dramatizing the story of Cinderella is not to cover a series of events but to discover in the playing what the story has to say to them. It is not just Cinderella scrubbing the floor while her stepsisters taunt her, but "What would it feel like to be in that situation?" "Do you know anyone else who has been taunted?" "How does it feel?"

Subjects for Dramatization

Dorothy Heathcotte speaks of the need to arrest students attention. Drama should not be watered down. It should not be fairies and flowers, but real situations and real problems to solve.

Start small. Start with one of the exercises suggested earlier, or a scene from a book you have just read to the class. When dramatizing a scene from a book, warm-up activities should be related to the scene and prepare children for further playing. Use a signal that the children have agreed to respond to with silence. "When you hear the bell, freeze."

Start slowly. Don't let children continue playing when their concentration is broken. Have them move in "slow motion." Start with short playing sessions. Sometimes only a few minutes. Children's ability to hold concentration increases with practice.

Evaluation of Creative Drama

Evaluation of creative drama is best done by the asking of questions between teacher and student, student and student, and teacher and teacher. These questions will center around the three elements most necessary to the success of a dramatic experience: concentration, social interaction, student involvement. Some possible questions are listed here.

1. Did all members of the group participate fully in the activity?
2. Did the group concentrate on the specific problem to be solved?
3. Could all members participate in ways that felt comfortable to each?
4. Did the improvisation depend more on narration (explaining) than on action (showing and doing)?
5. Was enough rapport established to permit each member to adjust to unforseen circumstances? If so, how? If not, why not?
6. Did the ideas used come from all members of the group or just a few?
7. Were people able to listen to each other's ideas, or were they more interested in presenting their own?
8. Could the group communicate to observers what it had set out to?
9. Where did the ideas for the work originate? How might they be developed further?
10. How were differences of opinion resolved? Did the means satisfy most people? How were they determined and used?
11. Did someone have to act as leader, or was the group able to function communally? How was this decided?
12. What was learned from this experience?
13. Did the group enhance the work by using sound, color, or texture where appropriate? How did the group decide to use or not to use these?
14. How would the group change the work, given the chance to do it a second time, having learned from the first? Why?

OTHER ORAL COMMUNICATION ACTIVITIES

Other oral language activities that enhance children's oral communication abilities include making announcements and introductions, giving directions and explanations, proper use of the telephone, planning and constructing interviews, and learning parlimentary procedure. Children should have experiences with each of these. Elementary language arts textbooks provide excellent examples and activity ideas for developing these oral communication skills. In addition, many can be integrated with other content areas.

ACTIVITIES

1. Prepare a card file of prose and poetry to be used for storytelling and choral speaking.
2. Select a poem for choral speaking. With a group of people in your class discuss how stress, volume, pauses, and enunciation will communicate the groups interpretation of the poem. Practice and present the poem to others in your methods class.
3. Practice telling a story. Present it to a group of children or to your methods class.
4. Plan a creative drama lesson based on the story "Caps for Sale." Make certain that you plan warm-up exercises and reflection questions.

REFERENCES

BLOOM, BENJAMIN. (1956). *Taxonomy of Educational Objectives.* New York: Longmans, Green and Co.

COODY, BETTY AND DAVID NELSON. (1982). *Teaching Elementary Language Arts: A Literature Approach.* Belmont, Calif.: Wadsworth Publishing Co.

ELLIS, ARTHUR K. (1986). *Teaching and Learning Social Studies.* Boston: Allyn & Bacon, Inc.

FARNSWORTH, KATHYRN. (1981, February). Storytelling in the classrom—not an impossible dream. *Language Arts.* 58, 2, 162-67.

FOX, SHARON E. AND VIRGINIA G. ALLEN. (1983). *The Language Arts: An Integrated Approach.* New York: Holt, Rinehart and Winston.

JACKSON, PHILIP. (1986). *Life in Classrooms.* New York: Holt, Rhinehart, and Winston.

JOHNSON, EDNA, EVELYN R. SICKELS, AND FRANCES C. SAYERS. (1970). *Anthology of Children's Literature.* Boston: Houghton Mifflin Company.

MCCASLIN, NELLIE. (1984). *Creative Drama in the Classroom* (4th ed) New York: Longman, Inc.

MOFFETT, JAMES. (1967). *Drama: What is Happening.* Champaign, Ill.: National Council of Teachers of English.

SIKS, GERALDINE. (1958). *Creative Dramatics, An Art for Children.* New York: Harper & Row.

STEWIG, JOHN W. (1983). *Exploring Language Arts in the Elementary Classroom.* New York: Holt, Rinehart and Winston.

STEWIG, JOHN W. (1978, March). Storyteller: Endangered Species? *Language Arts* 55, 3, 339-45.

WAGNER, BETTY JANE. (1976). *Dorothy Heathcotte: Drama As A Learning Medium.* Washington D.C.: National Education Association.

WARD, WINIFRED. (1957). *Playmaking with Children.* New York: Appleton-Century-Crafts.

WAY, BRIAN. (1967) *Development Through Drama.* Atlantic Highlands, N.J.: Humanitus Press.

Appendix

Stories and poems are taken from Geraldine Sik's book, *Children's Literature for Dramatization* and Winifred Ward's book, *Stories to Dramatize.*

POETRY

Ellison, Alice, "Sing a Song of Seasons"
Stevenson, Robert Louis, "At the Seaside"
Stevenson, Robert Louis, "Marching Song"
Boyden, Polly Chase, "Mud"
Baird, Phyllis Lee, "Picknicking"
"Riddle-Dee-Dee"
"A Star"
"A Candle"
"Baby Seeds"
Smith, William Joy, "Fish"
Shakespeare, William, "A Fairy"
Dickinson, Emily. "Morning"
Farejon, Eleanor, "Circus"
Child, Lydia Marie, "Thanksgiving Day"
Talbot, Ethel "Crab Apple"
Mackey, Vivian, "Hunting for a Halloween Cat"
Siks, Geraldine, "Women in Moss"
Horace "Country Mouse and the Town House"
LaFontaine "Grasshopper and the Ant"
Fontaine "The Turtle and the Rabbit"
Noyes, Alfred, "The New Duckling"
Tennyson, Alfred, "Charge of the Light Brigade"
de la Mare, Walter, "I Saw Three Witches"
Marryman, M., "The Pirate Don Durk of Dowdee"
Moore, Clement, "A Visit From St. Nicholas"
Thayer, Ernest, "Casey at the Bat"
Johnson, James Weldon, "Creation"
"King John and the Abbot of Canterbury" (ballad)
Justus, May, "Winds A-Blowing"
Hay, John, "The Enchanted Shirt"
Get Up and Bar the Door (ballad)

STORIES FOR YOUNG CHILDREN

Flack, Marjorie, *Ask Mr. Bear*
Potter, Beatrice, *Tale of Peter Rabbit*
Herford, Oliver, *The Elf and the Doormouse*

Dasent, G., *The Three Billy Goats Gruff*
Bryant, Sara, *The Little Pink Rose*
Bannerman, Helen, *Little Black Sambo*
Grimm, *The Musicians of Bremen*
Baily, *Little Rabbit Who Wanted Red Wings*
Grimm, *The Elf and the Shoemaker*
Southey, R., *Goldilocks and the Trhee Bears*
Harris, Joel, *Wonderful Tar Baby Story*
Brown, Margaret L., *Home for a Bunny Bunny*
McCaslin, Nellie. Creative Drama in the Classrooms 1986 *Peddler and the Monkeys*
(Hawaiian Legend) *Pua and the Menehunes*
Aesop, *Lion and the Mouse*
Gingerbread Boy
(Russian Tale) *The Big Turnip*

STORIES FOR OLDER CHILDREN

Perrault, Charles, *Cinderella*
Leuser, Eleanor, *Clown Who Forgot How to Laugh*
Siks, Geraldine, *A Legend of Spring*
Fyleman, Rose, *The Princess Who Could Not Cry*
Grimm, *Rumplestiltskin*
Grimm, *Sleeping Beauty*
Grimm, *Snow White and Seven Dwarfs*
Cooper, George, *The Wonderful Weaver*
Hans Christian, *Emperor's New Clothes*
Alden, Raymond, *Why the Chimes Rang*
Grimm, *The Frog Prince*
(Norwegian Folktale) *Boots and His Brothers*
Grimm, *Snow White and Rose Red*
Anderson, Hans Christian, *Ugly Duckling*
(French Fairy Tale) *Drakestail*
(Greek Myth) *Pandora*
Sawyer, *Voyage of the Wee Red Cap*

MUSIC

Three main series:
Adventures in Music, R.C.A. Victor
Bowmar Orchestral Library, (#51, 52, 54, 59, 61, 64)
R.C.A. Record Library for Elementary Schools

Giants, trolls, bears, etc.

"Wheelbarrow Motive", Anderson, R.C.A. *Record Library*
"The Comedians", Kabalensky, R.C.A. *Adventures in Music*

Happy mood, lyrical, smooth, beautiful

"The Lark Song", Tchaikowsky, *Bowmar #52*
"Flying Birds", Anderson, R.C.A. *Rhythmic Activities*
"Vale", Walton, R.C.A. *Adventures in Music*
"Anna Lucia", Lecuona, R.C.A. *Adventures in Music*
"Ballet of Sylphs", R.C.A. *Adventures in Music*
"The Swan," Saint Saens, R.C.A. *Adventures in Music*
"Aquarium", Saint Saens, *Bowmar #51*

Waiting, growing, hatching

"In the Hall of the Mountain King", Greig, *R.C.A. Adventures*
"Wheat Dance", Ginastera, R.C.A. *Adventures*
"The Anxious Leaf", Donaldson, *Bowmar #52*
"Ballet of Unhatched Chicks", Moussorgsky, R.C.A. *Adventures*
"Poet and His Lyre", Donaldson, *Bowmar #52*

Light, gay movement (small creatures)

"Tiptoe March", Anderson, R.C.A. *Adventures*
"Anna Lucia", listed above
"Music Box", Lisdov, *Bowmar #64*
"Les Pifferari", Gounod, R.C.A. *Rhythmic Activities*
"Bouree and Minuet II", Handel, R.C.A. *Adventures, Gr. 3 Vol. 1*

Reflective mood: characterization of older people

"Traumeri", Schuman, R.C.A. *Adventures*
"Poet and Lyre", Donaldson, R.C.A. *Adventures*

Big, slow moving creatures

"March", Follaender, R.C.A. *Rhythmic Activities*
"Pantomime", Kabalensky, R.C.A. *Adventures, Vol. 1*
"Byb", R.C.A. *Adventures, Vol.2*

Horses

"Galloping Horses", Anderson, R.C.A. *Rhythmic Activities*
"Running Horses", Anderson, R.C.A. *Rhythmic Activities*
"High Stepping Horses", Anderson, R.C.A. *Rhythmic Activities*

Music for Marching (clocks, pumpkins, soldiers)

"March of Tin Soldiers", Tchaikowsky, R.C.A. *Rhythmic Activities*

Mice

"Etude Joyeuse", Kopylow, R.C.A. *Rhythmic Activities*, Vol. 7
"Non Presto", R.C.A. *Adventures, Gr. 4, Vol. 2*

7

LISTENING
The Other Half of Oral Communication

Listening is the first form of communication that an individual engages in and it remains an essential skill throughout life. We spend 45 per cent of our waking hours listening—listening to friends, co-workers, family members, and the media. The products we consume, our political and economic philosophies, how we relate to one another are all affected by the way we listen (Wolvin). Employers recognize the importance of listening. Business, government, and human relations professions teach listening skills. One international company advertises that it instructs each of its employees in listening. It is apparent that listening is an important life skill.

Listening is also important within the educational setting. Listening is at the core of the teaching-learning process. Students listen between 42 and 58 per cent of their classroom time (Bird, Markgraf, Wilt). Unsurprisingly, students who listen well, learn. Listening is also fundamental in the development of other communication forms. As children listen, they experience language, become acquainted with concepts and ideas, and develop a vocabulary to be used in speaking, reading, and writing. It is, therefore, important to help children become effective listeners.

LISTENING IN THE ELEMENTARY SCHOOL

While the importance of listening is readily acknowledged among educators, listening instruction is largely ignored in the classroom. This is evidenced by research, surveys by Goldstein and Anderson, a lack of textbook attention observed by Landry, and the frequency with which teachers ask children to "listen" and "pay attention." Lundsteen suggests four reasons for this neglect.

She states that it is assumed because children have two ears, they can listen. In other words, listening skills develop naturally and there isn't any need for instruction. While it is true that children enter school having acquired considerable listening ability, to leave the development of these skills to evolution is to hope that all goes well. If school children had acquired listening expertise, teachers would not have to repeat directions or request that children "listen carefully." The listening abilities of young children are rudimentary and they vary greatly depending on individual language-listening backgrounds. Effectiveness in listening is developed through ongoing organized instruction.

Secondly, because teachers have had inadequate listening training themselves, they are uncomfortable and uncertain about planning listening instruction. As a result, listening instruction is either omitted or teachers turn to the security of a commercial program. While the few commercial programs available identify skills and procedures to facilitate listening development, they lack the flexibility and tailoring of a teacher designed program.

A third reason for the neglect of listening instruction is the "hidden behavior of listening." That is, we are unable to observe what someone does when they listen. Despite the numerous investigations of this complex, cognitive process, it is incompletely understood. We, therefore, find ourselves in an interesting situation. While we know what affects listening, we are uncertain about listening as a process (Pearson).

Since listening is clouded by confusion, it is not surprising that teachers are uncomfortable about what to teach or how to teach children to listen. They may even ask if it is teachable. Researchers have investigated this question thoroughly. Trivette (1961), in working with fifth grade students, demonstrated that children who received specific training in listening for main ideas, details, and inferences made significant gains in these skills and showed improvement in other skills, such as, listening to directions and understanding word meaning. Hollow, Edgar, Fawcett, Canfield, Norwich, Childers, and others cited in literature reviews (Russell, Devine, Duker) have concluded that children's listening abilities improve with instruction.

Lastly, Lundsteen suggests that listening instruction receives so little attention because the school day is aleady overcrowded. While children spend the majority of their school day listening, instruction in listening is the last priority. Van Wingerden found, within the language arts, teachers devote the most instruction time to reading, followed by writing, speaking, and listening. This dominance of reading and writing is currently supported by an emphasis on "basics." Under PL 95-561, the Office of Education has recently added listening to the list of basic skills. This action stresses the importance of learning to listen effectively and encourages teachers to make room for the teaching of listening within their crowded day.

LISTENING THEORY

Helping children to become effective listeners begins with an examination of what is involved in listening. As previously stated, listening is a complex mental process about which we are uncertain; however, after much study and careful analysis, researchers have provided us with a theoretical framework. While the vocabulary varies with each writer, the process of listening has been consistently divided into the following components.

The first component is *hearing*. The terms hearing and listening are mistakenly used interchangeably. Hearing refers to the physiologic process of receiving sound waves through the ear. Listening involves both the process of hearing and interpreting what has been heard. This is an important distinction for teachers as they must be careful not to misdiagnose a child's inability to hear as his or her failure to listen.

The second component, *attending*, refers to selecting and focusing on a specific aural stimulus. This requires that the listener filter out other environmental sounds and concentrate, in order that the message may be comprehended.

Comprehension, the third component, is a complex cortical process by which meaning is obtained from the message. While we are uncertain about the exact process, we do know that it requires an understanding of the language code at four levels, the phonological, syntactic, semantic, and text structure level (Pearson, 1982).

At the phonological level, listening demands that one be able to process discrete segments of sound. For example, the child who cannot distinguish between /tap/ and /top/ will have trouble listening. Other phonemic demands include a sensitivity to rising and falling voice patterns, or intonation ("You are going swimming?" or "You are going swimming!"); to stress ("You are going swimming?"); and to pauses, so that sounds are not missed or distorted (I saw vs. ice saw).

Listening at the syntactic level, in general, requires an understanding of language elements and their relationship to one antother. For example, one must be able to recognize surface structure cues (past tense, plurals, subject, verb, and object locations); and be able to "disambiguate" or recognize that sentences such as "The missionaries are ready to serve" have more than one interpretation.

At the semantic level, listening includes both knowledge of individual and lexical items and the interrelationship of lexical items within a sentence.

At the text structure level, listening demands that one understand the typical organization of narration (central point, sequence of events, location or setting, cause and effect, supporting ideas and details).

By integrating all of these fundamentals to the process of gaining knowledge, the listener is able to obtain meaning from the message and he or she then correlates this with previous knowledge and experience.

Effective listening involves the simultaneous coordination and organization of each of the components. In order for comprehension to occur, one must hear and pay attention to what has been said. A listener not adept at any one of the components will require increased processing time or attain only partial comprehension. The school must, therefore, be concerned with the reinforcement of hearing, attending, and comprehending.

CLASSROOM ENVIRONMENT

One of the most important steps in developing effective listening is to minimize physical distractions within the environment. In any classroom, there are a number of competing stimuli that affect a child's ability to hear and/or attend. Hall noise, insufficient ventilation, nearby classmates talking, an overheated or underheated room, all inhibit hearing and attending. These factors are a particular concern for the child with a limited attention span. Attending requires effort, it requires that the listener maintain concentration and follow the speaker so he or she moves from one idea to the next. As the child with a short attention span has difficulty maintaining attention (rather than an inability to attend), physical distractions compound this listener's problem.

While it is not possible to control all distractions, some conditions may be improved by the way we structure our classrooms. An open or closed door or window will help regulate noise, ventilation, and heat. A rug placed in the room will diminish sound. Specify quiet times. Schedule activities that demand careful listining when the band will not be rehearsing.

Additionally, children need to understand that the acceptable classroom noise level is relative to the activity. If the children are practicing a play, the acceptable noise level will be high. On the other hand, listening to guest poet necessitates a quiet classroom. Children will readily become sensitive to variances in noise levels if you consistently pre-establish and enforce an acceptable minimum.

TEACHERS AND LISTENING

As a teacher, you need to be aware that the way you listen, plan, and present significantly shapes your students' listening attitudes and skills. Whether you are cognizant of them or not, your everyday actions serve as a behavior model for your students. Therefore, we need to consciously evaluate our own listening habits to make certain that they are what we want children to emulate. Stammer suggests three self-check questions.

1. Do you maintain eye contact with the speaker? Within the majority of western cultures, looking at the speaker shows that he or she has your undivided attention and that you value what that person is saying. Maintaining eye contact demonstrates attentive listening and instills self-confidence in the speaker's ability to communicate.

Evidence of listening, however, is not consistent among cultures. The American Indian child, for example, is taught to listen and show repect by looking away (Maccoby). Within the Black culture, being in the proximity of the speaker implies listening. There is no reason to demonstrate it. Teachers need to be aware of and sensitive to such cultural variations.

2. Do you respond to the speaker quickly and thoughtfully? Not all listening situations require an overt response, (in fact, by responding verbally, you become the sender of communication and are no longer the listener) but by quickly answering a child's question or acknowledging that

you hear what someone said, indicates that you were listening and that listening is important to you. Too often, however, teachers are preoccupied with their many responsibilites and only half-listen to children. As an unfortunate example demonstrates: During "sharing time" a boy was eagerly relating an event when in the midst of his dialogue, the teacher filled out the daily attendance slip and sent it, via another child, to the office. This not only deflated the boy's self image, but such unconscious actions convey an apathetic attitude toward listening.

3. Do you listen to what children mean as well as to what they say? A good listener uses context clues to gain insight into a student's listening and thinking skills. For example, if you ask who was the first president, the child who answers "Washington" listened well and answered correctly. The child who answers "cherry tree," heard the question but, perhaps could only remember the story about young Washington chopping down a cherry tree. Or, he or she went from thinking about Washington to the story about young George. If your response, to the second child, indicates that you understand the association between their confused answer and the correct one, you will be modeling conscientious listening.

ORGANIZATION AND PRESENTATION

As you plan instruction, remember to consider the listening skills that are demanded of each situation. In doing so, you will insure against inadvertently promoting poor listening habits. One of the first considerations in organizing for instruction is to set appropriate time estimations, don't expect children to listen beyond their ability to attend. Second, it is important to carefully organize directions and explanations. Comprehension is facilitated and you avoid wasting time reiterating information. In addition, clean, concisely stated instructions convey your enthusiasm and knowledge of the subject. Children see that you put a premium on the task at hand and that you expect them to listen carefully. Conversely, a disorganized presentation tells listeners that you do not understand or value what is being said and that it doesn't really matter if they listen. This develops sloppy listening habits.

Sometimes it becomes necessary to plan or alternate ways of presenting a topic or giving directions. When you can anticipate that the comprehension of a tack or subject will be difficult, it is a good idea to paraphrase (not repeat) your original statements. Occasionally, one or two children will not understand the instructions. In this case, it is better to privately rephrase the directions for these individuals rather than lose the attention of the rest of the children.

Fourth, attention is improved when teachers make a conscious effort to add a variety to their speech. Variances in volume, pitch, tempo, style, and gestures make what you have to say more interesting and can also facilitate the comprehension of oral instruction.

In contradistinction, unnecessary mazes ("ah", "um") make attending tedious and comprehension difficult. Mazes also slow the rate of speech and allow some children to be distracted. Research has demonstrated that children can comprehend oral material at twice the rate of normal presentation and that with instruction and practice they improve in comprehension (Orr, Fiedman, Miller).

A REASON FOR LISTENING

The primary aim of the listening experience is to understand what the speaker is saying. Comprehension, however, is limited by the information that is attended to. Listeners will not attend to the speaker's words unless they perceive them to be of interest or importance. An effective way to facilitate paying attention is to provide children with a reason for listening. The teacher may do this by indicating what the children are to focus on. For example:

> "Listen to the story and see if you would have done the same thing that Anita did."
>
> "There were three major differences that triggered the dispute. Be prepared to discuss them later."
>
> "As I read, please determine which items are fact and which are opinion."

Statements such as these, set a purpose and guide children's listening experience.

A pre-listening discussion will also motivate students and establish a purpose for listening. To begin a pre-listening discussion, the teacher introduces the topic and as children share what they know about the subject, they become aware of gaps in their knowledge and/or areas about which they disagree. This stimulates a need for listening. Most importantly, however, " . . . students know *why* they are about to listen and *what* they are expected to learn from listening" (Gold, p.139).

In the larger sense, establishing purposeful listening extends beyond the immediate task. It involves establishing a purpose for learning. By making content material relevant to children's lives ("this is how you would determine what baseball hat is less expensive"), involving them in decisions about learning (one child may decide to write a report about the Japanese life style while another may want to put on a play), and challenging students to learn through problem solving. You are establishing a purpose for being in school and paying attention to what is heard in the classroom.

BACKGROUND

An individual's background is an important factor affecting listening comprehension. Unfamiliarity with the speaker's regional terminology exemplifies how the listener's comprehension can be handicapped. A teacher from the midwest, talking to children in Phoenix, asked them to stand near the "bubbler." Some of them remained at their desks. While these children had paid attention, they lacked the background knowledge to understand this midwestern term for drinking fountain. Similarly, when talking about subject matter, children who have background knowledge about the topic find it easier to comprehend than do those deficient in previous topical knowledge. While it would not be practical to preassess each child's background knowledge for every topic discussed in the classroom, there are many instances where it would be advantageous to do so. One way is to informally question the students about their previous experiences with the topic at hand. In doing so, you learn about their existing knowledge, make a prediction about their ability to comprehend the forthcoming lecture or discussion, and decide either to continue or provide the necessary informational base. Another means of preassessment is that of recognition questioning. In a study by Hare and Devine, the researchers found that asking children multiple choice questions about a topic reflected the children's breadth and depth of their previous knowledge, required very little time for administration or evaluation, and simplified response requirements for younger and poorer students.

IMPROVEMENT THROUGH INSTRUCTION

It is evident, from the previous discussion, that the teacher is a key factor influencing the development of listening. By minimizing environmental distractions, demonstrating attentive conscientious listening, careful planning and presenting of lessons, providing feedback, establishing a reason for listening, and determining and building upon the student's knowledge, the teacher has set the stage for effective listening instruction. While every oral situation presents an opportunity for improving listening skills, an effective listening program includes planned activities. Research has demonstrated that direct listening instruction is more effective that incidental approaches. Direct instruction focuses the student's attention on their individual listening abilities (Pearson). For this reason, listening activities need to be planned carefully with attention to the following guidelines:

1. Activities ought to be flexible, allowing the teacher to structure them to children's varying abilities.
2. Activities ought to be based on the children's previous knowledge and experience. This allows them to concentrate on the listening task and minimizes

distractions caused by introducing unfamiliar concepts or vocabulary.
3. Activities which require a verbal response from the listener are more effective than those which do not.
4. As there are different types of listening for different purposes, instruction in the varying skills is needed.
5. Provide for evaluation.

Among the many possibilities, the following examples have been selected as they comply with the above guidelines. Teachers need to consider the capabilities, previous experiences, and needs of the children prior to adapting and utilizing such activities.

Discriminative Listening

Discriminative listening refers to the ability to distinguish likenesses and differences among sounds. The ability to discriminate auditorally varies considerably among children, especially those just entering school. At one end of the continuum are children who need practice differentiating among gross speech sounds. Many young children who are able to discern individual speech sounds and have adequate hearing, are unable to discriminate between similar sound phonemes. For example, a child may not have had sufficient exposure to speech sound variations to distinguish between /bill/ and /pill/ or /bomb/ and /balm/, thereby reducing comprehension. Since comprehension is the goal of listening, adequate auditory discrimination is fundamental to all listening situations. There are many elementary school children whose skills in this area need instructional attention. A good way to begin this is by listening to environmental sounds.

Sound specification. Working in small groups or with partners, one child creates a sound—ringing bell, tapping pencil, two pieces of sandpaper rubbed together, various animal sounds—and another child identifies the source of the sound. These sounds may be pretaped and used by individuals in a listening center or with the small group organization.

Sound pairs. Here, the children listen to, identify, and compare similar sounds. Pairs, such as tapping an empty glass and tapping a glass full of water, ringing sleigh bells and ringing a single bell, turning on an electric razor and turning on a vacuum cleaner, are pre-taped. As the tape is played back, the children identify the sounds and discuss the similarities and differences of the sounds.

Which word? Ask the children to listen to a series of words and have them identify the one that does not belong with the others.

boy	bag	balloon	shell	(initial sound)
calf	dog	puff	off	(final sound)
can	laugh	rat	pill	(medial sound)
switch	hitch	itch	tree	(rhyme)
shine	ice	toad	iron	(long vowel)

This may be done in partners or in a group where the children respond by writing their answers.

Same or different? Children are to listen to pairs of words, raise their hands if the words are the same or keep them down if the words are different (can, car; car, tar; sat, mat; sat, sat).

Voice identification. Audio tape each child's voice. While recording, instruct them to use their natural voices but to speak nonsense words. In doing so, the other children will not be able to identify them from the content of what they said. Play the tape back and have the children identify their classmates.

COMPREHENSIVE LISTENING

Comprehensive listening refers to accurate, uncritical listening for the purpose of understanding and remembering the content of what was said. Comprehensive listening is listening to learn. It is an important skill utilized daily in the classroom. As children listen to instructions, lectures, discussions, and announcements, they are engaged in comprehensive listening.

The focus of comprehensive listening varies. One may listen to learn the sequence of events, to follow directions in order to complete a task, to obtain the main idea, to learn specific details, and for other purposes. Children need practice in each of these areas of comprehensive listening, as research has found little transfer among them (Pearson). The following activities are representative of the many possible exercises that might be used to enhance comprehensive listening abilities. They will be most effective when adapted to group interests of ongoing topics of study.

ENHANCING SEQUENTIAL MEMORY

Sound imitation. Clap out a sound pattern (clap—clap, clap) and ask the children to imitate what they heard. Standard patterns may also be created by tapping a desk, stamping a foot, clicking the tongue, or vocaling (la, la,—la, la).

Sequencing stories. After reading a short story to the children, have them verbally relate the order of events. Sequentially arrange pictures depicting the course of action, or arrange sentence strips describing the sequence of events.

Variation: Tell a short story out of order, and then ask students to unscramble the story and arrange it in a logical sequence. (Again, this may be done verbally or by arranging pictures or sentence strips.)

Variation: Instead of a story, read a paragraph relating to an area of study, such as a series of events that lead to the Revolutionary War, or the steps in a science experiment.

Variation: Have the students unscramble sentences which you read aloud. For example: rain I today it doesn't hope.

LISTENING FOR DIRECTIONS

Do as I say. Ask a child to carry out three or more directions given at one time. For example, "Go to the chalkboard, pick up an eraser, and take it to Shanna." Or, "Walk backwards to the window, turn around three times, and return to your desk." As the children become more skillful, increase the complexity of the directions and allow more than one child to follow the directions at a time.

Textbook directions. For this exercise, each person must have a copy of the same book. Pre-tape or read a set of instructions that will help the children solve a puzzle by using information in a book or magazine. For example, "Turn to page 126 and count the number of pictures. Stay on that same page and find the fourth word in the second column and write down the last letter in that word. Count the number of words in the first paragraph, subtract 5, and turn to the page of the same number. Write down the first letter of the first word on the page. The instructions continue until the students spell out a word, such as "chocolate" (Adapted from Burnham, 1981).

Where next? The children are grouped in pairs, with a divider visually separating them. Each child has a map in front of him or her. For example, a map of the local neighborhood containing the school and several homes and landmarks along different roadways. One child decides on a route to get from school to home and traces it out on his or her map. The second child asks questions about how to get home and the first child provides directions. When the imaginary child is home, the students reverse roles (Adapted from Dickson, 1981).* See page 142

LISTENING FOR SPECIFIC INFORMATION OR DETAILS

Pass it on. This activity stresses the importance of listening carefully to details. Select a group of five children, ask four of them to leave the room. The class and the remaining participant then view a simple drawing, which the participant will describe to one of the other group members. Ask one participant to come back into the room and listen carefully to a description of a drawing as he or she will be asked to describe it to the next participant. Have the class note changes in the original description as it is passed on from one person to the next.

News notes. Tape, from the radio, the summary that is broadcast at the beginning of each hour. Tell the students that they will be hearing the news and are to listen for specific points. To focus their listening, write key questions on the board, "What bill is currently being debated in Congress?" "What was the outcome of last night's hockey game?" After listening to the tape, discuss the previous day's events using the questions as guidelines. As children become familiar with this format, the focusing questions can be eliminated and students can note the main idea in each news story (Adapted from Burnham).

LISTENING FOR MAIN IDEAS

Finding the main idea. Preselect a paragraph or short story to be read to the class. Write on the board three or four sentences containing subordinate ideas within the selection and one sentence identifying the main idea. Cover the sentences. Tell the children you are going to a selection and they are to listen for the main idea. Uncover the sentences and ask the children to identify the one that expresses the main idea.

ENHANCING SUMMARY SKILLS

Summarizing stories. Provide a two or three sentence summary of a familiar story and ask the children to identify the story. For example: "A girl visits a house when the owners are not there. She tastes the porridge, sits in the chairs, and naps in the beds. When the owners come home, she becomes frightened and runs away."

OBTAINING INFORMATION THROUGH INFERENCE

Comprehensive listening often involves listening to context in order to obtain understanding. The listener must be able to infer information that is not explicitly stated. To facilitate the development of this skill, read a selection, such as the one which follows, and then ask the children questions that require "listening between the lines." Prior to reading the students should know that they will be questioned about inferred information.

> As I looked across the cornfield, the frost covered stalks glistenend in the sun. Geese could be heard overhead. The wind began to blow and the leaves swirled and danced along the ground. Suddenly my cap was whisked from my head.
>
> What is the season of the year?
> What caused the speaker to lose his cap?
> Does this take place in the city or the country?

CRITICAL EVALUATIVE LISTENING

After meaning is obtained, the critical-evaluative listener then makes judgments regarding the message. In today's technocratic society, evaluating what we hear is especially important. Radio and television have become our primary sources of information and entertainment. Through these mass media forms, speakers have the ability to reach millions of people and thereby shape public opinion and significantly affect behavior. Devine writes:

> The professional persuaders, whether politicians, advertisers, or bakers at county fairs, have learned with Hitler, that it is in their listening that people are most vulnerable! Yet while speakers have developed the skills of persuasion, listeners, in general, have not learned to listen, especially listen carefully.

Critical-evaluative listening involves the ability to distinguish between relevant and irrelevant information, fact and opinion, inductive and deductive arguments, and verifiable and erroneous information; discerning and hasty generalizations, one-sided information, emotion, biases, and progaganda techniques; and an awareness of the effects of language, appeals, and spokespersons. There are many ways to develop these abilities. The following are but a few activities which nourish critical-evaluative listening.

Relevant-irrelevant information. One way to help students discern relevant and irrelevant information is to pre-tape a series of directions (e.g. putting a model together or playing a game) and include extraneous information. Then ask the students to identify necessary and unnecessary information.

Children's literature. Literature may be used to model emotions, biases, and opinions. Narration on character dialogue may be selected as examples of feelings, stereotypic attitudes, or viewpoints. Read the selection aloud and ask the students to identify, for example, what the character is feeling, how they were able to recognize those feelings, and what words convey emotion.

Variation: Have two students read a dialogue selection and then discuss the reading.

News Notes II. As a variation of News Notes, ask two or three children to tape different network's news broadcasts. When comparing the same news item, note the different methodologies of presentation and discuss the following questions. Is information presented objectively? Are statements backed up by verifiable data? Are hasty generalizations and/or stereotypic assumptions made? Are opinions presented as facts? Are conclusions drawn inductively or deductively? Are editorial arguments emotion-charged or logical?

Variation: the same questions may be asked of oral presentations, taped speeches, or articles read aloud.

Advertising. Analyzing advertisements such as television commercials and magazine ads helps children to develop many critical listening skills. The purpose of advertising is to present information that will cause the listener to think a certain way. This is accomplished through a variety of techniques.

Through the manipulation of language advertisers, consumers are led to believe many things that have only been implied. "Weasel words" (Tutolo, 1981) or ambiguous statements such as "can be," "virtually," "the feel of," or "refreshes" convince the listener that he or she hears things that have not been said. Words are also used as attention grabbers. "Announcing," "magic," "last chance," and many others are especially effective when combined with motivating music and/or scenes. Use of the simile and metaphor imply positive associations between the product and a consumer's need or desire. Repetition of key words or phrases tend to make them memorable and believable.

Advertisers also empty famous spokespersons to present their product. Listeners tend to feel that a celebrity or an accepted authority is trustworthy, thereby making his or her endorsement more credible. Similarly, an emotional response may be elicited by appealing to the listener's sense of adventure, guilt, pleasure, achievement, or sexual attraction.

Other techniques include only presenting one point of view, using sweeping generalizations, and implying that everyone uses the product.

Children need to be aware of these techniques. Wright and Laminark outline a unit they use to develop critical listening. They begin by discussing the purpose of and techniques used in advertising. The second step is to examine print media and taped television commercials to identify the commercial language and techniques used. Thirdly, test the product. That is, identify the producer's claim and test it. Lastly, draw conclusions about the validity of the claim.

ACTIVITIES

1. Write a lecture-listening lesson. Write out prediscussion questions that will give students a reason to listen.
2. Ask a group of friends to discuss the outcome of a football game, a movie they have recently seen, or any topic of interest. Tape the conversation. In your methods class listen to the tape and evaluate your friend's listening habits. Did speakers have an opportunity to finish their sentences or were they interrupted? Were comments made in response to previous statements or were they unrelated comments? Did one or two people dominate the conversation?
3. Look at several elementary language textbooks and evaluate their treatment of listening. Do they devote much attention to listening instruction? Which activities would you use? Why wouldn't you select others? How would you supplement the listening activities?

REFERENCES

ANDERSON, HAROLD A.. (1954, April). Needed research in listening. *Elementary English*, 215–24.

BIRD, DONALD., (1955, April). Are you listening? *Office Executive*, 18–19.

BURNHAM, LARRY D. (1981, January). To hear or not to hear. *Teacher*, 96, 5, 68–69.

CANFIELD, ROBERT. (1961, December). How useful are lessons on listening? *Elementary School Journal*, 62, 146–51.

CHILDERS, PERRY R. (1970, summer). Listening ability is a modifiable skill. *Journal of Experimental Education*, 38, 1–3.

DEVINE, THOMAS G. (1978, January). Listening: what do we know after fifty years of research and theorizing? *Journal of Reading*, 21, 296–304.

DICKSON, W. PATRICK AND JANICE H. PATTERSON. (1981, January). Evaluating referential communication games for teaching speaking and listening skills. *Communication Education*, 30, 11–21.

DUCKER, SAM. (1969) "Listening", In *Encyclopedia of Educational Research*, ed. Robert L. Ebel. New York: Macmillan, 747–751.

EDGAR, E. K. (1961) The validation of four methods of improving listening abilities. Doctoral

dissertation University of Pittsburgh, Pittsburgh.
FAWCETT, ANNABEL E. (1966, May) Training in listening, *Elementary English*, 43, 473–76.
FRIEDMAN, PAUL G. (1978) *Listening Process: Attention, Understanding, Evaluation*. Washington, D.C.: National Education Association.
GOLD, PATRICIA COHEN. (1981, November) The directed listening-language experience approach. *Journal of Reading*, 138–41.
GOLDSTEIN, HARRY. (1940) Reading and listening at various controlled rates. *Contributions to Education*. New York: Teachers College, Columbia University.
HARE, VICTORIA CHOU AND DENISE A. DEVINE. (1983, January/February) Topical knowledge and topical interest predictors of listening comprehension. *Journal of Educational Research*. 76, 157–160.
HOLLOW, SISTER MARY KEVIN. (1955). An experimental study of listening comprehension at the intermediate grade level. Doctoral dissertation, New York: Fordum University.
LANDRY, DONALD L. (1969, May). The neglect of listening. *Elementary English*, 46, 5, 599–605.
LUNDSTEEN, SARA W. (1971). *Listening Its Impact on Reading and Other Language Arts*, Urbana, Ill.: National Council of Teachers of English.
MACCOBY, ELEANOR E. AND MIRIAN ZELLNER. (1970). *Experiments in Primary Education; Aspects of Project Follow-Through*. New York: Harcourt Brace Jovanovich, Inc.
MARKGRAPF, BRUCE R. (1957). An observational study determining the amount of time that students in the tenth and twelfth grades are expected to listen in the classroom. Masters thesis, University of Wisconsin.
MILLER, JOSEPH M. AND JOHN B. VOOR. (1965). "Effects of practice upon the comprehension of time-compressed speech", *Speech Monographs* 35 (November).
NORWICH, ANTHONY L. (1971, April). A career development program in the Chicago public schools, *The Elementary School Journal*, 71, 391–399.
ORR, DAVID B. ET AL. (1965). Trainability of listening comprehension of speeded discourse, *Journal of Educational Psychology* 56, 148–56.
PEARSON, P. DAVID AND LINDA FIELDING., (1982, September). Research update: listening comprehension. *Language Arts*, 59, 617–629.
RUSSELL, DAVID H. (1964, March) a conspectus of recent research on listening abilities. *Elementary English*, 41, 262–67.
STAMMER, JOHN D. (1981, March). Mapping out a plan for better listening. *Teacher*, 98, 37–38.
TRIVETTE, SUE E. (1961, March). The effect of training in listening for specific purposes, *Journal of Educational Research*, 54, 276–277.
TUTOLO, DANIEL. (1981, September) Critical listening/reading of advertisements, *Language Arts*, 58, 679–683.
VAN, WINGERDEN, STUART. (1965) A study of direct listening instruction in the intermediate grades in four counties in the state of washington, Doctoral dissertation, Pullman: Washington State University.
WILT, MIRIAN E. (1950, April). A study of teacher awareness of listening as a factor in elementary education, *Journal of Educational Research*, 43, 626–636.
WOLVIN, ANDREW D. AND CAROLYN G. COAKLEY. (1979). *Listening Instruction*. Urbana, Ill.: ERIC Clearinghouse on Reading and Communication Skills.
WRIGHT, JONE PERRYMAN AND LESTER LAMINARK. (1982, February). First graders can be critical listeners and readers. *Language Arts*, 59, 133–136.

**Where Next?* is a referential communication game. (One person describes a target referent and the listener tries to choose the described referent in a set of alternatives.) Referential communication games provide practice in knowing how and when to ask questions or for additional information—skills important to comprehensive listening. See Dickson for additional referential communication games.

8

THE WRITING PROCESS

Writing is a problem solving process. Children must learn over a period of several years the steps they need to follow when they want to write. The major stages of the writing process are represented in the following model.

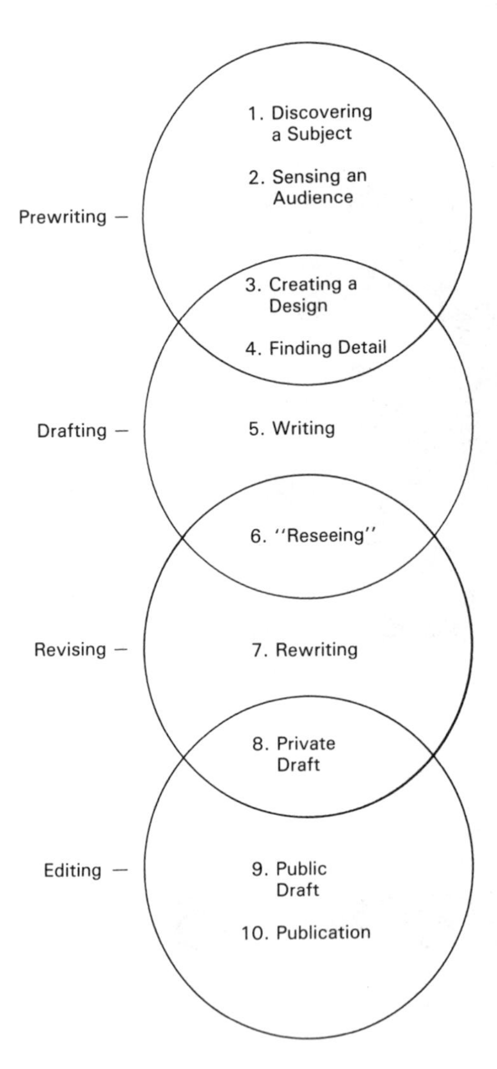

FIGURE 8-1 The Writing Process

The writing process is itself made up of a number of processes, as the model illustrates. As an act of conveying meaning, it assumes movement through these four stages: prewriting, drafting, revising, and editing. This movement is not linear. We move recursively, shifting among the processes using strategies as needed. For example, prewriting is an initial stage;

however, a writer may discover during the revising process that new ideas are necessary, thus returning to the strategies that initiated the writing activity in the first place. Thus we may view any one of the four major processes as a matter of emphasis. Although we may be engaged primarily in one process, we often revert to one or more of the others throughout the writing period.

Students need consistent experience with all four major processes if they are to develop writing strategies, learn to consider alternatives, and mature in the writing process. It is important for teachers to write with their students, modeling the major processes and teaching the strategies which enable students to grow in writing skill. Students who understand writing as a thinking process most often demonstrate confidence in the act of writing. They know how to use many strategies from which they can choose for a given purpose. Just as important, they most often *like* to write.

CREATING AN ENVIRONMENT FOR WRITING

Learning to write is essentially learning to make choices in the writing situation, but in order to make choices, writers must generate many ideas from which to choose. Read the following descriptive composition by a second grader and describe the prewriting strategies which his teacher helped him to use (see Figure 8-2 on page 146).

The child who wrote this piece was given the purpose of describing a peanut clearly for the rest of his classmates. The children were given time to observe the peanut with their senses and then were helped to list words describing their observations in the organized form that follows:

Sight	Smell	Touch	Sound	Name	What is it like?

Before listing, the children shared many sensory words describing their peanuts. After writing some words in their columns students shared again. They were also asked to give their peanuts names. This prewriting activity took a whole class period and students saved their peanuts and their lists in their writing folders for the next day. The following day before writing students shared their words with a partner, told their partners what they were going to say about their peanuts, and started to write.

What do you think is the most important part of this boy's description? Yes, the last line. Children express their feelings through story and in this last sentence the child's feelings come through. This is the emotional heart of the story. However, he would never have written the last line (which wasn't on his list) if he had not spent the time in class on careful observation, generation of many words and ideas about the peanut, and oral sharing. The prewriting stage is where the most thinking occurs for children and is the source of detail in their writing. Time spent in prewrit-

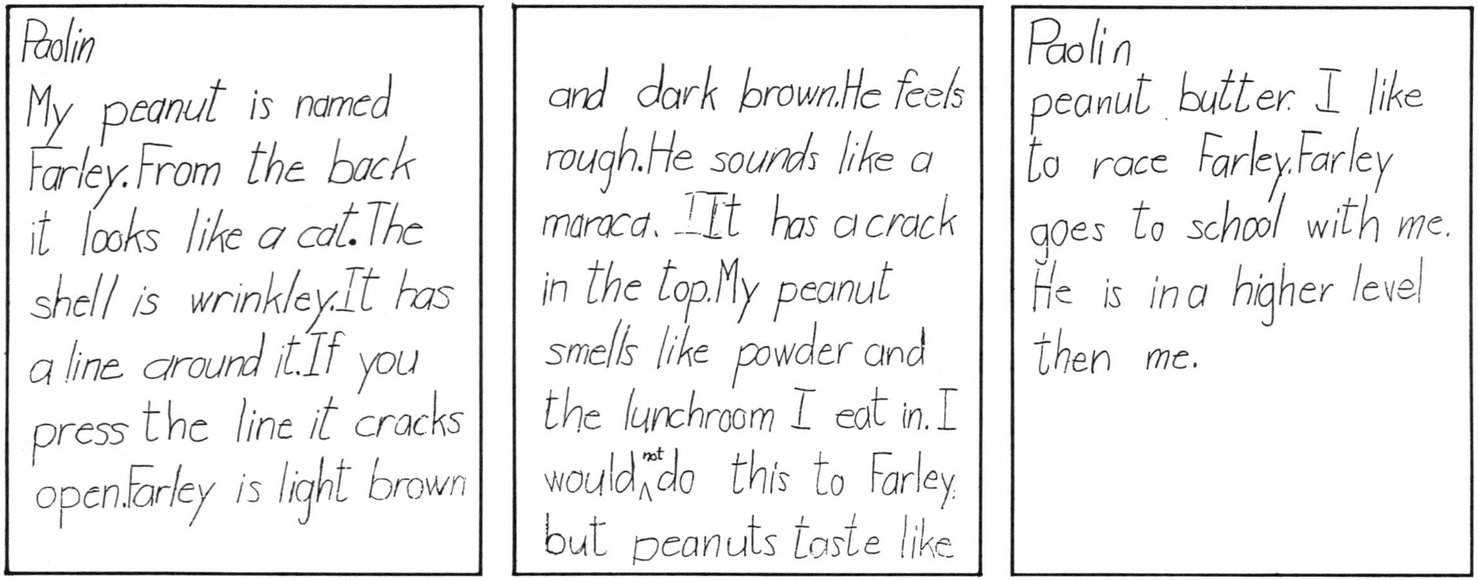

Paolin
My peanut is named
Farley. From the back
it looks like a cat. The
shell is wrinkley. It has
a line around it. If you
press the line it cracks
open. Farley is light brown

and dark brown. He feels
rough. He sounds like a
maraca. I It has a crack
in the top. My peanut
smells like powder and
the lunchroom I eat in. I
would not do this to Farley.
but peanuts taste like

Paolin
peanut butter. I like
to race Farley. Farley
goes to school with me.
He is in a higher level
then me.

FIGURE 8-2

ing will help them become mature writers. However, you the teacher must guide them carefully through prewriting in order for it to be effective.

Another child in the same group wrote the following description:

Kim
My Peanut
look like part of a
snake head. It feels
crunchy. It is brown
and dack brown. It's
name is Candy.

FIGURE 8-3

Up to this point in second grade this writer had only copied words and sentences written by the teacher and had written nothing on her own. She was very specific and clear in her description of the peanut.

A fifth grade teacher taught her students to do sensory writing after a visit to a John Deere manufacturing plant. She asked them to describe what they had seen as a way of processing their learning. Their audience was to be the men at the plant. This description is adapted from one written by three children.

A Feel for John Deere

People we depend on for producing . . .
Mechanics, designers, secretaries, assembly line workers,
Var-r-room comes the sound of the forklift
As it shifts, ships, and screeches.
Dry-nose smell of smoke + coughing smell of oil
= one big clogged nose!
Greasy hot machines like sunburn weather,
Makes me feel a warm comfortableness.
Robots following white lines like
Turtles putting for home,
As I, myself, putt for home wishing to return.

The work of Donald Graves and his colleagues suggests that three conditions are necessary for children to make progress as writers. First, they must be allowed and encouraged to write on topics they really care about, with the expectation that their work will be read seriously for its content. After all, why should they sustain the effort of writing and revising if they are not personally involved with their topics or do not expect to be read? Second, there is a developmental aspect to writing growth. Children need time and frequent practice to get better at writing. Third, children need sensitive guidance from adults to become good writers. Donald Graves (1983) suggests some of the following teacher strategies for creating an environment conducive to writing in the classroom:

1. Set up times and places in the classroom for sharing interests, descriptions of personal objects, and experiences.
2. Have children keep journals and write every day.
3. Set up partnerships or groups for children to share this writing, receive feedback, and begin to revise.
4. Arrange for teacher-child conferences during writing periods. Try to reach at least five children a week.
5. Introduce many different types of stimuli for writing.
6. Keep writing folders for each child.
7. Focus on revision instead of recopying, always building a sense of audience.
8. Have children keep in notebooks things they know and might write about someday.
9. Socialize writing. Have places in the classroom where children can go if they want to share it.
10. Help children to start out gradually by making lists or labeling.

The most important thing you can do to be an outstanding teacher of writing is write yourself and share your own writing with your students. As you are working through the rest of this chapter and the following one, keep a personal writing journal in which you can try the strategies and activities suggested. The following section will describe some of the most commonly used prewriting strategies with ideas for their implementation in the classroom.

PREWRITING

Finding a Topic

This is a part of prewriting. Writing is a way of finding out what we know about a topic. However, children need guidance in finding topics for writing. They should keep lists of possible topics in their journals or writing folders. Lists of favorite foods, sports, or TV shows are a good place to start. Sometimes you may want to assign a topic so students can compare their ideas on the same subject or in order to structure a lesson to help them explore particular data (as with the peanut). Children generally write best when they are guided to find their own topics and write about what they know. Donald Graves (1983) states, "Children don't learn to make their own decisions and choices of topics in a vacuum. The teacher works to provide a cumulative record of what a child can do; topics written about, future topics to be considered. Books are published, the child hears others share their topics and the reasons for those decisions, as well as the same from the teacher in her modeling" (p. 31). This takes time.

Brainstorming and Classifying

During the brainstorming process students generate words and ideas around a topic either individually or in groups. The purpose of brainstorming is to get out all possible ideas. The goal is quantity, uninhibited participation, and uncritical acceptance. It is important, however, that you guide students through the next step of classifying and organizing their ideas. This is a skill that needs to be taught directly and reinforced many times in small group situations. For example, have your students brainstorm all the possible sources of conflict between children their age and parents or teachers and list their responses on the board. Divide them into groups and have each group organize their answers into different subgroups and then share their organization with the rest of the class, or as a large group experiment with different ways of organizing the data. Then have students choose one subtopic to write about.

Keeping a Journal

The essence of journal keeping is that it must be done on some regular, fixed basis without fail. Journals can be narrow in focus (how I feel today; what I saw today) or broad in focus (some sort of entry for each designated day, even if it is only a carefully illustrated "yuck").

Just before journal writing time, you might want to talk a bit about some event in the day's news, show a picture, read a short story or poem, suggest a focus word (love, hate, ambition, rear, warmth, goodness, and so on), talk about an upcoming school, city, or national event, or simply announce that it is journal time. Personal writing in journals is tremendously valuable for the practice it gives. It should not be evaluated by the teacher. You should not read journals without permission of the student. However, personal comments written by the teacher in a situation where the teacher is the audience for the student writing in the journal can directly improve student writing. Encourage children to refer to their journals for topics and starts in writing. Many first grade teachers find journal writing the most effective way to begin the writing process.

How often should children write in journals? In fourth grade and above, a daily schedule is effective. For primary children two or three times a week with other writing structured for the other days. How much should they write? Decide upon the amount you want written. Schedule journal writing for early in the day so children who don't finish can finish later. How can you monitor journal writing? You just need to check up that it was done. If you have minimal criteria share it with children at the beginning of journal writing. Some starters for journal writing are listed here. Try some of these in your own journals. Remember, if you are going to have your students write about a topic, you should write about it yourself.

1. What would I like to know?
2. What would I like to do?
3. What are my favorites (food, places, people)?
4. What have I read that I can't forget?
5. What are the most important (exciting, frightening) things that have happened to me?
6. What do I love?
7. What title would make me buy a book or see a movie?

Topics for Journal Writing, Grades 3–6

Personal Reminiscences

My First Allowance
A Very Important Decision and Why I Made It
My Narrowest Escape
I Changed My Mind
I Was in a Hurry, and . . .
My Big Moment
My Ancestors
The Origin of My Family Name
A Tradition in our Family
The Dog in My Family
Moving into a Strange Town
The Prize Memory of This Year
If I Could Do It Over
Clouds in the Sky
An Unusual Incident
Keeping a New Year's Resolution
Houses I Remember
He Who Hesitates is Lost
A Fishing Trip
A Trip to the Zoo
I Was Scared!
I Knew It Would Happen

Personal Reactions

My Name
My Favorite Sport
Why I Like Poetry
My Idea of Hard Work
My Favorite Color
What Animal I Should Like To Be for a Day
My Favorite Season
My Ambition
My Alarm Clock
Confused
The Most Important Day
A Book Character I Should Like To Meet

What I Like About Ohio
What I Really Enjoy Doing
If I Were President
My Hobby and Why I Like It
My Book of the Year
My Favorite Subject
How To Take Pictures
How To Grow Flowers
How To Set the Table
Things That Make Me Happy
I Am Afraid of . . .
Getting Something New
Man's Greatest Invention
If I Had a Million
Teaching a Parakeet To Talk
Making Something out of Nothing
How Books Are Classified in a Library

Comparison and Contrast

Two Christmases
I'd Rather Have a Dog
Before and After
Living on a Farm versus Living in the City
Plane versus Train Travel
Two Books by the Same Author

Persuasion

Live and Let Live
The Best State in the Union
The Best Sport to Watch
The Only Way To Travel
Foreign Customs We Should Borrow
Everyone Should Have a Hobby

Argumentative Topics

The Advantages or Disadvantages of Too Many Friends
The Advantage of Learning a Foreign Language
Should We Simplify Our Spelling System?
What Our School Needs Most

Sports

The Greek Olympics
America's Greatest Athlete
Football is the Best Sport
Swimming
What Is Sportsmanship

Science

Fabrics of the Future
The Automobile Telephone
Travel in the Next Decade
A Trip Through Space
A Useful Gadget
My Invention

Familiar Topics

Pet Peeves
An Important Decision
A Curious Dream
The Personality of a Shoe
A Rainy Day
Table Manners
A True Friend
Borrowing
If We Could Read Each Other's Minds
A Skeleton in the Closet
Mice
Counting Chickens Before They Are Hatched
Bad Habits—What To Do About Them
The Alarm Clock
What Is Humor

Character Sketches

Day Dreamer
Baby Sitter
The Average American
A Distinguished Ancestor
A Person Who Has Influenced
My Life
Meet My Family
A Person I Will Never Forget
Eyes of Blue
A Character from Fiction
I Should Like To Meet
An Interesting Historical
Character
Gum Chewer
The Most Wonderful Person
I Know

Description

A Crowded Restaurant
An Airplane Takes Off
A Lonesome Road
Main Street
Sounds at Night
My Favorite Haunt
A Mysterious Sound
The Corner of _____ Street
and ______ Street
School Sounds
January
Christmas Eve
Full Moon
A Snow Storm
Snowfall
Colors
Cats
An Autumn Day
Clouds in the Sky
Words
Music
An Elephant
The Smell
of Thanksgiving

How To's

How To Care For a Cat
How To Get Along with Your
Brother or Sister
How To Keep Friends
How a Band Moves into
Formation
How To Play a Game
How Seeds Scatter

Free Writing

The idea behind free writing is to conquer the fear of the blank page. To conquer students' fears of having nothing to say, free writing aims to help them get something on paper. Anything. Here again, the audience is the writer and the purpose is the writing. Freed from other constraints, the writer simply gets words on paper for some specific amount of time in list, phrase, or sentence form. The rule is that students must be writing something all during the free writing time. There is no ruminating, no editing, no rereading. There is only the scratching of pens, even if those pens are only scratching, "I can't think of anything to write" over and over again.

Five minutes of free writing can seem an eternity to a third grader, less formidable but still challenging to a fifth grader. Thus, it is best to start with a small amount of time and increase it gradually to no more than five or six minutes.

As with journal writing, the teacher may want to have some sort of pre free writing exercise. This writing is for the student only. After free writing when used as a prewriting activity, students need to go over the material they have produced and choose the parts they will use for a draft.

Directed Free Writing

During directed free writing, the teacher talks quietly on a given topic. The students are free to write along the lines he suggests or go off in any direction. For example, the teacher may suggest that students describe a place they love to visit. He helps them visualize the place, remember how it smells, think of sounds they hear, or remember things they do there. Many of the topics suggested for journal writing also are good for free writing. When used as a prewriting strategy, time must be allowed for free writing that is separate from the actual writing of a draft. Children get tired doing free writing and often are not ready to do more writing. They also need help in using material from a free write in a draft because they think that the free write is the draft.

Drawing

Drawing is an excellent strategy for prewriting especially for young children. Lucy Calkins (1987) states that "the act of drawing and the picture itself both provide a supportive scaffolding within which the piece of writing can be constructed (p. 50). She cautions however against letting drawings limit the writing.

Reading

Models from literature are used as part of the prewriting process in two major ways: To initiate a new writing experience and as a model for content and form. After hearing the poem, "Sweet Like a Crow" by Michael Ondaatje, a fourth grade girl wrote this poem based on her personal experience:

"Bugs"

When my brother bugs me
it's like a bird bobbing
on my head.
It's like a mouse crawling
in my hair.
It's like living with a gerbil.
It's like a fish eating my big toe.

Raini, gr. 4

The teacher in this case used the poem as a springboard for personal or imaginative writing by asking the students to write about the place they would like to visit on a terrible day.

After reading and analyzing a descriptive paragraph from *Charlotte's Web,* a fourth grade class in an urban school wrote a group composition:

> The barn was very large. It was very old. It smelled of hay and it smelled of manure. It smelled of the perspiration of tired horses and the wonderful sweet breath of patient cows. It often had a sort of peaceful smell—as though nothing bad could happen ever again in the world. It smelled of axle and grease and of rubber boots and of new rope. And whenever the cat was given a fish head to eat, the barn would smell of fish. But mostly it smelled of hay, for there was always hay in the great loft up overhead.
>
> E. B. White, *Charlotte's Web*

> The school room was very large and old. It smelled of chalk dust and children's clothes. It often had a quiet smell—as if nothing bad could happen in school. It smelled of pencil lead, ink, ink paste, water-color paints and crayons. Whenever it rained or snowed, the wet coats and boots in the dressing room smelled like a skunk. When the children walked into the room, it smelled like potato chips, candy, nuts, and pumpkin seeds. Most of the time it smelled like smoke and dust. The dust came from the windows. The smoke came from the chimneys.
>
> Northwestern, *1967*

The influence of the model in the above piece of writing is obvious. However, the children did not automatically transfer learning from the model to writing. After discussing the specific detail related to smell in the description of the barn, the teacher guided the class in their attempt to write with the same focus. She helped them decide to describe their classroom, choosing it from many possible topics, observe carefully the details in this familiar place, gather and list those details, and select those which they wanted to use. You can never tell children to simply "write" but must show them how to think their way through each writing situation enough times so they learn how to do it on their own.

A model lesson in which literature is used as a stimulus for writing is outlined here. After reading the plan, find some examples of children's literature and describe how they could act as prewriting models.

Model Lesson

Objective: After hearing a story about a stuffed animal and sharing information about their own stuffed animal, students will write a short description.

Purpose: To describe clearly.
Audience: Classmates.
Materials: "Ira Sleeps Over," by Bernard Waber.

Prewriting: Read the book aloud to the class. Discuss the book. Have the children bring in their favorite stuffed animal and show it to the class. Put all the animals in back of the room and have the class face front. A volunteer comes up and gives clues about one of the animals by describing it to the rest of the class. The teacher writes the descriptive words on the board. Do this several times while the other students guess the animal being described. After the game, review the words on the board and have volunteers use some of the words in sentences. Write the sentences on the board.

Organizing: Put the following questions on the board to help the children choose words to describe their own animals.

A. What kind of animal is it?
B. What is its name?
C. What color is the animal?
D. What does it feel like?
E. What do you like to do with it?

Drafting: Have children put their own animal on their desks and write some sentences describing it.

Revision: A focus on revision may not be appropriate in this learning situation. It can be done as a part of sharing. Students share their descriptions with partners and partners look to see if the above listed questions are answered. If they are not answered, students can add information.

Editing: Editing would be appropriate only if the children make final copies for display or publication.

Mind Mapping or Clustering

A map provides a visual frame for the student's thoughts and ideas around a single topic. It also gives them a visual aid for organizing their ideas. You must use this process yourself in order to understand it so pick any single topic to explore with a mind map as you read this section. Your topic may be a concept such as circles or love, or a place or a particular person. Figure 8-4 on page 156 shows one person's mind map of the topic *circles*.

Some rules for the effective use of mind mapping in the classroom are listed below:

1. Use a large piece of paper and colored markers or pencils.
2. Begin by putting a key concept, word, image, or idea in the center. It is best to draw a representation of the concept if possible. For example, draw a sailboat for the concept *sailing*.
3. Print, using color now or later to circle the main related ideas.
4. Draw whenever possible.
5. If you get stuck add more branches then go back to fill them in.

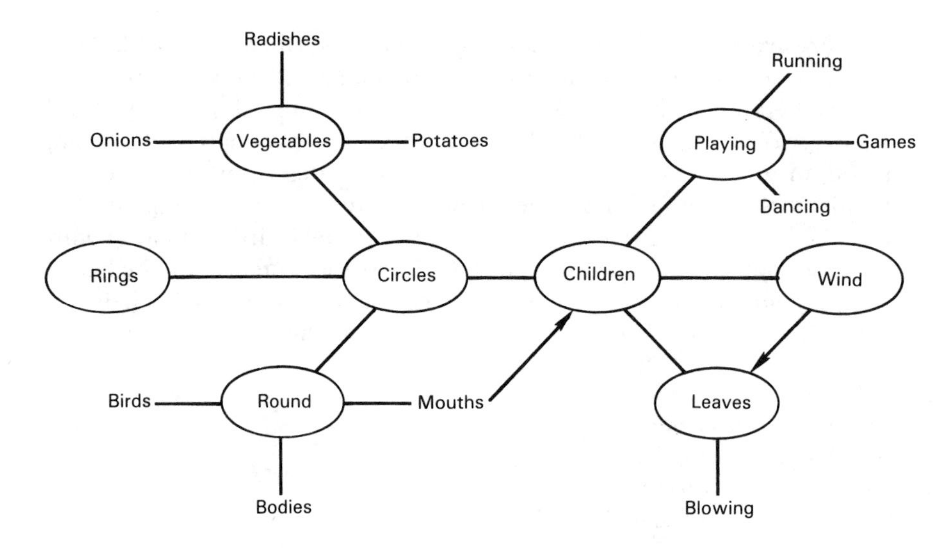

FIGURE 8-4

6. Keep adding to the pattern until you can dredge up no more ideas. (This usually takes about ten minutes.)
7. Use arrows or lines to connect related ideas from different branches of the pattern.

Mind mapping will help you see connections within and between related ideas. It will help you identify the key ideas since the less important ideas will be further from the center. The parts of the mind map which you choose to use may need further development through another map or free writing. Analyze the following piece of writing on circles and the mind map from which it took shape.

of circles and my sons

This poem is for Timmy
for he is onion mouthed
his words can make me cry
his mouth always is   always was open
he describes and catalogues each moment
a geologist examining the ancient hills
with his exact eyes
his words are like the round bodies of birds
that hit against my window in October
and fly away again without being dazed
for he winters without me
and returns in spring
growing shadows
only slightly familiar

this poem is for Andy
for he is radish warm
a flamingo in his cool home
he runs like a scurrying mouse
his voice a trail dragging behind him
he swims outward turning his head backward
he sees earth and flowers in the frosted winter windows
his hand fits in mine as a place where it plans to stay
for his is the warm country
and he never travels far

I don't know yet if we are leaves swirling in a great wind
or the wind itself
I circle them as they circle me
we dance around each other in ever growing orbits
we wear each other
like tight rings
impossible to remove

Mary Kay Rummel, (1989)

What parts of the finished piece did the writer take from the prewriting map?

Mind mapping should be taught to children as a strategy for exploring topics and doing memory searches when they need to prepare for essay writing in test situations. It is probably the fastest method for generating information on a given topic because each section of the map can lead to new ideas.

Oral Interviewing

Donald Graves (1983) presents this strategy as a powerful means of helping children find out what they have to say about a topic before they write. Follow these steps:

1. Choose a topic you would like to write about, a favorite activity, for example.
2. Choose a partner.
3. Partner A interviews partner B about the topic. Partner B answers A's questions.
4. B then interviews A.
5. After you and your partner have interviewed each other, write about your own topics.
6. When you are finished share your draft with your partner. Is there anything that you said which you did not include in your draft? Would it make your writing clearer?
7. Oral rehearsal or just plain talk is essential as a prewriting activity for children. They compose orally before they compose on paper.

Observing and Writing

Hillocks (1987) uses this strategy as an example of a focus on inquiry in teaching writing. Inquiry strategies include recording and describing, generalizing, presenting evidence, hypothesizing, discriminating using criteria, and so forth. According to Hillocks, teachers using this focus present students with data (objects, drawings, scenarios, problems), designate a task to be performed using the data, and provide guidance in performing the task. The procedure is repeated using similar tasks but different data until students become proficient in using the strategy required by the task. This approach has shown to have a strong effect on improving quality of writing. The activity with the peanuts described at the beginning of this chapter is an example of such a task.

The objective of a given writing lesson may include only prewriting. This is personal writing for the exploration of the self and a topic. Since it is personal, it frees us to explore and experiment without worry over spelling, punctuation, and syntax. The audience and purpose are served by the act of writing itself. Personal writing is tremendously valuable for the practice it gives. Such writing should not be evaluated by the teacher. Children should keep their prewriting and personal writing in a notebook or writing folder.

DRAFTING

Organization of Prewriting and First Draft

Often prewriting will, as in the oral interviewing example, lead to a first draft. The child must be helped to decide where to start in with a draft and what material generated in prewriting to use. Is the purpose to describe a peanut? What words give the clearest picture? Will your reader or partner be able to "see" that peanut which you are describing?

The drafting stage of the process produces ideas written in a form that allows for later revision. Encourage young writers to leave spaces between lines for later additions and changes. Encourage them to write without fear of error. The writing or drafting stage includes: provision of time for composing, attention by the teacher to individual progress, some time for teacher writing, teaching of organizational types and patterns of development through use of models, and opportunities for students to practice and experiment with writing.

Drafting, like other aspects of writing, is highly personal. The following methods and variations (McDougal-Littell English, 1987) seem to be the most common. Help students to discover the style with which they are most comfortable.

1. The highly structured writer works from very complete prewriting notes, changing little of the content or organization.
2. The loosely structured writer works from rough notes experimenting with ideas and organization during writing.
3. Some writers build bridges by beginning with two or three main points or situations to be covered and build logical bridges between the points during drafting.
4. Some writers compose quickly, not stopping to refine ideas or rework copy until the "revising stage."
5. Other writers work meticulously, carefully drafting one sentence or paragraph at a time, revising continuously and reworking the piece in its entirety when the draft is complete.

Which of these five descriptions fit your style of drafting?

Young children often talk aloud to themselves while writing. This is a form of rehearsal for them and is necessary for them in order to write. It is normal for there to be quiet buzz in a classroom full of young children as they are writing. It is best if feedback can be given to young writers as soon as they are ready for it. This can be done by having students share in pairs or small groups at the end of writing time. Encourage children to use invented spelling during the first draft stage rather than stop writing to get a correct spelling from the teacher or even to look it up. It is most important at this stage to get the flow of ideas onto the paper.

A given writing assignment may end at the first draft stage. Children can add a draft to their folders. After they have many starts to pick from, they can choose one to develop further. They should not be expected to create finished products from every draft.

REVISION

We revise our writing the way we revise our thoughts, naturally, from the time we start writing. The concept of revision or reworking or "reseeing" a first draft is one that develops slowly in children over many years and through many writing experiences. Children do not see writing as temporary at first. Donald Graves (1980) describes the development of the concept of revision in many individual children. Some of his findings about the development of revision skills are listed below.

1. Children revise in other media forms such as block building, drawing, and painting before they revise in writing. Children who demonstrate an overall learning stance toward revision in one area are more likely to demonstrate it in another.
2. When children try a new approach to writing, other areas in which they have been competent may suffer temporarily.

3. Beginning writers do not revise.
4. Invented spellings go through stages of development along with the child.
5. Young children find it easier to revise topics about personal experiences than the experiences of others.
6. Revision begins when children choose their own topics. Children who quickly arrive at a number of topics and learn to exclude some topics and write on others are learning to revise.
7. Children who can quickly list personal topics for writing, and write a series of leads about the same subject, demonstrate a strong capacity for revision.

It is important to separate skills that relate to revision of content from editing and proofreading skills when working with children. They begin to edit for spelling and punctuation errors quite quickly but are slow to make changes in content unless they are taught how to do it and unless they receive feedback on content from their peers. Children should make revisions on their first drafts instead of immediately beginning to rewrite. There are strategies which children of all ages should learn as they focus on revision. Lucy Calkins (1986) recommends looking at the component strategies we use when we revise. The following is a list of those strategies (Calkins, p. 186).

1. Change a piece from one mode to the next (personal narrative to poem, journal entry to published narrative).
2. Rework a confused section, the ending, the title, the lead, etc.
3. Try a different voice.
4. Take a long piece and make it shorter.
5. Take a short piece and expand it.
6. Experiment with different leads.
7. Predict a reader's question, then revise in order to be sure they are answered, ideally in the order in which they are asked.
8. Read the draft over, listening to how it sounds.
9. Put the draft aside for another day.
10. Talk to someone about the topic, then rewrite the draft without looking back at the previous versions.
11. Take a jumbled piece and rewrite it in sections.

Some of these strategies and others will now be developed more fully.

Sharing

The most effective way to help young writers develop a sense of authorship and audience and to improve writing skills is to include sharing with peers throughout the total writing process. Students of any age can learn to respond to the writing of others if they are taught how to do it. Begin by sharing some of your own work on a transparency. Ask your students for their responses. Teach them the following simple rules for discussion of each other's work.

1. Remember, you are not seeing a finished product.
2. Balance the negative with the positive. Do not simply discuss what is wrong. Discuss what is right.
3. Avoid making value judgments. "That's a dumb idea" is an inappropriate criticism because it is not the task of the reader to judge the strength or weakness of the ideas. The task is only to help clearly communicate the idea. (It is also an inappropriate criticism because it is impolite. That might also be worth mentioning.)
4. Try to offer concrete suggestions. If the word choice does not seem right, try to offer other words from which the writer might choose. If the idea, purpose, and/or audience seem vague, try to offer specific ideas for making them clearer.

At this point in the process, writers first test their work against the opinions and understanding of others. It should be a positive experience. Rather than jumping into this part of the process on an individual basis, it might be less threatening to practice, first, as a whole group or small group activity. The teacher can use made-up examples to demonstrate to the class and then ask volunteers to share copies of their work or to write sections of it on transparencies. Children can learn to think about content by learning to ask and answer the following question: What questions come to your mind that aren't answered in this piece? For example, Andy shared the following personal experience with his fourth grade classmates.

> My first airplane ride was nice. I liked the feeling of taking off into the air. I might be a pilot someday. I was lucky to have a seat next to the window I could watch everything on the ground grow smaller and smaller and I could also see the clouds float buy. I enjoyed every bite of the delishous breakfast. soon I could feel the plane touch ground.

After the children shared the things about Andy's story that they liked, the teacher asked them, "What questions come to your mind that aren't answered in Andy's story?" She listed these questions on the board as the children asked them:

> What did you have for breakfast?
> Where were you going?
> Who were you with?

The whole class helped Andy decide how he would answer the questions in composition.

Only after content has been dealt with should attention be given to the solving of minor editing problems such as misspellings or forgotten capitals.

After several weeks of large group practice in talking about writing and practice in content revision, students can learn to use other revision practices and strategies.

Small Group or Paired Revision Groups

In order to teach children to be specific and focused in their responses to each other's work you must give them specific things to look for as they read. Their responses should be oral and written on an accompanying questionnaire sheet. Some examples of questions to be given to children to answer as they practice giving feedback to one or more partners are given here:

1. What is your partner's writing about?
2. List the three most interesting words that your partner used.
3. Write your partner's most important sentence . . .
4. Write one word that tells how your partner feels in this story. Don't use "good" or "bad."
5. Could you draw a picture of this story? What parts are missing?
6. Write one question about this paper which you would like your partner to answer.
7. Should more details be added? Where?

Rating scales are also effective for improving student writing if the students are given much practice in using the scales to rate papers, their own and others.

Even first grade children can get quite good at reading the work of a partner and answering specific feedback questions about that work.

Revision as Reseeing

Because revision involves the cognitive task of looking at what is written in a new way it can be helpful for children to find the "emotional heart" or most important part of what they have written and present that in a new way by reading it out loud or incorporating it in artwork. In this way a child may start out writing a personal experience and end up with a poem.

Developing a Sense of Audience

It is awareness of audience that leads to revision in writing. The child must learn to view his work the way his audience will view it. You can help children develop this sense by teaching them to treat each other as authors. Activities such as having children draw the picture another child has described with words will increase the sense of writing for an audience.

EDITING AND PROOFREADING

Editing for errors in spelling, punctuation, capitalization, and sentence construction has a very real place in the writer's craft. Children as young as second grade quickly learn that after they have finished drafting and revising a piece they can take it to the editor's corner for proofreading. Most teachers use check lists as a guide for editing. An example is included here.

EDITOR'S CHECKLIST (CALKINS, 1986, P. 206)

Author:

Title:

Date began: Date ended:

Editor: Peer editor:

Does it makes sense?

Spelling:

Punctuation:

Periods, question marks, commas, exclamation marks, quotation marks

Capitals:

Excess words:

Teacher comments:

Proofreading cannot be taught in one lesson but needs to be repeated at frequent intervals. Little progress is gained by having the teacher proofread student papers. The job of proofreading belongs to the child who wrote the composition. Help from others should come only after each has made initial efforts to improve his own paper. You need to give students practical and specific suggestions about what to look for and teach them to look for only one thing each time they read through a paper. For example:

Time 1: Read for sentence sense
Time 2: Read for punctuation
Time 3: Read to make clearer word choices
Time 4: Read for capitalization
Time 5: Read for misspellings
Time 6: Check name, title, etc.

One way to improve proofreading ability is the group correction lesson, based on the same model as Cramer's editing workshop described earlier in this chapter. Have students write sentences from their papers on transparencies and, as a group, edit them for the aspect of mechanics on which you are focusing. After group work, students edit their own papers for the same purpose.

Word Processing

Word processing software makes the microcomputer a valuable tool in the writing program. The great advantage of word processors lies in their capacity for revision and editing. Conferences with teachers and peers can take place right around the word processor.

Even young children can learn to use the computer keyboard for composing. Composing at the keyboard is easier for them than handwriting.

TEACHER CONFERENCES

The heart of the revision process is the writing conference. There are two kinds of teacher conferences with individual students: scheduled and unscheduled. Scheduled conferences are planned in advance; each student knows when his or her conference will be and prepares for it bringing a composition in progress to discuss. Scheduled conferences are short—four to five minutes. During that time most or all of these things will happen:

- The student shares a current piece of writing in progress.
- You ask what is going well and receive an answer.
- You ask what is difficult and receive an answer.
- You ask where the student wants to go next.
- You point out one skill or aspect of writing to be checked.

Graves (1983) suggested that the teacher keep a notebook with a tabbed divider for each student's name and a few sheets of paper divided as in the sample below:

date	title
Oct. 10	A Skunk I Saw
run-on sentences	+
skill	rating
strong involvement	
note	

Students could also keep a list on their folders of the goals they set during their conferences.

Unscheduled conferences take place as you move about the room speaking to children as they work. These conferences last about two minutes and provide opportunities for children to speak and you to listen and encourage.

In any conference the key to success lies in asking questions that teach, questions that help children discover what they have to say. Here are some suggestive types of questions.

How is it going?
What are you writing about now?
Where are you now in your draft?

To help explain and elaborate:

Can you tell me more about this?
How did you learn about this?
How did this happen?

To help focus on the writing process:

Where do you think you'll start?
What do you think you'll do next?
If you started again with that lead, what do you think would come next?

To help writers see their own progress:

What's your favorite or strongest part?
Why did you choose this lead?
How could you include your new idea?

FINAL DRAFT

The final draft is the finished product. The final draft is presented to its intended audience. Language ability, interest, motivation, and sheer willingness to work hard will ensure variation in quality. Even though quality will vary greatly, it is good to keep in mind that the process of writing is what is being taught and is, therefore, what is important. Remember, not everything started will reach final draft. Children should not be expected to rewrite everything that they start, but instead should be allowed to choose from many starts something to develop for publication in a book or on a bulletin board or a class newspaper.

TEACHER EVALUATION

If you expect children to approach writing as a process, you need to give them credit for their work at all stages of the process. If children are assigned a fifty point paper, for instance, they should get ten points for prewriting, ten points for a first draft, one to twenty points for numbers of revisions, and ten points for a final draft. Obviously, this kind of grading is something you need to do periodically, not constantly, with children in the intermediate grades.

Teacher evaluation of writing assignments should be very specific. Your students should know from your specific objectives, directions, and check lists exactly what you will look for in their papers. Don't demand too much from one assignment. For example, in a description you might look for specific language as your main objective. Another time it may be narrative organization. Another time it may be mechanical skill such as punctuation.

As time goes on, you may increase the skills looked for but don't overload. The least effective method of evaluation is for the teacher to take home thirty compositions, correct every error on them, and hand them back to her students to rewrite.

It is best to evaluate children's composition skill from a developmental perspective. That is why it is so helpful to have students keep writing folders in which you and their parents as well as themselves can see development over a long period of time. The following check list will aid you in assessing skills belonging to different stages of the writing process at selected times during the school year.

FIGURE 8-5 Developmental Checklist for Writing Process Skills.

	Often	*Sometimes*	*Seldom*
Precomposing			
1. Draw	____	____	____
2. Construct (clay, sculpture, etc.)	____	____	____
3. Talk (Questions, answers questions, shares experiences)	____	____	____
4. Drama (Fine arts)	____	____	____
5. Brainstorming	____	____	____
6. Note taking	____	____	____

Postcomposing (continued)	*Often*	*Sometimes*	*Seldom*
7. Outlining	____	____	____
8. Non-visible rehearsing	____	____	____
9. For reporting—reads, paraphrases reading material, repeats to someone	____	____	____
Postcomposing			
1. Shares writing with others	____	____	____
2. Acts on feedback from others	____	____	____
3. Revises	____	____	____
a. Words	____	____	____
b. Sentences	____	____	____
c. Sections/Paragraphs	____	____	____
4. Can choose a title from several selections	____	____	____
5. Proofreads	____	____	____
a. Mechanics	____	____	____
b. Syntax	____	____	____
c. Spelling	____	____	____
6. Makes one draft and revises	____	____	____
7. Makes two drafts	____	____	____
8. Evaluates work and can set own writing goals	____	____	____
9. Final drafts	____	____	____
a. Appearance of paper	____	____	____
b. Indents	____	____	____
c. Margins	____	____	____
d. Legibility	____	____	____
e. Correct side of paper	____	____	____
f. Heading	____	____	____

When grading children's compositions follow these guidelines:

1. Allow students to select the writing to be graded.
2. Let them revise and edit work to be submitted for a grade.
3. Use a grading method that shows what they did well.
4. Let them select criteria for grading.
5. Grade mechanics separately from content.
6. Use written comments that are very directed, not general, or a conference to accompany a grade.

Remember that grading is different from analysis which is what you would do with a developmental check list. It means assigning a rank order and should accompany only a small portion of what children write. Children will actually learn much more from your reactions on a regular basis and the reactions of peers to their ongoing work.

THE HIGH ANXIETY WRITER

Anxiety results when children are asked to do too much at once. When young children receive negative feedback on mechanical problems such as spelling or handwriting, they may believe that they have nothing to say and cannot write. This is just not true. The most important thing you can do to help the high anxiety writer is to focus on one skill at a time and be sure the child knows your objective. As children write, keep the task manageable. Don't say "Spell everything correctly and watch your capital letters and punctuation." Instead, say "Find two words that you think you may not have spelled correctly."

Practice will help the high anxiety writer improve, especially if it is directed practice and you encourage him at each step. Children should write every day and as a part of every subject.

Let your students see many examples of "messy" first drafts, your own and those of others. Have visiting writers bring examples of their prewriting and many "messy" drafts. At the end of this chapter there is a poem written by the author with its many almost unreadable drafts. This is how we write and children (and their teachers) need to understand this process.

Provide models for children that can be used as a starting point. Let them rewrite tales from another point of view or use the pattern that an author has used or even a beginning line. Many writers get their ideas from the work of other writers.

Let children work together during the prewriting, revision, and editing stages. This will give the anxious writer support. Teach many types of prewriting strategies so that students can find one or two that work well for them.

Have students rehearse their writing orally or visually through drawing before they start to write.

Have all your students read their work aloud so they can "hear" their writing and encourage, encourage, encourage.

SUMMARY

The writing process consists of three recursive stages: prewriting, drafting, and revision. In prewriting children discover what they have to say about any topic. In drafting they learn to approach the same topic in a number of ways. In revision, they look at the work in a new way through receiving feedback from others in group and individual conferences with the teacher and especially with peers. These stages may be called different names and may be combined in different ways. Very young children may not go beyond the stage we have called rough draft writing. Older students may spend relatively less time on prewriting.

Evaluation of children's writing should include analysis of children's work over time. Only a portion of their writing should be graded and content and mechanics should be graded separately. Suggestions for dealing with high anxiety writers include always responding to content first, daily writing practice, and focusing on one writing skill at a time. In other words, hold their hands through each step of the process.

ACTIVITES

For Teacher Education Classes

1. Choose several prewriting strategies described in this chapter and practice them in your journal.
2. Choose a classmate for a revision partner and analyze a first draft using a check list you have devised together.
3. Go through children's literature books and find model paragraphs such as the descriptive paragraph from *Charlotte's Web* that you can use for teaching writing skills. There is a bibliography of such books at the end of the following chapter.
4. Plan a series of writing lessons for a chosen grade level which would take students through each stage of the writing process. Your plan should show your understanding of different parts of the process by following a format like the one shown in Figure 8–6.

FIGURE 8-6 Writing Process Lesson Plan Outline

Goal: ______________________________

____

Objective: ______________________________

____

Materials: ______________________________

____

Prewriting: ______________________________

____

First Draft: ______________________________

____

Revision: ______________________________

____

Editing: ______________________________

____

Presentation: ______________________________

____

Evaluation: ______________________________

____

5. Analyze a few student papers using the developmental format included in this chapter. Give a picture of overall student development.

6. Study an English textbook for children at one grade level. Is writing taught with a process approach? Analyze it for number and extent of

strategies taught for both prewriting and revising. Are revision of content and editing separated? To what extent?

For the Elementary Classroom

1. Consult the end of the following chapter for ideas for teaching different forms of writing.
2. Read *How a Book Is Made*, written and illustrated by Aliki (1986) to help children understand the long process involved in getting to a final product. Explain that you are interested in the steps along the way, not the final product.
3. Spend several weeks working on prewriting skills. Have students practice brainstorming, mind mapping, free writing, and oral interviewing. Have them classify and organize their material but only do one or two rough drafts.
4. Have children compare the steps of the process of writing with the process they use to solve problems in math or science.
5. Create a center in your classroom where children can go in pairs or groups to share writing and give and receive feedback or response.
6. Connect the visual with the teaching of revision by having children draw pictures of a writing topic, add detail to the pictures, and then compare details in their pictures with details included in their writing.

REFERENCES

BELL, PADEN, SCHAFFRATH. (1987) *McDougal-Littell English, level 5*. Evanston: McDougal-Littell & Company.

CALKINS, LUCY MCCORMICK. (1986) *The Art of Teaching Writing*. New Hampshire: Heinemann.

GRAVES, DONALD. (1983) *Writing: Teachers and children at work*. New Hampshire: Heinemann.

GRAVES, DONALD. (1980, September). What children teach us about revision. *Language Arts*.

HILLOCKS, GEORGE. (1987, May). Synthesis of Research on Teaching Writing. *Educational Research* 45.

Lessons in Composition for Elementary and Junior High Schools. (1967). Chicago: Northwestern University Press.

RICO, GABRIELE. (1983) *Writing the Natural Way*. Los Angeles: J. P. Tarcher, Inc.

RUMMEL, MARY KAY. (1989) *This Body She's Chosen*. St Paul: New Rivers Press.

WHITE, E. B. (1952). *Charlotte's Web*. Harper & Row.

Two night herons
fill the pond with silence
I hand binoculars to my
children
"There they are"
Those white holes
that radiate light into
the morning
light collected while we ~~slept~~ sleep
One is carried onto a
branch
the other ~~takes giant steps~~ giant steps
across the muck
eye on some elusive prey
Those are gripping claws
I say
claws that decide when
they will let go
The one on the branch
raises ~~it~~ one to scratch its
neck + back
Long bodies relaxed
only the jays can ~~[illegible]~~ [illegible] those
only the jays can [illegible]
~~them into [illegible]~~ alert then
while energy pours through
fills ~~[illegible]~~ the pond, [illegible]
~~[illegible]~~ like the bodies

I listen to night herons fill the
pond with silence
Hand binoculars to my
children say "There it is!"
Those white holes
that ~~send~~ light into
radiate
the morning
light collected ~~during~~
~~the long dark~~
while we sleept
~~like the faces of~~
like the faces of
my ~~[illegible]~~ teenagers
each morning
back from some
~~far~~ inward ~~roamings~~
gleaning
One heron carried
onto a branch
the other ~~slow~~
~~giant steps across~~
~~the~~ giant steps in
slow motion across
the ~~mulch~~ mud
~~bottom~~
eye on some elusive

~~thing~~ in the murky bottom
Those are gripping claws
I say
claws that decide
when they will let go
The one on the branch
raises it to scratch its
neck + back
~~Yes those what~~
~~Yes energy [illegible]~~
~~Only the~~ bodies
Those long ~~[illegible]~~
~~wear contentment~~
~~are relaxed~~ relaxed
Only the jays can send
them into alert
~~[illegible]~~
while energy
pours through them
and fills the pond
like the ~~faces of~~ bodies
my teenage [illegible]

FIGURE 8-7

Appendix: 8-A
Poetry Development

Gatherers

Two night herons
fill the pond with silence.
Those white holes that radiate
light into morning,
light collected while we sleep.
One sits frozen on a branch.
The other slow steps across the mulch,
eye on some elusive prey.
The statue raises a claw
to scratch its neck and back.
Slow and easy, only a screaming jay
can rouse those long bodies.
They are like teenaged boys,
inert in the morning, faces silent,
shining with secrets gathered
during a dark gleaning.

Mary Kay Rummel
(1989)

9

FORMS FOR WRITING

One of our major objectives in teaching writing is to give children experience with many forms of writing so that they will have tools to use for all of their writing purposes. Choice of form depends upon our purposes for writing and the needs of the audience. There is overlap between forms and often a writer is not sure of the form when he or she begins. This chapter will focus on the characteristics of descriptive, poetic, narrative, and expository writing with methods for teaching and criteria for evaluating each. It would be helpful to keep a journal as you work through this chapter and try some of the ideas for teaching each type of writing as they are discussed in the text.

DESCRIPTION

Probably the basis of all writing, creative as well as practical, is accurate, detailed, specific, and full observation of the world. Observation is a participatory sport and description is the way we participate. Detailed perceptions must be learned. So must the need for them. It is not hard to imagine the many times when specific descriptions are necessary if communication is to be complete. One of the troubles our students have is that they can't tell when they can be general, and when they should be detailed. One reason may be that they are not given an audience, or that they have one that is interested only in how their papers look. The major goal in teaching language arts in the elementary school is to move the child from general statements, such as "The dog is big," to language so specific that an audience who has not experienced what the writer has experienced can share in the experience. This is the meaning of language maturity. In teaching children to describe what they observe you will be teaching them to find words which will classify and particularize. They will have to consider the uses of general and specific words and consider the whole complex idea of audience and communication situation. It involves all the stages in the writing process and leads naturally to other types of writing, poetry, and narrative as well as expository reporting. Description is an excellent way to begin composition. It requires no special knowledge or experiences. The material for description is all around us. Describing will give the beginning writer practice in observation of familiar material, gathering details, organizing and selecting ideas and words. This kind of activity should begin in grade one and be developed each year.

Children should begin describing the things that are closest to them: their stuffed animal, their favorite food, the class pet, the leaves which they collected for science. Figure 9-1 gives a guide for teaching children to observe details.

FIGURE 9-1 Model for Observing and Recording: Prewriting

QUESTIONS	*ANSWERS*	*DETAILS*
What do I see first?		
What do I see next?		
What do I see next?		
What do I see last?		

Here is a sample description lesson using a story, *Ira Sleeps Over*, by Bernard Waber, as a prewriting stimulus.

Materials:

Ira Sleeps Over, by Bernard Waber
Stuffed Animals

I. Prewriting

Read the book aloud to the class. Discuss the book. Have the children bring in their favorite stuffed animal and show it to the class. Put all the stuffed animals in back of the room and have the class face front. A volunteer comes up and gives clues about one of the animals by describing it to the rest of the class. The teacher writes the descriptive words on the board. Do this several times while the other students guess the animal being described. After the game, review the words on the board and have volunteers use some of the words in sentences. Write the sentences on the board.

II. Assignment:

Have children put their own animal on their desk and write a short paragraph describing it. Put the following questions on the board for assistance:

A. What kind of animal is it?
B. What is its name?
C. What color is the animal?
D. What does it feel like?
E. What do you like to do with it?

Models from literature can actually guide children in their observation and help them put their observations into specific language. The following selections are examples of the kind of specific writing which can guide children in their own descriptions.

From *Angelino and The Barefoot Saint*

In a valley near the foothills of the Little Alps in Tuscany there lived a boy whose name was Angelo. He was a quiet, good-natured, friendly boy, gentle with creatures, and of exceedingly simple heart. For all his ten years, he was small and slender. People who knew him called him Angelino.

Valenti Angelo

From *Pinky Pye*

Here in Cranbury it was nice. On misty days it smelled like the sea, for it was near the sea. And after a thunderstorm the town smelled particularly wonderful. The gutters gurgled merrily then, with the swift rain water racing to the drains, with sticks for boats and chewing gum papers for rafts bumping into each other as they were swirled along. A person could go barefoot in the wet and new-cut grass.

Eleanor Estes

Sensory listing, drawing, and mind mapping as described in the preceding chapter are all effective prewriting strategies for description. The following is a plan for writing a descriptive paragraph.

1. Begin the clustering for your paragraph as shown in Figure 9-2. Use the five senses as subtopics. You may wish to add feelings as a sixth subtopic.

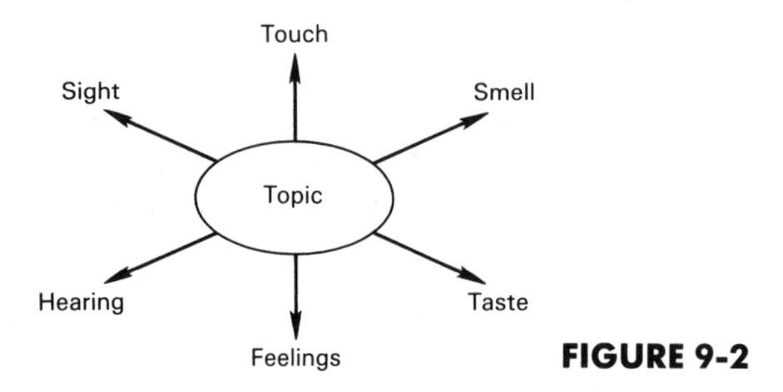

FIGURE 9-2

2. Add as many details as you can to your cluster. Imagine that you are experiencing what you describe. Name what you sense and feel as your cluster develops.
3. Write a topic sentence that gives a general introduction to your paragraph. This sentence may express the main idea.
4. Write your detail sentences using vivid and lively words. Create a realistic scene with your words.
5. Write a "clincher" sentence to complete your paragraph.

Here are other ideas for description:

1. Favorites

game
sport
season
relative
dessert
movie
animal

2. Myself

3. My pet

family
friend
neighborhood

4. I am an expert about

hockey
basketball
dolls
pizza . . .

You might want to try some of the following suggestions for helping children record sensory impressions.

1. Ask the children to bring to class pieces of different types of cloth. (You can get samples from drapery stores, rug sample books, and interior decorator's outmoded sample books.) In handling these materials, they should try to discover as many apt words as they can to describe the texture of the cloth they are working with. From the simple designations of texture as being rough or smooth they should try to be as specific as possible. A piece of burlap could be described as rough, prickly, scratchy, coarse. There are many extended activities which could be used at various times. From the adjectives they have chosen to describe burlap they could discuss what other items could be described with these words. They might compose similes or metaphors. They could compose sentences. They might think of a situation such as a boy in a sack race at a picnic and describe him hopping along with the rough fibers of burlap scratching his bare legs. If he fell, how would the coarse material feel against his skin?

2. Get sample cards from a paint store. Ask the children to find a word to accurately describe the color. From the known "ad" names: lime-green, avocado green, perhaps they could try some new combinations just as the advertisers do. They must be able to justify their choice.

3. Have a child walk across the room. Try to describe the way he walked. Ask another child to walk in a different way. Describe it. Do this as many times as it seems fruitful.

4. Tape record a number of sounds (or get a record from the library)—knocking at a door, ringing of a bell, a whistle, a dog's bark, the laughter of a child or an adult. Have the children identify the sound and describe it.

5. List some of the sounds you can hear at a football, basketball, volleyball game, and so on. Use a phrase which includes an adjective to describe the sound.

6. Describe the sensations you feel when stroking a cat, or dog, or any other animal.

7. Compose original similes for:

as big as
as hard as
as sour as
as fresh as
as tall as
as cold as
as loud as
as stale as
as round as
as sweet as
as soft as

Then compose a sentence: the moon was as round as . . .

8. List examples of trite phrases:

bright as a dollar
hungry as a bear
cold as ice
a dreary day

Discuss why these are so ineffective. Consider a person or object or place you could describe, and see how you could make these and other worn-out phrases you can think of more specific and original.

9. Describe a bonfire. Describe the colors in the flame, the sound of the flames, the movement of the flames, the smell of the smoke, the burning leaves.

10. Describe a "hot-rod" turning a corner.

11. Write a description of your favorite snack. Make it so "mouth-watering" we will all feel pangs of hunger.

12. Show a science film which shows a spider in action, spinning a web. Describe the pattern of the web, tell how the spider worked to design it. Describe the spider itself. (This would be a good time to read sections of *Charlotte's Web* by E.B. White.)

13. Describe a Thanksgiving dinner. Try to appeal to all the senses. Begin with phrases, then try to work out a short piece of writing together. Pretend you're a T.V. cameraman "zooming in" for a close-up. What will be central? The turkey? What will be peripheral?

14. Describe people in a circus: clowns, acrobats, tight-rope walkers. Describe a tight-rope walker. Try to appeal to as many senses as you can. Further, you could tell us about the personal feelings of the performer.

15. Describe the sound and sight and smell of bacon frying in a pan. Begin with the raw strips of meat. Finish with the bacon ready to serve.

16. List all the sensory impressions you experience when going into a bakery. Pretend you see a few people there. What are they buying? Why are they attracted to it?

17. If you were writing a suspense story that takes place in a "haunted" house, how would you describe the house so that your reader's spine would tingle?

18. How will (name of street) look 25 or 50 years from now? Write a description of how you think it will look.

19. Pretend you are setting up the ball for a critical shot in basketball or volleyball. Describe your actions and your feelings. (Use first or third person.)

20. Describe a girl or boy poised on the diving board, ready to dive. Describe the dive, the impact when he hits the water.

21. Imagine yourself sitting on the bleachers at a football game on a cold fall day. Describe how you would feel. Make us feel as you do, using as many sensory impressions as you can think of.

22. Describe what you do to get yourself up in the morning, or your feelings about getting up in the morning. Or, pretend you're lying in bed, gathering the courage to get up; describe what you see and feel and do.

23. Describe yourself in the act of squeezing toothpaste onto the brush. Appeal to our sense of sight, taste, and touch in this description. Perhaps you have a peculiar way of squeezing the paste from the tube. Do you press from the bottom, the middle, or the top? Do you screw the cap back? Do you apply the paste to the brush in a certain pattern? Do you hum or yawn as you're doing this? Make us *really see*.

24. Describe a monkey peeling a banana. Is someone watching him? Does he react to them?

25. Take four imaginary trips through the park: during spring, summer, autumn, winter. Describe the same area under these different seasonal changes. (One girl did this using her feet as a "focus," the various sounds she made walking over the slushy spring mud, the sharp tap of her heels over sun-baked stones in summer, the rustling sound of leaves under her feet during autumn, the crunching of snow under her feet during winter.)

26. Describe the feeling of snow blowing against your face. The feel of snow under your feet. Do the same with rain. Mud between your fingers and toes back in the days when you made mud pies. Sand on the beaches in summer between your toes and on your wet body. Try to weave into the description your reactions, feelings, memories.

27. Look for appeals to the senses in the ad writing for soft drinks, foods, clothes, cars and so on. Pretend you are writing the advertisement. Think of a caption to go with the picture, or write a T.V. commercial, or a parody to a modern song, or a dialogue.

28. Bring to class examples of literary passages which are good in sensory detail. Analyze and evaluate them. Have the children bring passages they think are good from books and magazines and newspapers.

Evaluating Description

What should you and your students look for in descriptive writing? Detail. Specific sensory detail. You can ask the following questions about a description:

Is the subject clear?
Are sensory details used to develop the topic?
Are verbs strong?
Is there a mood set by the description?
Is it so clear that you could draw it?

Just start. Once started children will find numerous subjects in their lives to share with each other through descriptive language.

How would you evaluate the following description written by a fourth grader?

> Baby Jack is about 5 months old. Ther's a curly one piece of hair on top of his head. that's all the hair he has. He has little blue eyes. Jack wears baby glasses. He has a little round nose and rosey red cheeks. When you tickle him he laughs and drools. Jack only has two teeth. He wears blue pajamas with feet. When he tries to sit up he acts like jello and falls over. His mother says he's chubby like a beach balll. People say he's always nice and cuddly to hold. Jack smells like baby powder almost all the time. His head is soft and smooth to touch. It feels nice to hold his little hands. He has little feet and toes. Sometimes it seems like he's a little dream come true to you. When he and his mother go shopping people always love to come and see the cute little baby, Jack and his mother.
>
> Nicole

CREATIVE WRITING

What is creative writing? How do you help children write creatively? It is very difficult to define creative writing as opposed to other kinds of writing since an element of creativity enters into many types of writing. However, one of the major purposes of writing which is creative is self-exploration and expression as well as communication. We usually consider poetry, fiction, and creative nonfiction as creative writing.

What is the best way to provide experiences in creative writing in the elementary school? Ideas for creative writing are countless. However, it is important that the activities you choose to do actually teach and are not just cute ideas. They should help children gain insights about the creative process and about the whole writing process that they can use in many situations. Teaching creative writing is teaching a way of thinking. The following eight principles are excellent criteria for choosing objectives, activities, and materials for teaching creative writing. If you use these principles in planning, your children will be learning thinking and writing skills and not just performing an isolated activity. They are:

1. Observe and write. Activities for this have been described in the section on description. More will be found in the poetry section.
2. Word association. This is word play and closely related to poetry. It is an activity that children can do in their journals.
3. Serendipity. In creative writing wonderful things seem to happen accidentally as connections are made. The "I Am" activity in the poetry section is an example of serendipity.

4. Alternative ways of looking at something. This skill is at the heart of creative thinking. Ways to teach it are described in the following poetry section.
5. Show—don't tell. This skill is essential for description, narrative, and poetry.
6. Making the ordinary extraordinary. This is also described further in the poetry section.
7. Picking the right word. This ability is essential for all good writing.
8. Metaphor/Analogy. The creative thinker is able to analogize.

This connection making is discussed at length in the poetry section.

POETRY

Take an object like an orange or a potato. Make a column for each sense and list sensory descriptors under the appropriate heading. Add a column titled "What is it like?" Whenever the object reminds you of something else, list it in the last category. Add a column, "How does it make me feel?" List words in that category. In the last two columns your thinking has moved from merely descriptive to the kind of thinking that produces poetry. Poetry begins in the senses and through metaphors expresses strong feelings in a compressed unified form. In teaching children to write poetry, it is the poetic experience that is important, not the final product. Can they use sensory language and metaphor to express strong feeling? Yes, with great alacrity and enjoyment. In order to elicit the poetic experience in children you usually have to tell them that they can't rhyme their poems. They are familiar with verse models and will sacrifice image and feeling for rhyme. Models from literature are an important aspect of prewriting in poetry. The following sections will describe specific methods for helping children write poetry and will include poems to help children get started and give them a sense of form.

Writing About Things

> Maybe we're here only to say: house, bridge, well, gate, jug, olive tree, window—at most, pillar, tower . . . but to say them in a way that the things themselves never dreamed of existing so intensely.
>
> R. M. Rilke, *Duino Elegies*

Concrete sensory objects such as vegetables, rocks, or leaves are a good place to start poetry writing with children. An exercise with an object such as the one described above is an effective way to begin. It helps children generate both sensory words and metaphors. The following lesson plan uses the poem, "I Write a Poem With Claire Who Is Almost Four," by Pat Barone (1983) as a model for this kind of imaginative sensory observation and writing.

Objective: Children will look at a common object in a new way and create a nonrhyming poem from their observations.

Materials: model poems, potatoes, radishes or other objects if desired.

I WRITE A POEM WITH CLAIRE WHO IS ALMOST FOUR

Remember? The winter bears
came out when it snowed—
when the river stopped.

I remember
trees on the island were
like broken teeth
on a black comb.

No! not a comb!
It's hair sticking up
from a giant bear.
He's not dead.
he's sleeping.
His head is cold
and his dreams got frozen.

Why are the winter bears awake?

Because. They are little
but they don't have naps.
They crawl around
and make snow angels
on the giant's head.

What does the giant hear?
Do you think white sounds
like a whisk broom

or the brush on a snare drum?

A bear drum is a big log.
I think when the mother sweeps

snow off the island's back?

I think she hits the log
and wakes the giant up.

Mother write this:
When it's summer, when
they are brown and orange,
the winter bears roll up
the snow and then come out.
They are hunting bears—no—
They are bumblebees!

Prewriting:

1. Read "I Write a Poem With Claire Who is Almost Four" and ask, "What did the writer make up in this poem?"
2. Give students an object and list sensory words that they use to describe the object.
3. Encourage them to "tell lies" about their object.

Drafting: Students write a short poem about their object. At this point or at the beginning it is helpful to read poems by both yourself and by other children using this same process.

The following is a poem written by a fourth grade teacher as a model for her students as they did sensory writing.

Marshmallow

Soft, delicately powdered like a tooth fairy pillow
A marshmallow begins so fresh and full of life
Shaped like a miniature soup can
Full of sweet, gooey delights
Changing
Rice Krispies are hushed by its presence
Ice cream graciously awaits its crowning
Changing
So tough it possesses the strength of
impenetrable snow fort walls
Soon like a lonely old man in the cold of winter
Nothing can change its heart
Rigid, solid, hard as convicts glare
What was once a wonderful impressionable baby
Has gone the way of mankind.

Sandy Fox, 1988
Randolph Heights Elementary

The following are poems written by Ms. Fox's students as they used this process in writing about their hands. For prewriting they traced their hands on drawing paper and made a mind map around them of words and ideas to use in their poems.

On my hands there are some rocks you can not throw.
Rocks that are as small as a beetle.
And they stick out like a red balloon
raised above a crowd.
My hands look like a turtle shell
without a turtle.
My hands will move anywhere I want them to
like a trained dog.

Jason

My Fingers

are
a
flash
in
the
sky
with
clouds
in
the
thickened
sky
my fingers
stand
with
the
thunder
and
lightning
and
they all
stand together

Claudine

Poetry does not mean writing with unusual, fancy words. It means looking at the ordinary in a new way. A class of first grade students wrote the following group poem about the sun with each student contributing one line. They had previously made up "lies" about radishes and snow so were very imaginative in their metaphors.

THE SUN

makes your clothes burn
makes the house hot
shocks you when you're lonely
makes you wet from sweat
pulls out its whiskers and
throws them down on you
boils down the buses
makes the houses jump up and down
makes the birds faint.
If it falls on you
the sun will break 10 times.
It kills the foxes
makes the clothes dirty.

If the sun falls down the moon comes up.
It makes the clothes whiter than snow.
When it goes down all the people run away
but they can't because it's bigger than the earth.
The sun sneaks in your desk when you go home.
It takes the number line down.
It takes a bath in the ocean.
It wears your shoes.
It shoots tomatoes down
when people tell bad jokes.
You can play baseball with it
because it's round.
The sun makes the pan burn so hot
it eats the cook.

Carol Master's poem, "Fly Ball,"* has been used very successfully with older children as a model for looking at a common object in a new way. As you can see, models by professional writers, teachers, and other students are absolutely essential to teaching the writing of poetry. Over and over again professional writers have attested to the fact that they learned to write through imitation. Why would children be different in their learning processes?

FLY BALL

a fly ball
has nothing of flight about it
it's pushed out there
its trajectory absolute
as the slap of the bat

but no one has ever seen
a ball go into the glove
it's true
follow the arc
unblinking   the slow climb up the last leg
of the mountain   the raising of a flag   salute
the sure sail home to the cup
of the mitt

suddenly the field breaks up
everyone running the same way
a terrible accident   Christ has landed
at International Airport
your presence is required

*In *This Sporting Life*, Milkweed editions (Mpls. 1987).

no it's just the game over
you missed it
in that last inch
the ball disappears

in fact there's a moment when the ball
never enters the glove
it decides to cock a wing
veer to the south
so long folks I'm off on a jet—
stream the sweet south
wind in my wingpits we're all going
all U.S. fly balls going to take off
like popcorn roll down the coast
and bloom like migratory monarchs
on the trees of Argentina

no it's still coming
a single headlight you below it
on the tracks

the ball ballooning
rides clear as an onion
breaking from its skin
that terrible moon

coming
the thing never stops
blazing with possibilities
and it's yours you claim it
whether you want it or not
it will come what matters
is where you are

Metaphor

Notice the way that feeling is expressed through metaphors written by children. Children use metaphor naturally. When teaching poetry writing to children, make sure they capitalize on their natural use of this thinking strategy. In writing metaphor children can begin with themselves. The *I Am* or identification experience is at the basis of much poetry. The following activity involves writing first group, then individual poems using the *I Am* metaphor.

Objective: Students will write group, then individual poems around metaphors.

Prewriting: Each person writes two sentences beginning with *I am.* To finish each sentence take something from two of the following categories:

a small animal
something from a garden
the weather
a liquid
a part of the body

Example: I am a small scurrying mouse. I am a tornado.

Drafting: In groups of four, each person contribute one sentence. One person writes for the group. After writing four *I Am* sentences, the group thinks of a title to connect them.

Sharing: One from each group shares.

Follow-up activity: Individuals write *I Am* poems.

The model used for the *I Am* poem exercise for second grade was *Moon Mobile* by Mary Kay Rummel. As you read the poem written by the second grader and by the sixth grader notice again the strong expression of feeling. The sixth graders were led by poet John Caddy to create a work of art that would express how they feel inside.

Moon Mobile

I am a bird song,
song of a bird, rising
over bodies asleep,
waking up hopeful at dawn.

And I am a stone,
a stone found by the sea
that you carry in your pocket
and squeeze when you are scared.

The truth is that I am neither
light nor heavy, singing nor silent.
I am no more than a sliver,
a sliver of moon in the morning sky
that outwaits the sun.

Mary Kay Rummel

Self Portrait

I am a painting
on a cloth of different patches of material.
In the center
a red banana on canvas,
In a corner
a wash of gray.

People ask each other
"What is that green circle?"
"Why a brown truck?"
The people laugh
at a low corner
where a child painted a ball
of blue, green, yellow,
orange, purple,
and red.
They seem to like
the picture of frightening faces weeping,
dark streets
and the dead.
I don't understand,
then I see the little boy.
He is crying.

Tim Rummel, grade 6

WHO AM I?

I AM A PAIR OF SHOES
RUNNING TO THE STORE
TO GET SOME FOOD.
THEN I COME BACK WALKING
TO MY HOUSE.
I AM A BED THAT LIKES
TO SLEEP IN THE MORNING
AND GET UP IN THE NIGHT.
I AM A PERSON
THAT IS WRITING A STORY
THAT IS ABOUT A RED CAT.

ANDY WEBSTER, grade 2

Using Models

It is teacher modeling that creates the atmosphere of sharing and experimentation with language that cause expressive writing to come alive in a classroom. A first grade teacher wrote a list poem as a model for her young students.

Things That Always Surprise Me

The first snowfall
the softness of a baby's skin
people that hurt other people
with words or actions
the smell of baking bread
sliding on ice in my car
the coldness of the water
in Lake Michigan
people taking someone else's
belongings
the enthusiasm of sports fanatics
the talent of a nine year old boy
called Mozart.

Carol Jacobsen, first grade teacher
Randolph Heights Elementary School

After listening to her poem and asking her questions about its content, the children contributed ideas for a class list poem. Individuals then wrote poems based on the list or poems that moved in a new direction. The following poem is the class list poem.

Things That Make Me Smile

When I get home making snowforts,
saying "I can do it."
My dog licking my face
my cat lying on my lap
my friends
my brother throwing me in the snow
my sister cleaning our room
sleeping under the Christmas tree
my friend's baby's smile
my sister grabbing my hands.

Grade 1

Poetry is primarily an expression of strong feeling. In the following poem, notice how the young poet played with lines in order to have the lines convey the emotion. Just showing models will help children do this.

How Do You Feel Being There?

I feel like an elephant when
he
goes
a
stomping
to
the
end
of the jungle, or a bee
who busies himself away
from getting pollen to the
flowers
by
buzzing
away
all
the
petals
to a
feeling
of new, the sun's feeling is brightness
of glow.

—Adapted from a fourth grade student

It is important to note, however, that reading a poem as a model for prewriting is not enough. As the sample lesson plans have shown, other prewriting activities (such as drawing and mind mapping) are also necessary in order for children to rehearse their ideas.

Compression in Poetry

Along with manipulation of line and repetition, compression gives form and power to poetry. Children often write their poetry like prose. In revision they can learn to set off their ideas by lines and to take out extra words that weaken the force of the poem.

Have students read through their lines, stopping at the end of each one. Then have them break up or combine lines by drawing a slash at the place where they want the line to end. Rewrite, making each slash the end of a line. Tell them that when they read contemporary free verse they should stop at the end of each line.

How Does it Feel Being Alive?

Being brought and cared for in a new world.
Air to breathe and the movements to prove you're there.
You can feel some of your movements like

The rhythms of your heart beating, the blood
Through your body or even your pulse.

Notice how much stronger and effective the compressed version of the poem is.

How Does it Feel?

Being brought
cared for
in a new world.
Air to breathe
movements to prove you're there
Rhythms
heart beats, blood pulses
through your body
You're Alive!

If you take some of these ideas and start your students writing and sharing poetry, it will feed itself. Their interest, enthusiasm, and creativity will grow as they succeed in creating poems that are concrete, true to feeling, and fresh in perspective. They will begin to find their own poetic voice.

NARRATIVE WRITING

Personal Experience Stories

The personal experience story is the natural beginning of narrative for children. The previous chapter discussed in depth the personal experience story as a medium for teaching writing process strategies. This is the type of writing in which children can most easily work on the detail that will make their writing more mature. This section will give a few more ideas for eliciting personal narrative and discuss the evaluation that is specific to it as a writing form.

All children can find topics for personal experience stories. It is the stuff of their daily lives. All they need to know is that you and their classmates are interested in hearing and reading those stories. Some suggestions for personal experience stories are listed here.

Personal Reminiscences

My First Allowance
A Very Important Decision and Why I Made It
My Narrowest Escape
I Changed My Mind
I Was in a Hurry, and . . .
My Big Moment
My Ancestors
The Origin of My Family Name
A Tradition in Our Family
Moving into a Strange Town
The Prize Memory of This Year
If I Could Do It Over
Clouds in the Sky
An Unusual Incident
Keeping a New Year's Resolution
Houses I Remember
He Who Hesitates Is Lost
A Fishing Trip
A Trip to the Zoo
I Was Scared
The Dog in My Family
I Knew It Would Happen

Personal Reactions

My Name
My Favorite Sport
Why I Like Poetry
My Idea of Hard Work
My Favorite Color
What Animal I Should Like To Be for a Day
What I Like About (Ohio)
What I Really Enjoy Doing
If I Were President
My Hobby and Why I Like It
My Book of the Year
My Favorite Subject
My Favorite Season
My Ambition
My Alarm Clock
Confused
My Most Important Day
A Book Character I Should Like To Meet
Things that Make Me Happy
I Am Afraid of . . .
Getting Something New
Man's Greatest Invention
If I Had a Million

Literature is another primary stimulus for personal experience stories. Children respond to literature by connecting it with their own lives. A second grade child wrote the following story in response to the poem, "Shadows," by Siv Cedering Fox (1979).

> Every morning my Brother wakes me up at 1:00. I say go to bed he goes and gets his pillow and brings it to my room. And then goes back to bed. Then he gets up at 3:00 and says get up and I say go back to bed the next time he tries to get me up is 10:00 but I am alrety at School. He screems for me and screems and screems for me. Then I come home he says ware were you. The next night it is nice and quiit. But the nest time it was so quiit I herd crecks on the flor I thot that it was goblins or gosts or even wiches. But then I remembed that goblins and gost were al falls. And it was just my Mom and Dad walking arond the House. The End

These kinds of extended stories that involve a number of events help increase fluency in young children.

What should you look for in personal experience narrative?

The most important aspect in this type of writing is the recording of the experience. You can ask these questions about the story keeping in mind that these are generic and mean something different for writers at different stages of development.

Does the writing show:

1. Direct and accurate recording?
2. Sensitivity to the meaning of the experience?
3. Relationship to the real world?
4. Observations of and response to happenings in the surroundings?
5. Precise sensory details of sight, hearing, feeling, touching, tasting?

How would you rate the story by the second grader on these characteristics?

Personal experience has a specific narrative organization that involves a sequence of events. These questions look at the organizational aspect. Does the paper have:

1. A central idea?
2. A sequence of development?
3. Adequate scene setting?
4. Voice of the author?
5. Description of scene?
6. Time and place?
7. Description of problem

How would you evaluate the above story on these criteria?

Fictional Narratives

Story writing is probably the most frequent type of "creative writing" in elementary school. Yet children seldom write stories that are effective, satisfying, meaningful pieces of fiction. Often they respond to a topic or a stimulus such as a picture, writing in an associative manner and ending when they get tired writing with "They lived happily ever after" at age six and seven and "Then he died" at age 12. Children can learn strategies to help think their ways through stories, strategies beyond and better than the fragmented approach of teaching plot, character, and setting.

What are the qualities of good fiction? Traditional good fiction deals with universal themes in a particular situation in which the reader cares about what happens to the character. In good fiction the character changes in some way or solves a problem. A good story has a sense of completion or wholeness. One of the main differences between a good story writer and a poor one is that the good writer thinks in terms of possibilities. He or she doesn't even write, "He walked across the room" without thinking of the possibilities inherent in the situation. What possible things could happen as he walks across the room? What are the many possible consequences? Immature story writers don't see possibilities beyond their own associations.

Post modern fiction writers are experimenting with all these traditional qualities of good fiction, but for work with children they are still the ingredients of good fiction. Taberski (1987) suggests five strategies which would enable children to better understand the qualities of good fiction and use them in their own writing. They are:

1. Stress the importance of topic selection when writing fiction; stories should be related to topics children care about and not assignments such as "Write about being an ice cream cone."
2. Use literature to teach fiction writing; discuss the characteristics of the stories that they read and use them as stimuli for new stories; basing fiction writing on literature is especially important when working with young children.
3. Stress the importance of having the main character change or solve a problem; through literature children can learn that every story is about change, sometimes very small changes.
4. Emphasize that stories should be reality-based, or grounded in the writer's own experiences.
5. Encourage the children to research their fiction pieces.

Story telling and creative drama are excellent rehearsal strategies for story writing. The following visual frame called a Story Spider is an effective prewriting technique for teaching story writing because it promotes the concept of many possibilities and choices in writing. Begin with a start, a character, a happening, or a setting, and build the spider from it. Have

FIGURE 9-3

Story Spiders

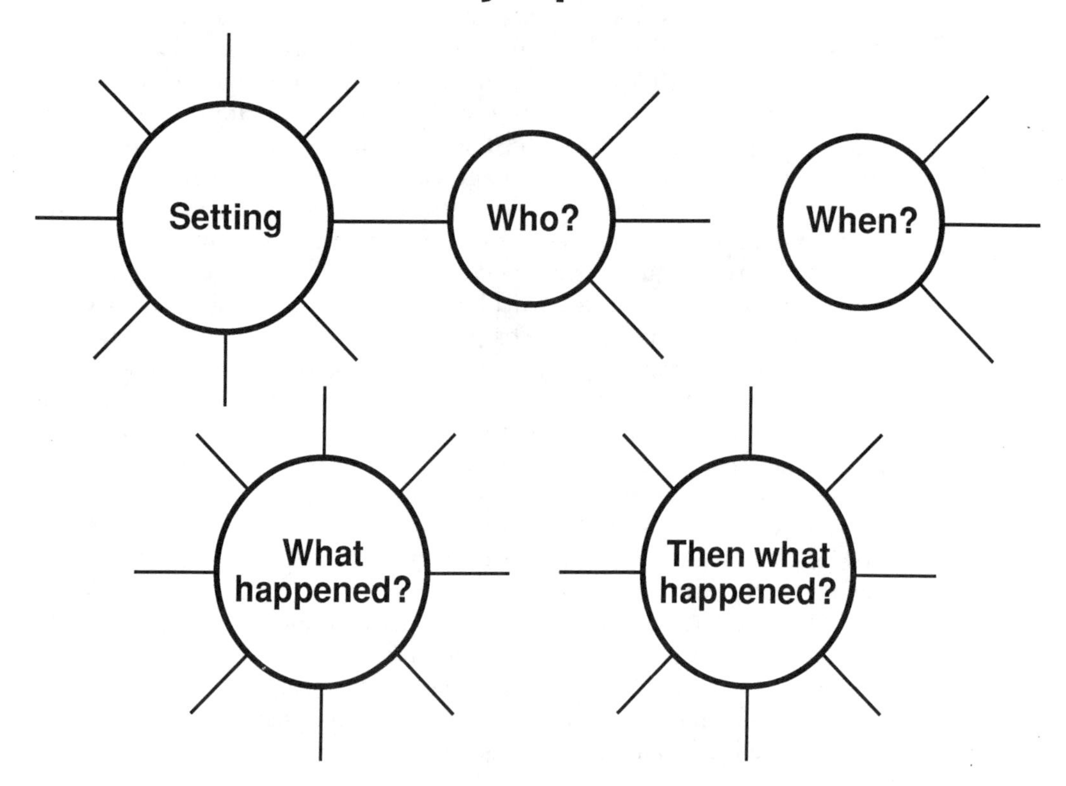

(Adapted from *McDougal-Littell English, Level 6*, 1987.)

students think of many possibilities for each part of the story instead of just one. They should come up with many choices in each section and then go back and select the ones they want to work with.

Character creating will also help children mature in story writing beyond a simple listing of events. Have children choose and create characters and then put them in situations where they run into conflict. If they have spent enough time creating their character, they will know what the character will do in a problem situation. Two character stories present a structure in which children can learn to add the detail that will give the reader a sense of character. Again, the characters and the situations should be close to their own lives or modeled on reading. Prewriting is as important in story writing as it is for every other type of writing.

The five points listed above will give you a sense of what to look for in children's stories. This sense is much more important than the traditional character, setting, plot evaluation.

How would you help the eight-year-old writer of this story?

Big Bad Bruce

One day Bruce, the dog, was playing with the cat. Roxy, the witch, was out picking berries in the forest. Bruce and Kinker the cat went inside. Kinker hit something over. It was some magic liquid. Bruce started to lick it up. He got tired so he fell to sleep. He started to grow bigger. He remembered his past life. Especially when he ate that pie!

He went outside and wrecked the garden. Then he left and went into the forest. When Roxy the witch came back, she saw her garden. She went to find Bruce but he wasn't there. She made a basket for Kinker. Then she went to find Bruce. He was scaring rabbits, squirrels, and other small forest animals. Then Roxy really got mad and set food out for Bruce. He was too smart and didn't eat it. It sat there all night.

When Roxy saw it still there she was really angry. She got all the men from the town. They scared him to another forest with their guns. There he lived. He scared the forest animals there. Big Bad Bruce lived there for the rest of his life. He moved from the forest evergreen to the black forest.

Andy Rummel, grade 3

EXPOSITORY WRITING

Report Writing

Children often write reports in the content areas, especially science and social studies. What is involved in writing a report? A report involves the same type of writing as description but includes the ability to get information from other sources. Report writing should start as simple description of observations for young children and the addition of information from reference sources should be added gradually. There is no value in the common practice of assigning reports to be done at home where children copy paragraphs from the encyclopedia. Students of any age should be led by the teacher step by step through the process of writing a report. The stages of the writing process are as important in report writing as in all other writing. We write the way we think.

Prewriting for a report on any topic should begin with a self search to help the students learn what they already know about a topic. This can be done by making a mind map on the topic as described in the previous chapter. They can then decide what areas they need to read about. A topic should be brainstormed by the class or individual students before they start studying for a report so that they can formulate questions which they need to answer about the topic. Students need to ask their own questions about a subject. The following steps will help them.

1. Decide upon a topic. (such as Earthquakes)
2. Brainstorm questions about it.
   How do they happen?
   Can they be predicted?
   How are they measured? etc.

3. Evaluate the questions.
   Do they expand or focus?
   Are the answers in the textbook or somewhere else?
4. Choose questions to be answered.
   Set limits. For example, choose six, only two can be easy.
5. Sequence the questions picked.
6. Set a goal. When we have answered these questions, what will we know (such as causes, results)? This gives a topic sentence to work with.
7. Revise. Are there any questions we want to add or subtract?
8. Assess. After study, ask, were the questions productive?
   Did they get the kind of information we wanted?

Students should get an assignment sheet with these steps on it.

Taking Notes

As practice for note taking, a short selection with a total of 150 to 200 words could be placed on the overhead with instructions to read and write notes about the topic. Comparison of notes written by the pupils would be encouraged, the discussion concluding with suggestions for note taking such as:

1. Read the whole selection before beginning.
2. Take notes only on ideas about the subject that are important and interesting.
3. Write notes in your own words without changing the meaning.
4. Do not copy notes that you don't understand.
5. Number each note.

References: It is advisable to have the pupils use only one reference source when they begin writing reports. Later they can use more than one. Reference books with which children should become acquainted include dictionaries, encyclopedias, biographical dictionaries, almanacs, atlases, and book indexes.

Bibliographies. Pupils make lists of books as they gather information from many sources. From the beginning, they are taught to note the source of information or quotation and to give credit to an author whose material they use in their writing. In the intermediate grades bibliographies should include publisher, place of publication, copyright date, and pages read as well as author and title. There is no standard form in general use and most districts use a common form. Pupils also need to learn to use bibliographies and to find reference books in the library.

Organizing. It is effective to have children take notes on notecards, titling each card. Then when they are finished they can list topics covered on the cards and organize the cards in the order they want to use them.

Mind mapping is another strategy for organizing report information. Students can make a mind map on everything they know about the topic and then organize topics on the mind map by circling them and numbering them. An example of such a mind map is shown on page in Chapter 2.

Outlining is an effective organization for some students if they are going to give an oral report. Outlines should be brief and are better than having students read from the report to the class.

Presenting a Report

This activity involves a whole new set of skills—those of oral presentation. Not all reports should be presented orally. Some can be posted around the room and read by others. Oral reports should include visual materials or they may be in the form of a panel or a dramatic presentation. They should never be given one after another but be scheduled over a long period of time. They should also be limited to a short time. When students give oral reports they should be given procedural instructions such as those listed below. They should also be given feedback from both teachers and peers. Children who are listening should be given a sheet with specific behaviors to look for such as "Was the speaker loud enough?" as well as content questions such as "What was the most important information in this report?" Both presenter and listeners need to work in this situation and both are evaluated.

REPORTING GUIDE

1. Choose a subject that is interesting to you and to those who will hear the report.
2. Gather information from various sources.
3. Take notes from your reading, putting them into your own words, if possible.
4. Select only the ideas essential to the subject. Arrange the ideas in a logical sequence.
5. Prepare an outline, noting the main and supporting topics.
6. Begin the report with an interesting sentence. Strive for varied ways of presenting the material. Use examples, pictures, objects, and diagrams to make the points clear. Plan an interesting conclusion.
7. Use acceptable sentence patterns and vocabulary, and speak in a clear, conversational tone.

Persuasive Writing

In one sense all writing for an audience needs to be persuasive. More formally, persuasive writing relates to argument or writing to convince others. It is difficult for elementary children to keep a sense of audience clearly in mind in the way that it is necessary in order to write persuasively.

However, in the upper grades children need to begin to learn how to write opinion and support those opinions. They also need to learn how to analyze language critically as it is used in advertisements to persuade them. The writing of persuasion and study of persuasion techniques go together. Advertising, since commercials are so familiar to children, is a good place to start this study.

FUNCTIONAL WRITING

The forms for other types of functional writing such as letter writing, card writing, thank you notes, telephone messages, and filling in forms should be taught as the need arises for them in the school year. Language arts texts include instruction in these life skills but the instruction is only meaningful if it relates to what is going on in the classroom or in other parts of the students' lives. Many opportunities for functional writing do appear during the year such as open houses, holidays, and school newspapers. A natural opportunity for instruction in letter writing should not be passed up since letter writing is so clearly audience directed. Writing a letter, like everything else, requires prewriting and planning.

Using Letters as Literary Form

After teaching the skills of writing friendly and business letters, try some of these activities.

1. Read letters from famous people. Discuss how letters describe the times in which people lived, their feelings, hopes, and ambitions. For example, letters of E. B. White and Beatrix Potter describe how some of their classic stories originated. Share old family letters if desired to show how family history and genealogy can be traced.
2. Try writing these kinds of letters.

a. Write a letter to a favorite author telling why you liked the story or book.
b. You are a historical character at a famous event writing to a family member or friend. For example, Harriet Tubman on the Underground Railroad, Neil Armstrong on the moon, and so on.
c. Write letters to the editor concerning issues confronting your community or school.
d. Imagine yourself a favorite character in a story and write about your adventures to another character. For example, Goldilocks writing about her encounter with the three bears.
e. Write a travel letter which can be used as a brochure to sell vacations.

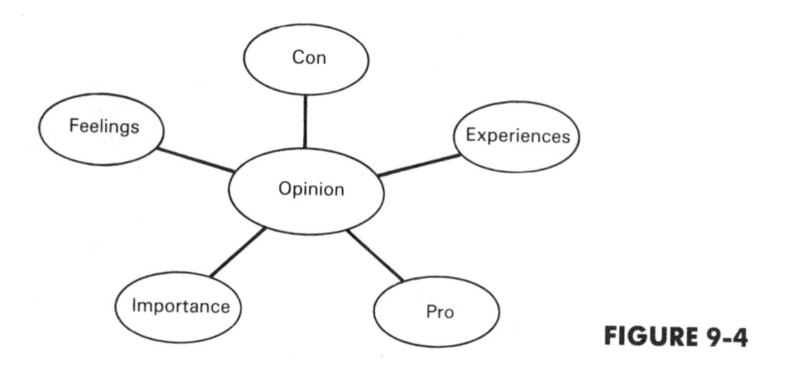

FIGURE 9-4

SUMMARY: LAYERING

Through the process of layering, students experience reading and writing in description, poetry, personal narratives, fiction, and report writing. As they move from the easier to more difficult forms, a solid foundation is being laid for them to write in many forms, choosing the form required by the situation, their own purposes, and the audience.

Different purposes lead to use of different genres although there is an overlap. A desire to inform may lead to a report, a persuasive paragraph, or a story. The demands of the audience may help decide which of these genres to use. These options make the writing process a joyous one.

This piece of writing by a fifth grade student is an amazing example of the layering process. It shows how forms for writing overlap and how the fluent writer chooses forms that will satisfy his purpose for his audience. In this case he was writing for his peers. "Huffy" is a response to an assignment to write an opinion essay. Figure 9-4 shows the frame given to the students to help in prewriting and organization:

As Kenneth wrote, the ideas that he wanted to express took the shape of a prose poem. The material that is required for the opinion essay but the compression and rhythm turn his work into poetry. Children, while writing, integrate learnings and create something uniquely personal when they are given time to prewrite, freedom to work with assignments as guides, not recipes, and the chance to share. Kenneth couldn't wait to share and "sing" his opinion essay.

Huffy

I believe that Huffy bikes are weak. I mean, the bikes are out of style man. Why did they have to bring Huffy's into business anyway? Skyway, Dominator, Predator, Diamond Back, Caliento, and Hutch are out-beating

Huffy. I have advice for you Huffians. Whatever you do, don't get one assembled or unasembled. Don't get one at all. They fall apart. The chain falls off. When you're going fast, the breaks don't work. the seats turn around too much. I know. I have one, which is too bad for me. One day I was riding my super-weak Huffy, when I patted it. I must of patted it a little too hard because the wheels and handlebars crumbled. I'm telling you, don't get a Huffy. *they are weak!* If you have a Huffy, destroy it! I'll get you a neww bike. This is a song for you Huffians: "Ain't it weak? It's coming down the street. Now I ask you very confidentally, ain't it weak?" Well anyway, you know the motto of Huffy? I think it should be changed from "Huffy, America's first choice" to "Huffy. America's last choice" or "Huffy. America's worst choice" or "Huffy. Rebbeca's only choice." The motto stinks. It's totally barforamma, man. I mean "PU!" If I was on Rated K, I'd give it a TS for "totally sucks." Here's some advice for you Huffians from Max Headroom. "Don't get a H-H-Huffy. They are c-c-cheap-cheap. I Had a Huffy, t-t-too. The bike fell a-a-apart when a fly landed on it. Don't doubt the fact that c-c-computers can get bikes. They can't." Here's a joke for you Huffians: "Found a Huffy, found a Huffy, found a Huffy just now, just now I found a Huffy, found a Huffy just now. It was rotten, it was rotten, it was rotten just now, just now it was rotten it was rotten just now. Rode it anyway, rode it anyway, rode it anyway just now, just now I rode it anyway, rode it anyway just now." Herron my Huffy. Smells musty, Don't it? I should sit my bike in a corner of a shack and let the cobwebs collect on it.

Moral: Take your Huffy to the
dump!!!

Kenneth Jarmon

REFERENCES

BARONE, PATRICIA. (1983, Fall). I write a poem with claire who is four. *Germination.*

MASTERS, CAROL. (1987). Fly ball. *This Sporting Life.* Milkweed Editions.

ANGELO, VALENTI. (1961). *Angelo and the Barefoot Saint.* New York: Viking.

ESTES, ELEANOR. (1958) *Pinky Pye.* New York: Harcourt, Brace & World.

McDougal-Littell English, Level 6. (1987). Evanston: McDougal-Littell & Company.

RILKE, M. R. (1977). *Duino Elegies and The Sonnets to Orpheus* (Poulin, Trans.). Boston: Houghton Mifflin.

RUMMEL, TIM. (1985). Self-portrait. First published in *A Piece of the Moon Is Missing.* St. Paul: Compas.

TABERSKI, SHARON. (1987, October). From fact to fiction: Young children learn about writing fiction. *Language Arts,* pp. 586-592.

GENERAL BIBLIOGRAPHY

APPLEGATE, MAUREE. (1963). *Freeing children to write.* New York: Harper and Row.

ATWELL, NANCY. (1987). *In the Middle: Writing Reading and Learning with Adolescents.* Portsmouth: Heinemann.

BURROWS, ALVINA T. ET AL. (1962). *They all want to write.* Englewood Cliffs, N.J.: Prentice Hall.

CARLSON, RUTH. (1970). *Literature for children: Enrichment ideas.* Dubuque, Ia.: William C. Brown Co. Pub.

CARLSON, RUTH KEARNEY. (1965). *Sparkling words: Two hundred practical and creative writing ideas.* Berkeley, Calif.: Wagner Printing Co.

FURNER, BEATRICE A. (1973, March). Creative writing through creative dramatics. *Elementary English*. pp. 405-408, 416.

GIROUX, JOAN. (1974). *The haiku form*. Rutland, Vt.: Charles E. Tuttle Co.

GOLDBERG, NATALIE. (1986). *Writing down the bones. Boston: Shambala.*

HANSEN, JANE. (1987). *When writers read*. Portsmouth: Heinemann.

HILLOCHS, GEORGE. (1975). *Observing and Writing*. Urbana, Ill.: NCTE.

KELLOW, AND KRISAH, (Eds.) (1983). *Poetry and language*. Toronto: McGraw-Hill Ryerson.

KOCH, KENNETH. (1973). *Rose, where did you get that red?* New York: Random House.

KOCH, KENNETH. (1970). *Wishes, lies and dreams: Teaching children to write poetry*. New York: Random House.

LANDRUM AND CHILDREN FROM PS1 AND PS2 IN NEW YORK CITY. (1971). *A day dream I had at night and other stories: Teaching children how to make their own readers*. Champaign, Ill.: NCTE.

LARRICK, NANCY. (Ed.) (1971). *Somebody turned a tap on these kids*. New York: Delacote Press.

PETTY, WALTER T., and BOWEN, MARY E. (1967). *Slithery snakes and other aids to children's writing*. New York: Appleton-Century-Crofts.

RODGERS, D. (1972, March). A process for poetry writing. *Elementary school journal, 72*, 294-303.

RUPLEY, WILLIAM H. Teaching and evaluating creative writing in the elementary grades. (ERIC/RCS) *Language Arts. 5*, 586.

SMITH, FRANK. (1988). *Joining the literacy club: further essays into education*. Portsmouth: Heinemann.

TEACHERS AND WRITERS COLLABORATIVE (Eds.) (1972). *The whole word catalog*. Champaign, Ill: NCTE.

YATES, ELIZABETH. (1962). *Someday you'll write*. New York: E. P. Dutton and Company.

10

GRAMMAR AND USAGE

Teachers and administrators often tell parents, "We teach grammar," or "We give lots of grammar," as if this ensured quality of education. The teaching of grammar carries with it the weight of tradition so the myth goes on. "We studied grammar so this generation should study it." Often, however, people are unclear about what they mean by grammar and, even more, the reasons for its study.

When educators and parents say "grammar" they often mean usage, which relates to various styles of language; morphology, which is really vocabulary study including homonyms, homographs, root words, and inflectional devices; or mechanics such as punctuation, capitalization, and spelling. Grammar really refers to the rules which govern the sentences or syntax of language. Traditional grammar is the collection of grammatical principles and rules that have been and still are being used by most teachers and in most language arts texts. Some features of traditional grammar are:

1. Parts of speech. There are seven to ten parts of speech: noun, pronoun, verb, adjective, adverb, preposition, conjunction, article, infinitive, and interjection. Nouns and verbs are defined according to meaning. Prepositions, adjectives, and adverbs are defined according to function.

2. Functions of parts of speech. Parts of speech can serve several different functions. A noun may be a subject, a direct object, a subjective complement, an indirect object, or an object of a preposition.

3. Terms and explanations of larger units. Phrases, clauses, and sentences—particularly the subject-predicate concept of a sentence—are covered in traditional grammar. Sentences are categorized according to function (declarative, interrogative, imperative, and exclamatory) and structure (simple, compound, complex).

4. Sentence expansion by modification, subordination, and coordination. The problems with consistency encountered in traditional grammar result from the fact that it was originally derived from an inflected language, Latin. English isn't an inflected language; the endings don't change. The important thing about an adverb in English is not that it's an adverb but that it can be moved around to make a better sentence.

Why teach grammar in the elementary school? How do we teach it effectively? The two questions are related. There is a large body of research that tells us clearly and definitely that the study of grammar in itself does nothing to improve the speaking or writing skills of students (Hillocks, 1987). The hours spent underlining nouns and verbs, diagraming sentences, are a waste of teacher and student time and energy and only produce the negative effect of teaching students to "hate English." Why teach any grammar in elementary school? How do we teach it effectively? The only reason is that it gives children and teachers a language to use in discussion of written work, their own and others'. For example, the immediacy of action in "Gatherers" by Mary Kay Rummel is intensified by the use of specific active verbs. They form the spring of the poem and vivid accurate verbs are the spring that winds up a sentence.

Gatherers

Two night herons
fill the pond with silence.
Those white holes that radiate
light into morning,
light collected while we sleep.
One sits frozen on a branch.
The other slow steps across the mulch,
eye on some elusive prey.
The statue raises a claw
to scratch its neck and back.
Slow and easy, only a screaming jay
can rouse those long bodies.
They are like teenaged boys,
inert in the morning, faces silent,
shining with secrets gathered
during a dark gleaning.

It is helpful for children as they mature to have some knowledge of the nature of language, what words describe certain things.

The teaching of grammar must be done in the context of writing in order to be meaningful. There are several reasons for this. Frequent writing leads to growth in understanding of grammatical principles because children are learning them by using them. If the purpose of instruction in grammar is to give students a language for discussion of writing, instruction must be given in the context of writing. Knowledge will not transfer unless the transfer is taught.

Why are children who begin learning what a predicate is in grade two still unable to define or discriminate a predicate in grade 12? This common occurrence has to do with how we learn. Teachers may start teaching seven-year-olds about predicates, but unless the concept of predicate or noun or verb is somehow connected to the child's life, the learning is short term. Long term retention requires that the learner process learning in a meaningful way. Such activities as repeating information back to the teacher and underlining nouns or predicates in an exercise are short term memory kinds of activities. Any knowledge gained is lost before the class period is over.

Grammatical knowledge is not a skill like multiplication. Children come to it slowly through use over a long period of time. In elementary school a few basic grammatical concepts are taught to an attainment level, not a level of formal definition. To attain a concept at this "fuzzy" level of understanding, children must be able to connect the concept with sensory images and emotions. This is difficult to do with a concept like noun or subject of a sentence unless instruction occurs in the context of writing, reading, and life experience. This kind of grammar instruction in elementary school will prepare students for further development of concepts when they are older.

What concepts should be taught in elementary school? The following pages list suggested activities in the nature and structure of language for different grade levels. These include concepts in morphology, usage, and semantics, or meaning, as well as grammar.

A. Grammar (Phonology, Morphology, Syntax)
   1. Primary grades, K-2
      a. Expose children to the notion of units of utterance. Use and call attention to the terms word and sentence.
      b. Explore a word as an arbitrary symbol made up of sounds in accepted order. Explore different words for the same thing, differences in things called by the same words.
      c. Identify what is a sentence and what is not. Discuss characteristics.
         1) tells or asks something.
         2) don't expect to hear more.
         3) tells or asks about something or someone and something about it.
      d. Give experience in completing part sentences by adding noun phrase or verb phrase. (Can use picture stimulus.)
      e. Explore order of words in a sentence. Must be in accepted order.
      f. Explore relationship between oral and written forms. Letters stand for sounds which make up words.
      g. Explore the effect of intonation and stress on meaning. Give experience in saying things to give variant meanings.
      h. Explore relationship of intonation and stress to capitalization, punctuation, and word division.
      i. Explore the relationship between oral signals and the written signals: the period, question mark, comma (in dates, conversation, series, and between city and state) and the capital at the beginning of a sentence and in special names.
      j. Discover the concept of plurality and common ways of expressing it, both phonemically and graphemically (s, es, ies).
      k. Discover the concept of possession and ways of expressing it, both phonemically and graphemically.
      l. Explore the differences in time expressed in verb tenses and methods of expressing these differences (regular present and past).

m. Discover the various function of words used in different ways: to describe, to name, and to tell what is happening.

2. Middle grades, 3-4
   a. Explore the concept of a word as an arbitrary pattern of sounds recognizing that the same sounds are used over and over again to form different words.
   b. Explore common phonemic-graphemic representation, recognizing that letters are symbols for sounds.
   c. Explore variant meanings for the same morpheme, homophonous morphemes (play-V, play-N), and variant words for the same thing.
   d. Explore word building in the use of combinations of free bases, common prefixes, derivational suffixes, and hyphenation.
   e. Explore the concept of plurality and explore various ways of showing it both phonemically and graphemically (e.g., those which are replacives—man–men, those with no change—sheep–sheep).
   f. Explore the concept of possession and ways of expressing it, both phonemically and morphemically. Include phrases.
   g. Explore the differences in time expressed in verb tenses and methods of expressing them, both phonomically and graphemically (regular and common irregular verb forms).
   h. Explore the form and position of various inflectional classes: nouns, verbs, adjectives, adverbs, and pronouns. Note that some words which are not inflected like the form are used in its position.
   i. Explore the positions and functions of the common positional classes which serve as function words: determiners, prepositions, conjunctions, question words, and auxiliaries.
   j. Explore the accepted arrangement of various types of words in utterances longer than one word.
   k. Discuss criteria of a sentence and develop ability to distinguish sentences from nonsentences. Criteria to be developed:
      1) tells or asks something
      2) has a noun phrase and a verb phrase
      3) don't expect to hear more
      4) ends in a fading or rising terminal
   l. Explore various kinds of sentences: statements, questions, exclamations, and imperatives, noting word order and intonation and stress patterns.
   m. Develop ability to expand noun phrases and/or verb phrases to form sentences of various types.
   n. Develop ability to expand basic sentence patterns through modification or substitution and to rearrange movable parts.
   o. Develop the concept that different meanings can be expressed through use of different intonation and stress patterns.
   p. Develop awareness of the intonation and stress patterns used in various types of sentences.
   q. Explore the relationship between intonation and stress and capitalization, punctuation, and word division in a variety of types of uttereances (for example, headlines, signs, various sentence patterns).

r. Explore the relationship between oral signals and the written signals: period in a statement, question mark in a question, comma in dates, city and state, after an introductory word, in series, and in conversation, capitals at the beginning of a sentence, special names, initials, written conversations, and to show emphasis.

3. Upper grades, 5-6
   a. Explore language as a system of sounds in which words are made up of patterns of sounds.
   b. Explore the phonology of English by identifying some of the phonemes of English and realizing that they are used in agreed upon patterns to make words / p +/ /+ p/.
   c. Identify various free morphemes of English noticing how they are used to express meaning.
   d. Explore word building processes in combinations of free morphemes, derivational suffixes and prefixes, hyphenation, and close relationship of the adjective + N pattern. Discover the order of addition of suffixes.
   e. Discover the differences in free morphemes which carry lexical meaning and bound morphemes which carry syntactic meaning.
   f. Explore the concept of plurality and various ways of expressing it both phonemically and graphemically (for example, those which are replacives and loan words).
   g. Explore the concept of possession and ways of expressing it, phonemically and graphemically. Include phrases and when the plural ends in *s* or after proper names which end in *s*.
   h. Explore differences in time expressed in verb tenses and methods of expressing them both phonemically and graphemically. Include regular and irregular verbs, modals, and to be, have, and do as auxiliaries.
   i. Explore the form and position of various inflectional classes: nouns, verbs, adjectives, adverbs, and pronouns. Explore the groups of words which will fill the positions held by these words.
   j. Explore the positions and functions of the common positional classes: determiners, prepositions, conjunctions (subordinating and correlative, as well as coordinating), question words, auxiliaries, relatives.
   k. Explore the accepted arrangement of various types of words in utterances longer than one word. Try various possible arrangements noting their semantic effect.
   l. Discuss criteria of various sentences as in middle grades. Explore various intonation patterns in complex sentences which may have rising and sustained terminals in them.
   m. Explore various kinds of basic sentences noting word order and intonation and stress patterns.
   n. Develop ability to expand sentence parts by attaching modifiers and substituting or by rearrangement of movable parts.
   o. Explore ways to join basic sentences to form more complex sentences, through joining, subordination, and embedding (do it as a descriptive process).
   p. Explore the effect of various intonation and stress patterns and ways of showing these graphemically.

q. Explore the relationship of intonation and stress to capitalization, punctuation, and word division in items listed for middle grades and the following:
   1) comma in direct address, before a connective in a compound sentence, to indicate a pause, to set off a transitional phrase
   2) hyphen in compound words
   3) colon in listing
   4) semicolon in multiple listings and before a connective word in a compound sentence.

r. Develop facility in interpreting graphemic representation of intonation and stress.

B. Dialects
   1. Primary grades, K-2
      a. Make children aware of different languages and different ways of saying the same thing.
      b. Make children curious about differences in language.
   2. Middle grades, 3-4
      a. Develop awareness of different ways of saying things—differences in sound, words chosen, or order.
      b. Explore reasons for the differences due to geographic region, age levels, and background.
      c. Explore the idea that each person uses serveral varieties of language. Give experiences in using different varieties.
      d. Note dialectical differences which children hear or are exposed to in literature.

C. Change in Language
   1. Primary grades, K-2
      a. Observe any morphemes which are new or which have dropped out of the language. Discuss the reasons for this.
   2. Middle grades, 3-4
      a. Explore ways in which language changes by adding words, dropping words, or changing meanings for words.
      b. Discuss meanings of slang terms.
      c. Discuss meanings of words like victrola which are no longer used.
   3. Upper grades, 5-6
      a. Explore the ways in which a language changes to meet the needs of society.
      b. Note changes in syntax as forms like those are encountered.
      c. Explore the relationship of English to other Indo-European languages.
      d. Note changes in English as found in literature.

D. Semantics
   1. Primary grades, K-2
      a. Make children aware of the effect of language in the way they feel, for example cheery greetings as opposed to a sour greeting.
   2. Middle grades, 3-4
      a. Explore the dependence of communication on both sender and receiver by discussing what a certain utterance would mean.

   b. Explore the effects of certain words, for example, name calling, prejudice, and so on.
   c. Make children aware of propaganda through ads and other media.
3. Upper grades, 4-5
   a. Explore the effect of language symbols in propaganda, advertising, and essay. Generalize about the control function of language.
   b. Make lists of loaded words.
   c. Discuss reaction to symbols (as in name-calling) as opposed to facts or things.
   d. Try to use language of propaganda, advertising, and so on in its control function.

SENTENCE COMBINING

The following story was written by a sixth grade boy. Notice the structure of his sentences. How could he improve the quality of his written work?

> There once was a bean plant that grew six feet tall and his name was Beanie. Beanie was too tall to sit in a house so he had to go outside. Beanie then saw a dog and the dog ran after Beanie. When Beanie hid, the dog ran away. That was close said Beanie. But that wasn't the end. A storm came and large hail or big ice ball hit Beanie on the head. When Beanie came to he was in the plant hospital. When he got out another dangerous thing came on Beanie. A cold night came and it was 26 degrees out and Beanie froze. Again he went to the plant hospital to get defrosted. Then Beanie got out once again. While Beanie was minding his own business he ran into a poison ivy plant. And he got poison ivy. So he was itching and itching and itching and when he got over it he died of old age. After being chased by a dog and still living after a storm and after a cold night and having poison ivy he died. What a life!

A teaching approach called sentence combining has been shown to be very effective in helping students in fourth grade or above to write more mature sentences. As you remember from the chapter on language development in this text, the number of words per T-unit is the most accurate indicator of syntactic maturity. T-units measure sentence complexity. Sentence combining teaches children how to change run-ons and short choppy sentences into denser, complex sentences. According to Hillocks (1987), "The practice of building complex sentences from simpler ones has been shown to be effective in a larger number of experimental studies." Sentence combining is a grammar activity that has been shown to affect writing skill. It is combining sentence to make a single acceptable sentence. A clue is often included to help the student combine the given sentences. The following are sentence combining models for the elementary grades.

Sentence Combining Models
for the Elementary Grades

A. *Adjective*
He was in the house when it caught fire.
The house was *old.*
He was in the old house when it caught fire.

B. *Present Participle*
The plane crashed into the house.
The plane burns. (ing)
The burning plane crashed into the house.

C. *Past Participle*
The students did their homework.
The homework was *assigned.*
The students did their assigned homework.

D. *Compound Adjective*
He dated the girl.
The girl *loves fun.*
He dated the fun-loving girl.

E. *Preposition Phrase Embedding*
We sailed in the boat.
The boat was the one *with the blue sail.*
We sailed in the boat with the blue sail.

F. *Participle Phrases*
The runner wins.
The runner was *making the best effort.*
The runner making the best effort wins.

G. *Adjective Clause Embedding* (using who, when, which that, when, or where)
He read a story.
The story had a surprise ending. (that)
He read a story that had a surprising ending.

H. *Multiple Adjective Embeddings*
The girl went to San Francisco.
The girl was *tall.*
The girl was *slender.*
The girl won the beauty contest. (who)
The contest was *local.*
The girl competed in the finals. (where)
The finals were state-wide.
The tall, slender girl who won the local beauty contest went to San Francisco, where she competed in the state-wide contest.

I. *Noun Clause*
SOMETHING alarmed his parents.
He might not have grades high enough to get him into Mugwamp College. (the fact that)
The fact that he might not have grades high enough to get him into Mugwamp College alarmed his parents.
The pilot tried to explain *something.*
He had drifted so far off course somehow. (how)
The pilot tried to explain how he had drifted so far off course.

J. *Gerund Phrase*
He enjoyed *something.*
He wrote his name on fences. (ing)
He enjoyed writing his name on fences.

K. *Infinitive Phrase*
He tried *something.*
He avoided hitting the tree. (to avoid)
He tried to avoid hitting the tree.

L. *Adverb Clause*
The king became confused.
His daughter turned into gold. (when)
The king became confused when his daughter turned into gold.

SLOTTING

Sentence work in which children substitute more accurate specific nouns and verbs for general terms should begin in the primary grades. Begin with a simple statement such as: The boy walked down the street. Take the generic term walked. Make a list of more specific words to describe exactly how the boy walked. Next take the word boy and do the same. Try to arrive at specific nouns and verbs. Help the students avoid excessive use of modifiers. Example:

Noun	Verb
the snow	fell
snowflakes	dropped
flakes	drifted
crystals	fluttered
floated	

PATTERNING

Repetitive pattern books provide an excellent source of model sentences for young children. After reading a pattern book such as John Burningham's *Would You Rather,* help students practice the pattern by making up their own sentences. This type of sentence activity can give children experience using sentence patterns such as "If, then" or "Either, or" which may be new to them. Older children can learn by paraphrasing written models. Select a paragraph from a reading text or literature book. Omit all the adjectives and adverbs or put in general nouns and weak verbs. Have your class, in pairs or small groups, supply them to enhance the paragraph.

Groups can then compare their version with the original. These last two activities are examples of learning about the possibilities of language by doing what authors do.

TEACHING GRAMMAR CONCEPTS

If you are going to teach a grammar concept, you must teach it well. The instruction should be clear and congruent with your objective and it should always be integrated with writing. The following lesson plan demonstrates a lesson which would help students attain the concept of noun.

Objectives

1. The student will demonstrate the ability to pick out a noun in a sentence.
2. The student will know that a noun names a person, place, or thing.

Teacher Actions

1. The teacher states that a noun is a name for a person, place, or thing.
2. The teacher and students give examples of nouns.
3. The teacher writes complete sentences on the board, coloring the nouns in red.
4. The teacher asks the class to give examples of nouns.
5. The teacher asks the class to raise hands when they hear a noun mentioned in a sentence. Teacher reads sentences from students' own written work.
6. Teacher asks students to underline three nouns in something they have written. The teacher asks for volunteers to write their own sentences on the board, putting nouns in red.

Student Actions

1. Students state examples of nouns.
2. Students raise their hands when they hear a noun mentioned in a sentence.
3. Students write or find in their own written work at least two sentences and outline the nouns in red.
4. Students volunteer to write sentences on the board.
5. Students demonstrate understanding of the concept of noun by describing what a noun is in their own words at the end of the lesson.

Further Application

1. Students cut words and pictures out of the newspaper or magazines that represent nouns.
2. Students make sentences using the nouns they cut out.
3. Students make small notebooks using this procedure with one example per page.

This type of instruction involves much more than underlining nouns on worksheets, but if you want children to attain grammar concepts, you must take the time to teach them in this way.

USAGE

Language situations range from the informal to the formal. However, most students are not aware of or not convinced of the need for knowledge of standard as well as conversational language. The following activities develop awareness in students of the levels of both spoken and written communication.

Begin by listing a variety of language situations, for example:

social studies report
directions to your house
class discussion
speech to rest of school
letter to a friend
conversation with an adult relative
conversation with a good friend
conference with principal or minister

Ask students to rank these situations from the most formal to the least formal. Discuss the reasons why a friendly conversation differs from a formal report. Students will usually see slang as a barrier to non-peer communication. Spend some time investigating both local and age level slang and regional and group dialect differences.

Words with more than one meaning provide another introduction to the concept of language levels. Many times standard words are used in new ways, with new meanings. These words work on more than one level of language. Their meaning depends on how you use them. For example, think about these words: cool, dig, turkey, neat. All of them have at least two meanings. Each one is used as a slang word and each one also has a meaning in standard English. Have students listen to friends or a TV program and write down some of the language they hear. Listen for slang and for words with two meanings. Have students gather slang/dialect expressions from a particular set of words or pictures (that is, pancakes may be called flapjacks, johnny cakes, griddle cakes, and so on).

Another approach consists of creating a set of role playing situations. For example, students might role play the following:

job interview
conference with principal
conversation with a friend's father
lunchroom conversation

Ask students in the audience to note any differences in language use. Note sentence use. Do friends converse in choppier, less complete language than a student and principal?

THE CODE IN OUR CULTURE

The following sets of activities are designed to help children attain understanding of three major concepts about the levels in our language.

Concept: Language Use Is Influenced by Situation or Context

A. Consider what type of person might have said each of the following and in what situation. Consider whether the same person might have said each.

I reside in a penthouse at two hundred and ten West Fortieth Street.
I live in a townhouse at two hundred ten West Fortieth Street.
I live in an apartment at two-ten West Fortieth.
I hang out in a flat at two-ten West four-o.

B. Pair children for role playing. Ask each pair to create two different scenes in which one person expresses thanks to another for some gift. They are to determine who they are, their age, occupation, sex, where they live, the nature of the gift, and how they would say thank you. Encourage them to make their two scenes as different as possible.

C. Consider the cause of variety in each of the following groups. Complete those having open slots.

victrola
phonograph

icebox

refrigerator

employer
supervisor
manager

clothes
togs
duds
rags

film
movie

limousine
automobile
car
hot-rod
rod

bag	spider
sack	skillet
poke	frying pan
flat	lift
apartment	elevator

D. Guide children to conduct a survey of differences in language in both oral and written forms. Suggest they try to note the age of the person and what situation the language was used in. Ask them to record their reaction to the language and what they could tell about the speaker by the language used. To focus on different occupations ask each person to talk to their parents about their jobs, noting specific vocabulary used. Discussion of survey information should focus on nature of dialect (previous time, age level, socio-economic, education, occupational, geographic or political region, and situational context). Children should be guided to discover that each person by his language, and that use of the appropriate dialect for each situation, can aid oral and written communication by creating the desired effect.

E. Use of concepts can be provided through the following:

1. Ask children to role play various situations involving differing age, occupational, and formal-informal settings.
2. Guide children to identify samples in books they are reading where language differences create a desired effect.
3. Groups could be established to explore the dialect of various occupational groups, such as the space agency, farmers, secretaries, or the medical professions. They could attempt to find words or phrases not in common use by the public or which have a different meaning.
4. Children can be given a set of statements such as the following. After discussion of various possibilities for each statement, develop motivation by asking children to picture the incident in their minds and to write a few paragraphs choosing their words and language patterns to indicate just what type of person he is, the setting, and what happens to him.

   There is a male who does yardwork.
   He is going home.
   He wears unattractive clothes.
   He lives in a rented place.
   He is forty-five or fifty.
   He is tired and carries a large package.
   He has a misfortune on the way.

Concept: Oral Signals

Oral signals such as pitch, stress, pauses and stops are part of the structure of English since they aid in expressing meanings. Listening for these oral signals and thinking what meaning is given can provide a basis for capitalization and punctuation in the written system.

A. Mark capitalization and punctuation as indicated by the speaker for each sample. In samples 4-8 try also to show the meaning of each utterance.

1. he lives in the white house doesn't he
2. he lives in the white house doesn't he
3. he lives in the white house doesn't he
4. I'm going home
5. I'm going home
6. I'm going home
7. I'm going home
8. I'm going home

B. Oral signals used in expressing meaning

1. Stress	2. Juncture	3. Pitch
Primary	pause	extra high
Secondary	fading terminal	high or stress
Tertiary	rising terminal	normal
Weak	sustained terminal	low

Listen to how these are used in combination to express meaning by determining order and meanings of taped sentences.

C. Capitalize and punctuate the following sentences in various ways to reflect various intonation patterns (pitch, stress, pauses, and stops) and various meanings. Listen to yourself as you say them.

tommy the turtle said mother has escaped
tommy the turtle said mother has escaped
tommy the turtle said mother has escaped
tommy the turtle said mother has escaped

D. Read the following sample to establish a meaning. Then show that meaning by using capitalization and punctuation to show how it sounds.

tom and cliff were walking down the main street in their town tom said cliff i'm going to punch you in the nose if you don't move over i don't want to fall in that hole over there it is a steep drop after a gentle nudge is heard the sound of the shuffle of sand and cliff.

Ideas can be shared to stress ability to think of meaning, listen, and encode. Children could also exchange papers to read aloud for practice in decoding.

Concept: Expressing Ideas

English permits choice in the manner of expressing ideas to indicate attitudes, positive and negative feelings, and perceived relationships.

After each indicate the kind of feeling each word arouses, using these responses: F (favorable), U (unfavorable), and N (neutral).

A.	B.	C.
1.	boy	dancer
2.	athlete	petite
3.	musician	young lady
4.	reader	athlete
5.	mannerly	tall
6.	teen-age	quiet
7.	cool	neat

D. Give one word with an unfavorable connotation for each of the following:

1. slender
2. verbal
3. big
4. yellow
5. injustice
6. nonsuccess
7. play
8. chatty

E. List several words for each of the following which show a positive or negative attitude, a feeling, or a relationship.

1. large size
2. slender
3. dark-colored
4. sudden
5. daring
6. creative
7. quiet
8. careful

F. Think of a school problem about which you have strong feelings. Write an essay or letter to the principal or school paper expressing your point of view with use of emotionally toned words. Next write a second letter expressing the same ideas in objective and impersonal language. Consider to whom each letter would appeal.

Write an accurate description of a friend in such a way that your words give a favorable bias. Then describe the same person, again accurately, using facts and words that will create an unfavorable bias.

G. Have children listen to a literary selection containing effective sensory imagery to discover sight, sound, feeling, taste, smell, movement, and emotional images. They may wish to share such selections of books they are reading.

For further background see "The Environment of Language" by Norman Cousins, in *Introductory Readings on Language,* Wallace L.

Anderson and Norman C. Stageberg, editors (Third edition, New York: Holt, Rinehart and Winston, Inc., 1970), pp. 155-158, from which many ideas were drawn.

ACTIVITIES FOR THE METHODS CLASS

1. Examine an elementary school language arts textbook. What is the nature of the grammar content: topics, scope, sequence, and teaching suggestions.
2. Plan a lesson for one grammar concept using the form given in this chapter related to each of the following.
3. Plan a lesson on the levels of language using ideas given in this chapter.
4. Choose a repetitive pattern book written for primary children and use it as a basis for a written or oral lesson on creating sentences using the same pattern.

REFERENCES

HILLOCKS, GEORGE. (1987, May) A synthesis of writing research. *Educational Leadership.*

JOOS, MARTIN. (1967) *The five clocks.* New York, Harcourt, Brace, Jovanovich.

GENERAL BIBLIOGRAPHY ON LINGUISTICS AND LANGUAGE

CAHN, WILLIAM AND RHODA. (1963) *The story of writing, from cave art to computer.* Irvington-on-Hudson, N.Y.: Harvey House, Inc.

DAVIDSON, JESSICA. (1972). *Is that mother in the bottle?: Where language came from and where it is going.* New York: Franklin Watts, Inc.

DELMAR, MAXINE. (1968). Language books for the library. *Elementary English,* January. p. 55.

FARB, PETER. (1974) *Word play: What happens when people talk.* New York: Alfred A. Knopf.

FOESTER, LEONA M. (1974, January). Idiomagic. *Elementary English.* pp. 125-127.

FOESTER, LEONA M. (1974, March). Teaching children to read body language. *Elementary English.* pp. 440-442.

FURNER, BEATRICE A. (1971) The nature of the elementary school language curriculum: The importance of problem method unit teaching. in Bradley Loomer, Jerry N. Kuhn, and Beatrice A. Furner. Eds., *The Problem Method* (p. 45). Iowa City: College of Education and Division of Extension and University Services, University of Iowa.

HODGES, RICHARD E. AND E. HUGH RUDORF. (1972) *Language and learning to read: What teachers should know about language.* Boston: Houghton Mifflin Co.

KIRTLAND, ELIZABETH. (1968) *Write it right: A handbook of homonyms.* Golden Press.

KOHN, BERNICE. (1974). *What a funny thing to say!* New York: The Dial Press.

LAIRD, HELENE AND CHARLTON. (1957). *The tree of language.* World. pp. 30, 37-38, 46, 79-83.

LAMBERT, ELOISE. (1955) *Our language.* Lothrop. chap. 11.

LODWIG, RICHARD R. AND BARRET, EUGENE F. (1973). *Words, words, words: Vocabularies and dictionaries.* Rochelle Park, N.J.: Hayden Book Company, Inc.

LUDOVICI, JAMES L. (1965). *Origins of language.* New York: G.P. Putnam's Sons.

OGG, OSCAR. (1971). *The 26 Letters.* (Revised Ed.). New York: Thomas Y. Crowell Co.

REED, CARROLL E. (1973). *Dialects of american english.* Amherst, Mass.: University of Massachusetts Press.

RUDDELL, ROBERT B., ET AL. (1974). *Resources in reading-language instruction.* Englewood Cliffs, N.J.: Prentice Hall.

SAUER, L.E. (1970, October). Fourth grade children's knowledge of grammatical structure. *Elementary English, 47*, 808-813.

SAVAGE, JOHN F., (ED.) (1973). *Linguistics for teachers: Selected readings.* Chicago: Science Research Associates, Inc.

STEWIG, JOHN WARREN. (1974). *Exploring language with children.* Columbus, Oh.: Charles E. Merrill Publishing Company.

STRICKLAND, RUTH G. (1965, November). The teaching of grammar. *The national elementary principal.* pp. 58-62.

STRONG, WILLIAM. (1987). *Sentence combining.* Champaign, Ill.: NCTE.

11

SPELLING

From Mark Twain's insistence that he had no respect for a man who could only spell a word one way, to a large banner proclaiming "Welcome to Forth Werth," we are surrounded with a concern for "correct" spelling. There is no escape. Those who are good spellers are probably only marginally aware of their skill. Those who are not good spellers, but need to be, find spelling a curse and a mystery. That is understandable. There is a social cost of poor spelling and its origin is this: Were we to receive an important, even profound, message in language badly misspelled, we would discount it, perhaps ignore it. Even if the misspellings did not render the message mysterious in any way, we would think less of it and of the person who wrote it than we would if all the words were correctly spelled.

The teaching of spelling skills is important because ability to spell affects a student's sense of competence as a writer. Spelling skills can be taught and there is a strong body of research that tells us how to do it. This research and the resulting suggestions for classroom application focus on three different aspects of spelling: the orthography or system of rendering our language in print; the development of the speller; the best methods for teaching spelling to children at different stages in their development.

ORTHOGRAPHY

Our system for rendering our language in print may seem a crazy jumble with its "silent" letters and multiple spellings of the same sound. It has been seen as wildly inconsistent by generations of spelling reformers. However, in the recent past, a new school of thought has emerged. This thought, starting with the work of Chomsky and Halle (1961), suggests that our orthography is near optimal when we look beyond the symbol to sound fit. Looking only at symbol-sound correspondence, grapheme-phoneme regularity, the language does appear hopeless. The problem is summed up very well in this poem.

ENGLISH

I take it you already know
Of tough and bough and cough and dough?
Others may stumble, but not you
On hiccough, thorough, slough and through?
Well done! And now you wish, perhaps,
To learn of less familiar traps?

Beware of heard, a dreadful word
That looks like beard and sound like bird.
And dead: it's said like bed, not bead;
For goodness sake, don't call it deed!
Watch out for meat and great and threat,
(They rhyme with suite and straight and debt).
A moth is not a moth in mother.
Nor both in bother, broth in brother.

And here is not a match for there,
And dear and fear for bear and pear,
And then there's dose and rose and lose—
Just look them up—and goose and choose,
And cork and work and card and ward,
And font and front and word and sword.
And do and go, then thwart and cart.
Come, come, I've hardly made a start.

A dreadful language? Why, man alive,
I'd learned to talk it when I was five,
And yet to write it, the more I tried,
I hadn't learned it at fifty-five.

Anonymous

These examples make a very sound argument for reform if you assume only the need for symbol to sound regularity. (Spend a moment with a classmate and see if you can come up with more examples of the bad fit between symbol and sound in English.)

What if we required of our orthography two things beyond a high grapheme-phoneme correspondence? What if we wanted the orthography to preserve the visual similarity between and among related words and, thereby, to have the orthography itself carry some share of the burden of conveying meaning? How then would our present orthography shape up? Very well, it seems. For that is the basis for the argument that orthography is near optimal. For example, consider the seemingly useless *n* tacked onto autumn and hymn. The optimal orthography argument suggests that they are not useless at all. They are place holders that clearly demonstrate the relationship between "hymn" and "hymnal" and "autumn" and "autumnal," a relationship that would be less obvious in a one-to-one phoneme-grapheme system. Further, the optimal orthography argument goes, in word pairs like "nation" and "nationality," a one-to-one correspondence would, because of the change in the first vowel sound, destroy the relationship between the words that our present orthography makes clear.

Another aspect of this argument is that the present orthography preserves the historical background of the word. "Knight" is spelled that way because at the time of the invention of the printing press, which slowed change in the orthography, the word was pronounced "kuh-nickt." In addition, our orthography uses a within words pattern principle which explains why the *gh* in words such as laugh, through, and ghost is pronounced differently. Sounds that letters or particular groups of letters represent depend on their position within words. The sound *gh* digraph represented depends on its position within the word or the pattern of the letters making up the word.

Meaning also is important in determining how words are spelled. For example, the different spellings of the homophones whole/hole, see/sea, reed/read, and sell/cell avoid confusion in writing and reading. It is meaning that explains the *n* in hymn, the *g* in sign (signal) and many other words that are similar in meaning.

Spelling reform movements have never been successful. The orthography, of course, has changed, but it has been an evolutionary, rather than revolutionary change. Still, there will come a time when today's orthography will be as out of reach to that future generation as Old English is to the present generation. In fact, the most potent argument against a very rapid change in the orthography may be that it would unduly hasten the arrival of the day when the writing of previous generations is impenetrable to the modern eye.

HIGHLIGHTS OF RESEARCH

Templeton, in a recent review of the research (1986), sums up what is known at this time about the learning and teaching of spelling.

1. Learning how to spell follows a developmental progression.
2. Learning how to spell is primarily a conceptual process rather than a rote memorization process.
3. Words selected for study should reflect students' level of conceptual understanding of words as well as the frequency of the words and word patterns.
4. Learning how to spell depends on interaction with the other language arts of reading, writing, and vocabulary development.

As for the spelling system of English, linguists have pointed out that it makes a great deal of sense when viewed from the perspective of how well it represents meaning rather than simply how well it represents sound. The remainder of this chapter will discuss how to apply these findings to the classroom teaching of spelling.

DEVELOPMENT IN SPELLING ABILITY

Study of the writing and spelling of young children has yielded the understanding that children develop strategies which they use systematically and predictably to help them spell (Marsh et al., 1980; Read and Hodges,

1982). Their invented spelling progress through about five rough stages as they grow toward correct spelling. Henderson (1980) comments on the child who wanted to write "built," did not know how to spell it, but did know someone named Bill and so spelled the word "billt." Very logical and reasonable but outside the conventions of English orthography.

The notion of symbol-to-sound correspondence is, however, grasped amazingly early by most children. They do not spell randomly, and as they are exposed to more and more print, their spellings begin to approach conventional orthography. For example, in the chart below, note two things. First, how sensible the invented spellings are, and secondly, how those invented spellings begin to approximate and equal conventional spelling in discernible stages.

HENDERSON'S CHART

Word	Preliterate Prephonetic	Preliterate Phonetic	Letter Name	Vowel Transition
dog		D or DJ	DIJ	DOG
candy		K or KDE	KADE	CANDE/CANDY
bit		B opr BT	BET	BIT
Cinderella		S	SEDRLI	CINDARILA
went	———	———	WAT	WENT
table	———	———	TABL	TABEL/TIEBLE
bitter	———	———	BEDR	BITER
bake	———	———	BAK	BAIK

Prephonetic Spelling

Because, although these spellings are made up of recognizable letters, the letters bear no relationship to sounds in these words, they are prephonemic. This type of spelling shows that the child is aware that words are made up of letters and that print is arranged horizontally. It is typical of older preschoolers, kindergarteners, and many first graders.

Phonetic Spelling

Phonetic spelling shows that the child has discovered that letters in print represent sounds in spoken words. It is typical of beginning readers whether in kindergarten, first grade, or older.

S S t K (This is a truck.)

Letter Name Spelling

Letter name spelling shows children's firm awareness that letters represent sounds, so the letters they use stand for sounds with no silent letters included. It is typical of children who can read a little but are not yet fluent. Most first and second graders are included in this group.

in the morning wen I
Woc My Feet are rainbow
colored
Wen I wet toscool for
Sheo and tel I Sheod My
feet the clss lafd
the ned morning evrething
Was all rit

Transitional Spelling

Transitional spellers incorporate more features of standard spelling. Their words look more complete and adultlike. Young children who are beyond the beginning reading stage and older pupils who are unfluent readers are usually transitional spellers.

A strang lite a vary strang vistgin. And after that a space sip. and I hade to hide ondr the cavrs and it Just disperd. But the goblensare comeing to tacke me away away. Thar comeing to tacke me away.

Mark Mitchell, gr. 2

Derivational Spelling

According to Henderson (1984) derivational spellers have mastered the phonemic system of spelling. They have learned spelling rules such as consonant doubling. What they still lack is knowledge of how spelling reflects historical and meaning relationships. Children who have this understanding view words as members of related families with common roots. In the derivational stage children need wide exposure to language. Teaching spelling is teaching vocabulary skills.

All of this illustrates two major points to be made in this chapter. The first is that from the very beginning, children attempt to represent language in print systematically. That is, they think carefully about how the language should be represented. The second point is that spelling is not a separate mechanical skill. It is totally involved with language and language development and, in fact, represents quite dramatically stages of psychological and language development. This development takes time and includes many attempts and failures before mastery is achieved. One of the most important ways we can support students in their development is to provide the opportunity for them to do a great deal of writing at all levels and to accept their best guesses or invented spellings for words.

When a child who is stuck asks "How do you spell ______?" he should be encouraged to attempt the spelling himself even if it is only one letter. He should write *d* for dog. This attitude of encouragement and acceptance on the part of the teacher will give the young writer a sense of competence. To do otherwise is to restrict children to writing only those words that they are sure of and to cause them to miss opportunities for their own development of skill as they learn what works through experimentation.

FOUR PRINCIPLES FOR SPELLING INSTRUCTION

The concern for correct spelling should go beyond the formal spelling program. Good spelling is born as much from an attitude as from anything else. Promoting that attitude is an essential part of the Language Arts teacher's job. That job is something of a balancing act. Consider this: You will want your students to be aware of the importance of good spelling. Correct spelling is, as Hillerich (1977) so aptly put, "a courtesy to the reader." That is, correct spelling is an aid to communication. It may be difficult to believe, but students are often unaware that poor spelling diminishes the message intended. And yet, along with the concern for correct spelling, you do not want your students to fear incorrect spelling so much that they resist writing, resist taking a chance on a new word. How can the balance between concern for correctness and the need to take a chance be attained?

First, the classroom spelling atmosphere must be established. Discuss with your students the point made above by Hillerich: Correct spelling is a courtesy to the reader. Show some examples of instances wherein poor spelling ruined the communication either because an important word could not be deciphered or because a crucial word was misinterpreted.

Second, encourage students to use in their writing the words they want even if they do not know how to spell them. This can be done by showing them how to make a guess at the spelling by writing out the first few letters of the word and/or its ending and putting in lines for the parts they do not know. This allows them to finish what they are writing without interruptions and then go back and fix it up. For younger pupils, the fix up may involve asking the teacher for assistance. For older pupils, the words can be looked up in the dictionary.

Third, reward correct spelling but, in cases where "fixed up" papers still contain errors, do not punish incorrect spelling. In fact, it is a good idea to acknowledge partial success. If a child has attempted the word "neighborhood" and transposed the "i" and the "e," acknowledge how much she got right. Don't ignore the mistake, of course, but don't dwell on it.

Fourth, where possible and as time allows, expand spelling instruction by suggesting different forms of words and similarly spelled words.

Thus, using these principles, a classroom day might include such teacher-student exchanges as a "fix it up" session where students get, from the teacher or the dictionary, the correct spellings for a number of words, praise for a student's attempt to spell "ecology," a brief discussion of the word's origin. In a very tight teaching schedule, you might think these activities too time-consuming. They are not. They take little time and pay off handsomely.

EFFECTIVE METHODS FOR TEACHING SPELLING

Richard Hodges (1982) observed that older children who are good spellers have wide morphological (word building) knowledge. To spell an unknown word they use a spelling by analogy strategy in which they relate the word they have to spell to words that they already know. Spelling is no longer considered a low order memory task. It involves complex thinking skills as children learn to understand the relationships among the words in our language. The study of spelling should be the study of families of words so that children can easily see relationships and make generalizations. An effective spelling program should include these three key factors:

1. It must be organized to aid learning and retention.
2. It must teach students a strategy for remembering words through understanding relationships among them.
3. It should reinforce this strategy with purposeful activities that focus on relationships among words.

Let's look at each of these factors in more detail.

ORGANIZING TO AID LEARNING AND RETENTION

Educational theory tells us that we more easily remember things in which we see patterns or relationships. For example, which sequence is easier to remember 8-2-64-1-16-4-32, or 1-2-4-4-16-32-64? The second number sequence is easier to remember because it follows a pattern. The first number sequence is a random ordering of the same numbers. The second sequence takes into account our natural instinct to seek relationships and to organize information into logical patterns. What strategy would help you learn the following list of spelling words?

receive
siege
sieve
believe
foreign
wiener
Caribbean
Jamaica

As haphazard as this list looks it is typical of how spelling lists have traditionally looked. It shows no awareness of the consistent structure of our language or of an understanding of how we learn. With this type of list students must memorize the spelling of each word individually. Words learned this way are hard to remember and learning to spell becomes basically a low order memory task.

Learning to spell should be much more than rote memorization. Zutell's (1978) investigation into how spelling knowledge is acquired demonstrated that words are not learned in isolation but are learned together with a growing understanding of structural relationships between and among words. The importance of perception in learning to spell is discussed in a research monograph, "Spelling Research and Practice" by Fitzsimmons and Loomer (1977). Their research shows that spelling ability is primarily based on a person's ability to perceive relationships between words, especially visual relationships.

STRUCTURAL RELATIONSHIPS

Bohen (1980) analyzed student misspellings and found that they revealed predictable patterns of errors: "Major spelling problems resulted from phonetic inconsistencies and soundproof spelling patterns." According to Bohen spelling programs should improve visual and associative memory and should formulate word lists that demonstrate predictable patterns and simplify learning. For example, extensive error analysis proves that silent letters are one cause of high-frequency spelling problems. If a list were made of -ough words, a phonetic inconsistency would become a structural consistency:

rough
tough
cough
enough
though
thought
through
fought

PRESENTING WORD FAMILIES

Bohen's error analysis (1975) also provides insight into additional organizational patterns that could aid thinking and learning. Some of the most common errors in spelling occur when students add affixes to words. An effective spelling program presents base words with other related forms, thus encouraging students to see relationships between base words and their affixes. Part of such a word list might look like this:

procure	procuring	procures	procurement
amaze	amazing	amazes	amazement
measure	measuring	measures	measurement

In addition, spelling lists should also show how the related word is formed (ir + regular = irregular). This reinforces the visual perception of each word and aids understanding of the meaning relationship.

MEANING RELATIONSHIPS

Many words in our language have common Latin or Greek roots. These meaning relationships among words in or language need to be learned in spelling. For example, the root scrib/script has given birth to the following words: scribe, scribble, scribbler, script, scripture, conscript, nondescript, subscription, inscribe, describe, ascribe, circumscribe, manuscript . . . . How many more can you add to the list (Hodges, 1982)?

Organizing lists in these ways helps focus on similarities among words and aids students in perceiving relationships, thus making learning easier.

TEACHING STUDENTS A STRATEGY

We have seen that spelling lists can be organized to aid learning and retention. Students must also be taught a strategy for remembering words and applying the knowledge they have learned to similar words and in written activities. This means students must learn generalizations about list words that apply to other words. It is the making of generalizations about words that helps students process their learning and make it a part of their long-term memories. This is a plan for teaching spelling words in a way that will lead to generalization.

1. Begin instruction with a self-corrected pretest. Research strongly supports the teacher guided student self-correction of the pretest as the single most important factor in learning to spell (Loomer, 1977).

2. Note that self-correction needs to be teacher guided. During this time, the teacher should point out the similarities in the words and lead students to understand a generalization about the words. For example, assume a class is correcting a pretest on a list of words such as the following:

badge	page
edge	huge
bridge	change
dodge	garage
fudge	arrange

The students would see that the common structural characteristic in the first group of words is *dge*, and in the second group is *ge*. During the correction of the pretest the students would also be led to see that the *dge* is found in one syllable words and follows a single short vowel. They would see that *ge* is used in the words that don't follow this pattern. By the end of the self-correction, students would come to the generalization that when they must decide on the correct spelling of words that fall into these categories, they use *dge* immediately after a single short vowel in a one-syllable word, and use *ge* in most other words. This would give them a strategy for remembering not only these words, but also for spelling other similar words in written work. Students will mentally store the associated list of pattern words along with the generalization.

ACTIVITIES FOR MEANINGFUL PROCESSING OF SPELLING WORDS

Spelling activities for children should be designed to focus on the relationship among the words which they are studying. This will aid long-term retention.

Activities should provide instruction and practice in the three modes of learning—the auditory, visual and kinesthetic modes. Richard Hodges (1981) states "Spelling is a multisensory process. The study of written language . . . brings into play visual, auditory, and kinesthetic processes."

Examples of activities that reinforce skills in all three learning modes are:

1. Activities that provide visual reinforcement such as configurations and proofreading;
2. Activities that provide auditory reinforcement such as rhyming words, categorization by sound, listening to changes in stress to point out letters that are hard to hear;
3. Written practice is a kinesthetic activity. It should be extended to use of textures with poor spellers.

In addition to the above activities, students should use a study method as part of their spelling activities. The method should combine the auditory, visual, and kinesthetic methods in the study process. The following steps are an example of an effective approach to word study:

1. Look at the word.
2. Say the word.
3. Spell the word aloud.
4. Copy the word.
5. Close your eyes and picture the word in your mind.
6. Cover the word and write it. Check for mistakes.

If you have made a mistake, repeat (1) through (6).

Activities should teach and develop perceptual ability, especially visual perception and associative memory. Examples of these kinds of activities are:

1. Structural analogies such as, consider is to considerable as comfort is to comfortable.
2. Configurations
3. Proofreading activities to develop a sense for correct spelling.
4. Acrostic poems and puzzles that force the child to consider each of the letters in a word. For example, an acrostic poem causes the child to focus on the silent *e*.

   Lapping
   All around me.
   Kids swim
   Everywhere.

Activities should focus on word-building and related forms of words such as history and historical.

Activities should teach and develop vocabulary and meaning skills. Some of these kinds of activities are:

1. Dictionary work which encourages the perception of relationship, not merely looking up the definitions of words;
2. Work with suffixes and prefixes;
3. Study of language relationships such as the Latinate forms sign, signal, and medicine, medical;
4. Activities which encourage students to discover meaning relationships in words such as dejection, projection, and objection.

It is important to integrate spelling and writing. This can vary from use in composition to sentence writing to work with sentence combining.

TEACHING THE POOR SPELLER

Eight special points should be considered in teaching the poor speller.

1. Present a limited number of words to be learned each week. Cut the lists to five or ten words.
2. For spelling words, use the most commonly used words in writing.
3. Each child should keep an individual list of words most often used in writing or most often misspelled.
4. Use kinesthetic techniques in word study such as tracing words written with crayon and visualizing techniques to improve visual memory.
5. Give children practice in sensing when words are incorrect by asking themselves "Does it look right?"
6. Give poor spellers fewer words to learn. Success is most important in developing a sense of competence.
7. Teach them to use meaning as an ally.
8. Help them choose someone to consult.

THE GOOD SPELLER

The student who writes at least 90 percent of the words on a pretest correctly should not be given the same list again. These children can work on the same generalization that the other students are working with, however, by finding new examples and listing derivations of words found in the weekly spelling list. They can test each other while you are retesting the rest of the class. Other activities for this group could include:

1. Study of word origins;
2. Keeping lists of words used in writing;
3. Adding prefixes and suffixes to root words and writing an explanation of their effect on meaning;
4. Making charts of synonyms, antonyms, homonyms, contractions, and abbreviations;
5. Using spelling as a part of meaningful writing experiences, not just "write your words in sentences;"
6. Studying subject related words in content areas which they are studying and which they are using in writing. Good spellers should not be given isolated lists of "hard words" to learn unless they are related to a language understanding or are words they need to use in writing.

USING THE DICTIONARY FOR SPELLING*

"If I don't know how to spell it, how can I look it up?" Good point! Maybe. For younger students, grades 1 and 2, the teacher *is* the best source for correct spelling. However, for older students, grade 3 and up, who have had more experience with the language and its orthographic conventions,

* Adapted from Hillerich, 1977

the dictionary for spelling is not that difficult. Teach your students to follow these few, easy steps.

1. Make a guess about the beginning letter or letters.
2. Make a guess about the ending letter or letters.
3. Using the approximation, check the dictionary for the correct spelling.

Except in rare instances, where there might be a silent letter, steps 1 and 2 will yield a useful approximation of the correct spelling.

Here are three more points for the teacher. First, students will need to be led through the guessing/approximation process several times. Second, it would be worthwhile for students to see you use the procedure yourself. That is, actually use it to find the correct spelling of a word you want to use. Third, there is nothing very magical or mysterious about this process. It is what adults do when they need to find correct spelling in the dictionary. Why not let students in on the secret?

SUMMARY

The social cost of poor spelling is, chiefly, that the importance of a message poorly spelled is diminished or dismissed. If you want people to pay attention to what you write, you had better spell it correctly.

The orthography of English is, depending on what you expect from it, either wildly inconsistent or "nearly optimal." Its grapheme to phoneme correspondence is a bit rough, but it does preserve historical antecedents and establishes the relationship between variants of single words.

Recent studies in children's attempts to spell have shown a remarkable consistency of attempt, good grasp of the alphabetic principle, and stages of growth toward conventional spelling. Finally, various approaches to teaching spelling tend to share basic orientations with the various methods for teaching beginning reading. Unfortunately, in the area of spelling, the gulf between research and practice is great.

ACTIVITIES FOR THE METHODS CLASS

1. Prepare a list of spelling words on the basis of a structural or meaning relationship. State the generalization to be achieved.
2. Present a list of spelling words to a class or small group of children using the test-study and corrected-test technique.
3. Prepare a set of four study exercises to accompany the spelling list used for option (1) or (2).

4. Collect written papers from an elementary classroom. Analyze most common types of spelling errors.
5. Plan a mastery lesson for one of the kinds of errors located in the set of papers used in (4).
6. Evaluate a spelling text at the grade level of your choice. Identify generalizations presented in it and the congruence of activities in the lesson to the generalization. Judge whether the methodology recommended in the book follows the recommendations made in this chapter.

REFERENCES

BOHEN, DELORES. (1975). *Analysis of words misspelled in academic writing samples.* Fairfax Va.: Fairfax County Public Schools.

BOHEN, DELORES. (1975–1980). Stem Analysis of standardized test results for grades 4, 6, 8, 11. Fairfax, Va. Fairfax County public schools.

HENDERSON, EDMUND H. (1980). Developmental concepts of words. In Edmund H. Henderson and James W.Beers (Eds). *Developmental and cognitive aspects of learning to spell.* Newark, Del.: International Reading Assn.

HODGES, RICHARD E. (1981) *Learning to spell.* Urbana, Ill.: NCTE.

HORN, ERNEST. (1919) Principles of method in teaching spelling as derived from scientific investigation. In *Eighteenth Yearbook, Part II, Chapter II, National Socity for the Study of Education (p. 72).* Bloomington: Public School Publishing Company.

TEMPLETON, SHANE. (1986, March). Synthesis of research on the learning and teaching of spelling. *Educational Leadership.*

GENERAL BIBLIOGRAPHY

BEERS, CAROL S. (1980). The relationship of cognitive development to spelling and reading abilities. In Edmund H. Henderson and James W. Beers (Eds.), *Developmental and cognitive aspects of learning to spell.* Newark Del.: International Reading Assn.

BEERS, JAMES W. (1980). Developmental strategies of spelling competence in primary school children. In Edmund H. Henderson and James W. Beers (Eds.). *Developmental and cognitive aspects of learning to spell.*

CHOMSKY, N. AND HALLE MORRIS. (1968). *The sound pattern of english.* New York: Harper and Row.

CLYMER, THEODORE L. (1963). The utility of phonics generalizations in the primary grades. *The Reading Teacher, 16,* 79-82.

EMANS, ROBERT. (1967). The usefulness of phonics generalizations in the primary grades. *The Reading Teacher, 20,* 419-425.

FROESE, VICTOR AND STRAW, STANLEY B. (EDS.). (1981). *Research in the language arts: Language and schooling.* Baltimore, Md.: University Park Press.

GIBSON, E. AND LEVIN H. (1985). *The psychology of reading..* Cambridge, Mass.: MIT Press.

GILLET, JEAN WALLACE AND KITA, M. JANE. (1980). Words, kids, and categories. In Edmund H. Henderson and James W. Beers (Eds.). *Developmental and cognitive aspects of learning to spell.* Newark, Del: International Reading Assn.

GLEITMAN, L. R. AND ROZIN, P. (1977). The structure and acquisition of reading 1: Relations between orthographics and the structure of language. In A. S. Reber and D. L. Scarborough (Eds.). *Toward a psychology of reading: the proceedings of the CUNY conference.* Hillsdale, N.J.: Lawrence Erlbaum Associates.

GROFF, PATRICK. (1979, January). Speaking and spelling. *Language Arts, 56.* (1), 26-33.

HENDERSON, EDMUND H. (1980). Developmental concepts of words. In Edmund H. Henderson and James W. Beers, (Eds.). *Developmental and cognitive aspects of learning to spell.* Newark Del.: International Reading Assn.

HILLERICH, ROBERT L. (1977, March). Let's teach spelling—Not phonetic misspelling. *Language Arts, 54* (3) 301-307.

HODGES, RICHARD E. (1981). The language base of spelling. In *Research in the language arts: Language and schooling.* Victor Froese and Stanley B. Straw (Eds.). Baltimore, Md.: University Park Press.

HORN, ERNEST. (1919). Principles of method in teaching spelling as derived from scientific investigation in *Eighteenth yearbook, park II, chapter II, national society for the study of education (p. 72).* Bloomington: Public School Publishing Company.

MARINO, JACQUELINE L. (1980, February), What Makes a good speller? *Language Arts, 57* (2) 173-177.

NICHOLSON, TOM AND SCHACTER, SUMNER (1979, October) Spelling skill and teaching practice—Putting them back together again. *Language Arts, 56* (7) 804-809.

READ, C. (1975) *Children's categorization of speech sounds in english.* Urbana, Ill.: NCTE.

STEVER, ELIZABETH. Dialect and spelling. (1980). In Edmund H. Henderson and James W. Beers (Eds.). *Developmental and Cognitive Aspects of Learning to Spell.* Newark, Del.: International Reading Assn.

TEMPLETON, SHANE. (1980). Spelling, phonology, and the older student. In Edmund H. Henderson and James W. Beers, (Eds.). *Developmental and cognitive aspects of learning to spell.* Newarks, Del.: International Reading Assn.

TOVEY, DUANE R. (1976), November/December). Language acquisition: A key to effective language instruction. *Language Arts, 53,* (8) 868-873.

ZUTELL, JERRY. (1975, January). Some psycholinguistic perspective on children's spelling. *Language Arts*, 55, (7) 884-850.

ZUTELL, JERRY. (1980). Children's spelling strategies and their cognitive development. In Edmund H. Henderson and James W. Beers (Eds.) *Developmental and Cognitive Aspects of Learning to Spell.* Newark, Del.: International Reading Assn.

12

HANDWRITING

Handwriting, whether manuscript or cursive, is taught in every elementary school in the land. Oddly enough, however, there are few objective, reliable measures of what constitutes "good" handwriting. We suspect that is true in part because adults find widely divergent cursive styles to be legible. Thus, a single objective measure of "goodness" is not likely to emerge since it would unduly narrow the range of acceptability. For a graphic demonstration (pun intended) of this, collect 20 or so examples within your class. Most likely your group can achieve a level of agreement on which four or five are the "best." Yet, it would be difficult to say by what criteria your judgments were made. In addition, a comparison among the favored four or five would probably show them to be dissimilar to one another. The problem of systematic instruction and evaluation of that instruction persists. How should we teach handwriting and how should we judge our success (or failure) at doing so?

SOME AREAS OF CONCERN

In teaching handwriting, as in teaching any other aspect of the Language Arts curriculum, there are areas of concern. Generally speaking, the areas of concern in the teaching of handwriting are these:

1. The relationship of development to handwriting;
2. Best methods for teaching letter formation;
3. Sequence of learning letter names;
4. How to meet the special problems of the left-handed child;
5. How to come to some reasonable objective measure of legibility and how to (or whether to) encourage individuality of writing style;
6. How best to practice the skill whether it be manuscript or cursive.

Let us consider these one at a time.

THE RELATIONSHIP OF DEVELOPMENT TO HANDWRITING ABILITY

In recent work Donald Graves traced the journey of the child from the time when handwriting is very conscious to the time when the shaping of letters becomes automatic. What does this careful study of development tell teachers? From Graves' work we learn the importance of choice of topic, frequency of practice, some emphasis on speed, and attention to the physical aspects of writing.

Development affects handwriting in the child's use of space, pressure, control, and speed. Small muscles have a chance when the following occurs:

1. Placement of the work: The paper needs to be slightly to the right of midline and turned at a forty-five degree angle. In this way it is possible to maintain small muscle control from the top to the bottom of the page. Otherwise, as the writer moves down the page and the hand gets closer to the body, the pressure of large muscles come into play.

2. Pencil Grip: If the pencil is held at an angle to the paper, the full downward thrust of the pencil is reduced, thus allowing the pencil to have the right pressure. The grip is aided by the coordinate action of thumb, index, and middle fingers. It is not unusual to find children gripping the pencil like an ice pick or writing with a stirring motion.

The control of pencil motion is dependent on the development of small muscles and eye-hand coordination. Children interpret size as quality and use larger script naturally. According to Donald Graves (1983) there are two basic motions in working with letters in manuscript, the circle and the straight line. The circle is the more sophisticated in terms of small muscle rotation, the straight line more susceptible to problems of force.

According to Graves (1983) time spent in writing and choice of topic have as much to do with children's handwriting as any other factor—perceptual or motor. A constant theme troughout this book has been an emphasis on the need for the Language Arts to relate to the child's own experience. Part of establishing that relationship between what is new, what is to be learned, and what is known, that is, prior experience, is the need for integration. A skill is not learned in isolation. Reading skills, as an obvious example, relate to a child's success in virtually all school subjects. That is true also of handwriting skills. They are not mere mechanics. They are a part of learning to communicate. That is why Donald Graves found the strong relationship between desire to communicate and growth in handwriting ability.

READINESS ACTIVITIES

The following activities will help prepare young children for handwriting instruction.

1. Have children roll clay into "snakes" and use them to form real or imaginary letters.

2. Draw a stick figure of a child on a ditto and place an *X* on either side of it. Have children swing their pencils from *X* to *X* going underneath the child. Tell them they are helping the child to skip rope.
3. Draw a frog on a ditto and place an *X* on either side of it. Have children swing their pencils from *X* to *X* going over the frog. Tell them they are playing leap frog.
4. Cut narrow crepe paper into three-foot strips for children to wave in the air. Play music and have children make line or circle strokes using whole arm movement. (Adapted from Building Handwriting Skills 1987, 1982 by McDougal-Littell & Company. All rights reserved 1987)

LETTER FORMATION

Furner (1967) demonstrated that the development of handwriting skill was perceptual-motor learning, involving perceptual and muscular control; therefore, methods of instruction in handwriting should stress perceptual development. Children must learn to recognize form, notice likenesses and differences, and be able to infer movement necessary to production of form. Only one component of these skills should be taught at one time. Handwriting is improved when children are taught through a multi-sensory process that includes instruction and practice in all three modes of learning—the visual, the auditory, and the kinesthetic.

INTRODUCING LETTERS

The most effective method for introducing and reviewing letters with children follows these steps:

1. Present letters to children in small groups using an overhead projector so that they can clearly see how a letter is made and so you can watch their copying for errors in formation.
2. When children are working at their desks, they should have a sample of the handwriting task before them. Have them trace models with their fingers and then with erasers of their pencils before using pencils and making the letters themselves.
3. Involve pupils in establishing a purpose for each lesson. The primary purpose for handwriting is to express meaning.
4. Provide many guided exposures to the formation of letters: Teach students to make each part of a letter rather than the whole letter at once to help them build a mental image of the letter. For example, teach the letter A in the following steps:

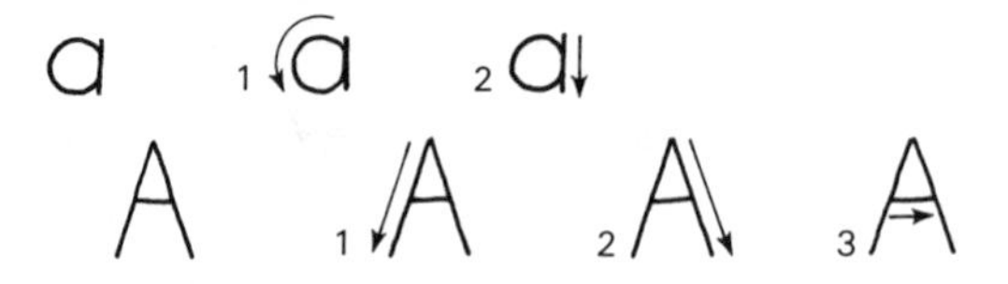

FIGURE 12-1

a. Begin at the headline. Draw a straight line that slants to the left and stops at the baseline.
b. Begin the second stroke at the same point as the first. Draw a straight line that slants to the right and stops at the baseline.
c. Begin the third stroke where the first line crosses the midline. Draw a straight line along the midline to the place where the second line crosses the midline.*

5. Encourage a mental as well as a motor response from each child during the writing process: for example, have the child describe the process while writing, or have the child visualize or write a letter as another child describes it.
6. Use handwriting terms so students can orally describe the letters with ease. Handwriting terms for cursive writing are given here.
7. Provide consistent letter form models. The teacher's writing should conform to the style adopted by the school.

Handwriting Words for Cursive Writing

baseline the line on which letters rest

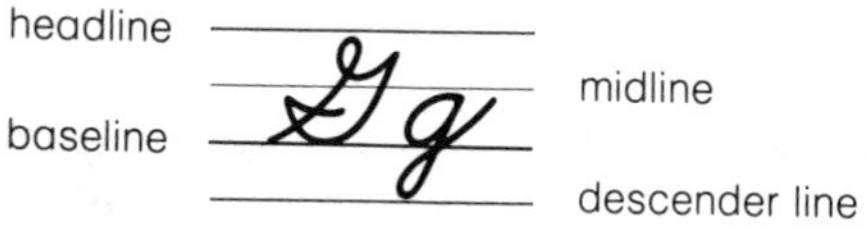

clockwise this direction

counterclockwise this direction, opposite to clockwise

cross-stroke a horizontal stroke, from left to right

cursive writing writing in which the letters are joined

descender line the line below the baseline. Descenders reach down to the descender line. See the picture for **baseline**.

downstroke a straight line made in a downward motion

full space the space from the baseline to the headline. Capital letters are a full space tall.

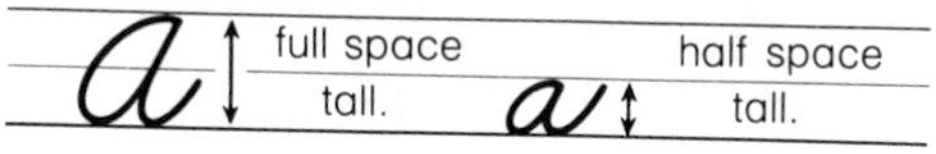

half space the space from the baseline to the midline, or from the midline to the headline. Most small letters are a half space tall. See the picture for **full space**.

headline the line at the top of the writing space. See the picture for **baseline**.

loop the shape made by a letter crossing itself

manuscript writing printing

midline the line in the middle of the writing space. See the picture for **baseline**.

oval this shape

overcurve the top part of an oval

slant the angle or tilt of the downstrokes of letters

spacing the distance between letters, words, and sentences

undercurve the bottom part of an oval

upcurve a curving line made in an upward motion

upstroke part of an undercurve

FIGURE 12-2 HANDWRITING TERMS

PRACTICE THROUGH A FUNCTIONAL APPROACH

Practice of the handwriting skills taught is absolutely crucial. It is doubtful that any literate adult gives much thought to letter formation as he writes. Getting to the point where letter formation is automatic or nearly so is the point of practice, but in what form should that practice be accomplished?

Endless drawing of a single letter is, ultimately, boring and unrewarding. Certainly this drill aspect of handwriting practice has its place, but it can easily be overdone.

It is also important that handwriting procedures be individualized from the beginning. Children should be helped to evaluate their own work and to find their own errors. They should not be required to practice repeatedly forms they have already mastered.

For beginners, getting to the stage of a word or phrase is satisfying. Children who can take home a picture that they have labeled for themselves and signed for themselves are thereby rewarded for the hard work they have done and careful handwriting is hard work for little hands.

TEACHING MANUSCRIPT

Manuscript is a writing form that uses simple curves and straight lines to make unjoined letters. Cursive is a writing form with the strokes of the letters joined together and the angles rounded.

After much discussion and study of the relative merits of manuscript and cursive writing, most authorities agree that manuscript writing has definite advantages for initial instruction and the addition of cursive writing should be made before the beginning of fourth grade. According to Herrick, there are three major arguments supporting the use of manuscript symbols for initial instruction. First, the motor development and eye-hand-arm coordination of young children enable them to form straight vertical lines and circles more rapidly and legibly. Second, the manuscript writing symbols are similar to these used in books. Children who are learning to read will be more familiar with them. Finally, manuscript writing is more legible that cursive writing. A sample of letters recommended by one publisher is shown in Figure 12-3. In some school systems an intermediate type alphabet, called D'Nealian, is taught instead of traditional manuscript symbols.

MULTISENSORY LETTER ACTIVITIES

One commercial handwriting program* suggests the following activities for increasing the beginning writers' sensory experience with letter forma-

*From *McDougal-Littell Handwriting*. Copyright © 1987, 1982 by McDougal-Littell & Co., all rights reserved.

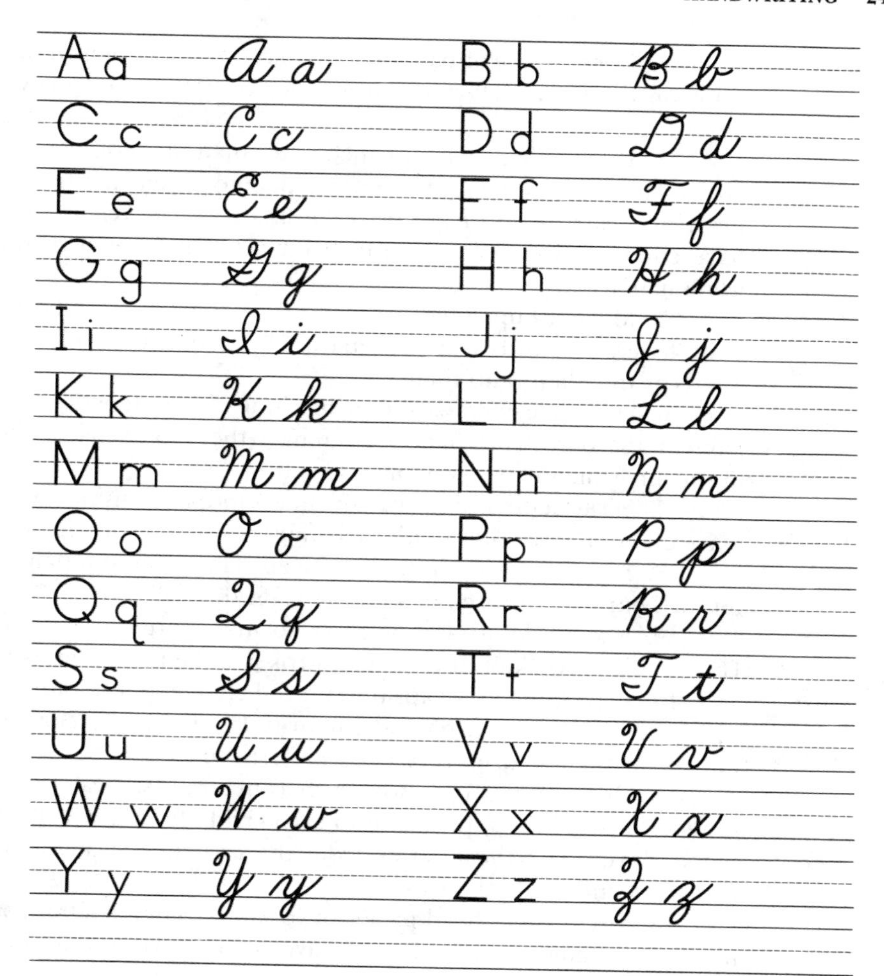

FIGURE 12-3

tion. These activities are particularly effective for children who are slower in perceptual development.

1. Have children "paint" freely on the board with their fingers or a larger paintbrush dipped in water, using whole arm movement. Older children can make letter strokes and letters. Children at desks can use shaving cream, fingerpaint, or crayons, on classified ad pages of the newspaper.

2. Make large letter patterns on classified ad pages, old telephone directory pages, or newsprint. Have children trace the pattern with their fingers while naming the letter. Then have them trace it several times with a crayon or pencil.

3. Place a piece of paper on a square of wire screen. Write a letter or word on the paper. Have children trace over the letter or word several times.

4. Draw a three- or four-inch letter on a piece of tagboard or cardboard. Have children trace the letter with glue. Then have them add beans, peas, rice, yarn, sand or beads to the model letter. When the glue dries, have children trace over the three-dimensional letter with their fingers while naming it.

5. Make a hopscotch pattern on the floor with chalk or tape, and write letters or words in each square. Have children name the letters or words as they hop onto them.

6. Have one child use his or her index finger to write a letter on the palm of a second child's hands. Then have the second child write the letter in the air while saying its name and sound.

7. Write letters or words on fine sandpaper using magic marker. Have children trace these with their fingers while saying the letter's name.

8. Dictate or write letters in the air. Have children paint each letter on the board or an easel, or point to it on the wall chart.

9. Use masking tape or chalk to make large letters on the floor. Have children walk out the letter's strokes while repeating its name.

10. Give students scraps of textured cloth about ten to twelve inches square. As you dictate, have them write letters on the cloth using their fingers. Young children may need patterns to trace.

11. Prepare sets of cards, each containing several letters children have learned. Pin or tape a card to each child's back. Let children work in pairs. Have one write a letter from the card in the air, and the other recognize and name the letter.

12. Use the overhead projector to show a letter, a letter combination, or a word. Remove the letter and have children write what they saw.*

TEACHING CURSIVE WRITING

The transfer to cursive writing usually takes place in the scond or third grade. Since cursive is thought by most children to be the more adult style of writing, there tends to be a great deal of enthusiasm for the switch. Again, the sequence of instruction and the practice of the skill in teaching cursive are similar to those of manuscript instruction. The progression is from the more easily formed letters to the more difficult. Practice is with meaningful words and phrases related to other skill areas such as social studies and creative writing in the final stage of drafting.

*From *McDougal-Littell Handwriting*, © 1987, 1982, by McDougal-Littell & Co., all rights reserved.

Upper grade children will begin to develop their own unique styles of writing. There may, in fact, be such experimentation with angle of slant, different forms of letters, and different size of writing (all of these sometimes on a single page, unfortunately). The goal, ultimately, of handwriting instruction is legible, pleasing to the eye handwriting. Referring back to the beginning of this chapter, we have seen that those twin criteria can be met in a variety of ways. How much or how far children should be encouraged or allowed to stray from an artificially perfect model should be judged by these criteria. The work done in other areas of the Language Arts and other segments of the curriculum can serve as an opportunity for handwriting practice. Integration of handwriting skills into the larger curriculum is the goal.

IMPROVING RATE OF SPEED

The teacher needs to be alert to students for whom handwriting speed is a problem. There is a direct relationship between speed in handwriting and fluency and maturity in composition. Timed tests can be administered to students who are writing slowly. They should be given in a relaxed atmosphere at regular intervals and the student should be aware of their purpose. The standard speed in second grade for manuscript writing is approximately thirty letters per minute. The average speed in fifth grade for cursive writing is approximately sixty letters per minute. The student should be speed tested with familiar material. Speed is closely related to practice because familiar motor pathways need to be built up. The slow writer does not have the same access to experience as the person who can write quickly about an experience. Donald Graves found that speed leads to a different text cohesion and completion.

CHANGE FROM MANUSCRIPT TO CURSIVE

Cursive writing requires a fairly high level of control over the small muscles and high degree of eye-hand coordination. Prudence and common sense suggest that there will be some children at age seven and eight who will be ready to change to cursive writing and some who will not be ready. The teacher can determine those who are not ready by watching for problems: inability to recognize cursive letters; problems with spacing; and relative letter size in manuscript writing.

During the transitional period, children may continue to use manuscript writing for some work, especially that done without close supervision by the teacher. Skill in manuscript should also be maintained through the elementary school years and used when this style of writing is more appropriate for the work being done. The main purpose of cursive writing is to increase speed.

FREQUENT TYPES OF CURSIVE ERRORS

It is important when teaching cursive to teach the combinations that cause the most difficulty. This is where older children make many errors. Some difficult combinations are:

b (followed by *e, i, o, r,* or *y*)
e (followed by *a, i, s,*)
f (followed by *r*)
g (followed by *r*)
n (followed by *g*)
o (followed by *a, c, i, s*)
v (followed by *e, i*)
w (followed by *a, c*)

TEACHING THE LEFT-HANDED CHILD

The horror stories told by left-handed adults of having their knuckles rapped with a ruler for trying to use their left hands for writing or of having their left hands tied behind their backs are relics of history. The real problem of handedness for the modern teacher is not whether a child is right or left handed. The left-handed child will need a few special instructions and perhaps a reminder now and again, but presents no real problem. The real problem is those few children who are truly ambidextrous or who have not yet settled into being either right or left handed. Since instuction does differ a bit depending on handedness, it is important that such children decide which hand they will use for writing so that they may receive consistent instruction. A few casual observations by the teacher on which hand is most preferred for coloring and scissor work should be sufficient. Once instruction begins, the child should not be allowed to freely change hands. If after two to four months of instruction, the child expresses a desire to use the other hand, allow it. But, again, that instruction should also be continued long enough for the goal of consistency of instruction to be served.

Once the dominant hand has been determined, certain steps can be taken to promote success in handwriting instruction. Left-handed children should be seated together for instruction.* This permits group members to model from and help one another.

*From *McDougal-Littell Handwriting*, © 1987, 1982, by McDougal-Littell & Co., all rights reserved.

Seating. Left-handed children should sit so that the light shines over the right shoulder. Right-handed children should have light shining over the left shoulder. This will minimize shadows on the paper. There should be sufficient space on the left side of the desk for left-handers, on the right side for right-handers. If armchair desks are used, left-handers should have a desk specifically designed for left-handed students.

Paper Placement. Placement for left-handed students is different from that for right-handed sutdents. For the left-handed child writing in either manuscript or cursive, the lower right corner of the paper should point to the left of the center of the student's body. For the right-hander writing in manuscript, the paper should lie straight, parallel to the edge of the desk. For the right-hander writing in cursive, the lower left corner of the paper should point to the right of the center of the body.

Grip. Left-handers, like right-handers, may hold their pens or pencils too tightly. A ball of paper held inside the hand when writing can correct this problem. Left-handers also have a tendency to hook their wrists as they write, preventing a smooth flow of letters and hindering the student from seeing the work. Wrist-hooking can be prevented by keeping the elbow off the edge of the desk, keeping the elbow close to the body, or holding the pen or pencil about 1½″ (4 cm) from its point.

Frequent evaluation by both teachers and students increases the legibility and speed of handwriting. Evaluation should take place after every handwriting lesson. The use of see-through overlays is recommended for informal student evaluation and teacher evaluation. The basic elements of legible manuscript and cursive handwriting are as follows:

1. Alignmant of all letters on a baseline.
2. Regular shaping of letters and numerals according to a recognized alphabet.
3. Uniform size of small letter parts, and uniform size of tall letter parts of lowercase letters.
4. Even spacing between letters in words, with regular wider spacing between words, and additional space between sentences.
5. Consistent proportion of small to tall letter parts.
6. Uniform slant in cursive writing.

Meaningful evaluation occurs when the student is assisted by the teacher to set goals for improving handwriting.

CHECKLISTS FOR SELF EVALUATION

Students should keep an example of their own best handwriting for evaluation after each lesson. This sample will change as handwriting improves. Figure 12-4 shows an example of a checklist that is suitable for students to use in evaluation of their own writing.

FIGURE 12-4 Checklist for Self Evaluation. Adapted from *Handwriting*, © 1987, 1982, by McDougal-Littell & Co.

1. I kept my letters on the baseline.
   ____
2. I shaped my letters correctly
   ____
3. I made my letters the correct height.
   ____
4. I slanted my letters in the same direction.
   ____
5. I spaced my letters evenly.
   ____
6. I left the correct space between words
   ____
7. I left extra space between sentences.

   Key: (1) Sometimes (2) Usually (3) Always

SUMMARY

Handwriting is a communications tool. Since absolute standards of goodness are probably impossible for formulate, the measure of "good handwriting" that seems most realistic is legibility—legibility based on consistency of letter size, slant, and spacing.

ACTIVITIES FOR THE LANGUAGE ARTS METHODS CLASS

1. Analyze the stories by hypothetical students (Figure 12-5) and evaluate them for handwriting qualities using the progress checklist (Figure 12-6).
2. Recommend a list of activities for a child who lacks handwriting readiness.
3. Prepare a class report on a scope and sequence chart of one commerical handwriting program.

The bean grew but it turned into a flower instead
1. of a bean. The next day a bird came and
sat on the flower. The flower said get
off of me the bird flew away. After while
a bee came and started to eat
my flower. Then the flower swated the
bee the bee got killed. When I touched
the flower he bit me so I left
him along. That night I heard a noise
I saw the flower fighting a one
eyed monster. He had three arms,
four legs, and one ear and no
mouth. The flower beat the monster
up I took him to jail. The
flower got three year suply of
food for himself.

---

2. The old woman cowld not
pay her rent. So she moved
to Kansas anc brought the
beans with her. She baught 500
beans and planted all of them.
"the summer is gone" $10,000!.. And she
gave $500. to the bean
association. And gave $200. to
the bean heart association. So
she had $300. left and lived
in a mansion and drove a
cadillac. And lived lived
happlly ever after.

FIGURE 12-5

4. Use a perceptual-motor approach to teach a manuscript lesson to a small group of children or peers.
5. Select what might be a major difficulty in cursive or manuscript writing and outline a set of procedures to alleviate it.
6. Develop one activity for a handwriting learning center, listing objectives, materials, and procedures.

FIGURE 12-6 Progress Checklist

1. Alignment of letters on the baseline
2. Shaping of letters and numerals
3. Size of letters
4. Slant
5. Spacing of letters in words
6. Spacing between words
7. Spacing between sentences

REFERENCES

GRAVES, DONALD. (1983) *Writing: Teachers and children at work.* Heinemann Ed Books.

FURNER, BEATRICE. (1967) The perceptual-motor nature of learning in handwriting. *Elementary English.* NTCE.

——. The Development and evaluation of a program of Instruction based on increased perception of Letters and their Formation. Unpublished Master's thesis, State University of Iowa, Iowa City.

FREEMAN, FRANK N. *What Research Says to the Teacher: Teaching*

McDougal-Littell Handwriting (1987). Evanston: McDougal-Littell & Co.

HARRIS, THEODORE L. "Handwriting." *The Encyclopedia of Education Research, 3rd ed.* New York: Macmillan, 1960. p. 616.

HERRICK, VIRGIL E. *Handwriting and Related Factors, 1890–1960*. Washington, D.C.: Handwriting Foundation (n.d.).

HERRICK, VIRGIL E., ed. *Handwriting*. University of Wisconsin Press, 1963.

McDougal-Littell Handwriting. Evanston, Ill.: McDougal-Littell & Co., 1987.

MYERS, HARRISON. *The Whys and Hows of Handwriting*. Columbus, Ohio: The Zaner-Bloser Company, 1963.

13

READING

BEGINNING READING

Anyone who has laughed aloud at a book, who has felt that special inner feeling from reading and knowing that this is the way s/he felt but couldn't put in words, who has come to understand something by reading about it, who has created something by reading how to do it, who has escaped the cares of the day with a fanciful romance, an improbable tale of space, an ingeniously crafted mystery or spy story, who has had any one or more of those experiences, does not need to be convinced of the value of reading. All those things are rewards for acquiring the skill of reading: the most basic of the basic skills.

Reading is more than a passport to personal reward. In a society which simply assumes total literacy, reading is a tool indispensable to modern life. Those who have the tool can use it in any way the see fit, or not at all. In short, they have a choice, or even more properly, they have choices. Those who don't have the skill, don't have the range of choice. It is the teacher's and the school's most important job, then, to provide the best, most effective instruction possible. How should that be done?

Reading Instruction

If teachers and schools were not faced with the task of teaching reading to groups of children, reading instruction would be a fairly easy task. On a one-to-one basis, instruction would probably consist of reading to the child, pointing out words learned. However, the sad fact is that in schools, reading instruction must be done in classes that may range from 18-20 and up to, in some cases, 35-40. Thus, reading instruction has to be done systematically. That is, rather than the one-to-one situation wherein instant feedback is possible, there needs to be a scope and sequence of instruction. Scope here refers to *what* will be taught and sequence the *order* in which it will be taught. Critics of instructional scope and sequence have suggested that any such sequence will be arbitrary. That is true. No one really knows what the best scope and sequence is for a child. If we could, be careful and patient observation, find what is best for one child, we suspect that we would find the next child needing a different scope and sequence. As Goodman has said, any sequence is arbitrary. However, the sequence is also redundant—that is, it is designed to do the same thing in more than one way. This redundancy builds, in effect, a unique scope and sequence for every child.

Speculate a bit about how you might go about designing a reading program. How would you choose the materials you would use? What prerequisite skills would you deem necessary? What words would you teach? In what order? How? Would you teach the pieces and then the whole? The whole and then the pieces? Just the whole? What sort of practice would you provide for? How would you reinforce your teaching? What would you do with those students who were beyond the present level of instruction? What about those who could not understand what you were presenting at all? Would you have discussions with your slower students about what they have read, or would you postpone discussion until they could read fairly simple material? These questions, each of which begets a series of questions of its own, have been answered in various ways at various times. The way they are answered, in part, leads to the various approaches to teaching reading.

Generally speaking, most systematic reading instruction falls into place along a continuum from code emphasis to meaning emphasis. Note that, for example, a meaning emphasis approach does *not* preclude the teaching of decoding. Of course, the reverse is true of code emphasis materials. Decoding is the focus, but meaning is not necessarily excluded. Whatever the emphasis of initial and subsequent instruction, the goal is the same: to produce readers who can and do read independently.

Code Emphasis Material

Code emphasis materials fall into several different sub-classes: Phonics approaches which are analytic, phonics approaches which are synthetic, "linguistic" approaches (misnomer) which introduce single-letter to single-sound, and augmented symbol system approaches.

Synthetic approaches emphasize the teaching of the sounds assigned to the various letters. When the students have learned the sound values of letters and letter combinations, they are expected to blend (synthesize) the letters into a word. This is the basis for the famous *C-A-T* example. The students have been taught that the appropriate sound value for *C* when it is followed by *A*, the sound value for *A* in the medial position, and the sound value for *T* in the final position. The word is decoded by synthesizing the whole from its constituent parts.

Analytic Phonics

Using the same standard example, "cat," the analytic process would work nearly in reverse. That is, the students would be told the word and then be instructed in analyzing it for the sounds appropriated to its letters. They would learn the sound value of *C* in the initial position, the *A* in the medial position, and the *T* in the final position. Notice that in each case, synthetic and analytic, the students end up with essentially the same information. It is just that they got there by different routes.

In the case of the controlled symbol presentation ("linguistics") method, the goal is to reduce the confusion inherent in a language in which, in a written form, a letter can have more than one sound. For example, consider the sound value of the letter *A* as it appears in the first two sentences of this paragraph: c*a*se, present*a*tion, go*a*l, *a*, langu*a*ge, *a*, c*a*n, h*a*ve, th*a*n, ex*a*mple, v*a*lue, *a*s, *a*ppe*a*rs, p*a*r*a*gr*a*ph. (See if you can agree with a friend about how many sounds are assigned the letter *A* in that series of words.) To produce the aforementioned reduction of confusion, in controlled symbol presentations, the student is introduced only to words in which a single letter is assigned to a single sound. Thus, staying with our abused "cat" example, once the students are introduced to the letter *A* as it sounds in the word "cat," they, at least initially, do not see any other words that contain a different sound value for that letter. (Go back to the series of words above and see how many of those words would be eliminated if only the *A* sound heard in "cat" were included.) Naturally, the *C* seen in such words as "city" and "cello" and the *T* seen in such words as "thunder" and "nation" would be similarly banned. The most common sounds assigned a letter are, in the controlled symbol approach, taught first, and variations are introduced later, one at a time.

Augmented Symbol Systems

Controlled symbol presentations and augmented symbol systems are similar in that they attempt to present students with one-to-one symbol to sound correspondences. The difference lies in the route to the goal. As you have seen, the controlled symbol systems artificially restrict the data the learner receives by including only those words which contain the sound assigned as the target sound. With augmented systems, the various sounds of our language (phonemes) are each given a unique symbol. There are 42-44 phonemes of English (the number varies dialect-to-dialect). In augmented symbol systems, there are typically 40 or more letters, instead of 26. The best known modern example of an augmented symbol system is the initial teaching alphabet (ITA). The use of expanded alphabets for teaching purposes can be traced back to the 1500's in England.

Naturally, each of these code-emphasis approaches, as well as the notion of emphasizing the code over meaning, has its adherents and its critics. Some of the criticisms are discussed at the end of this chapter. Prior to reading those, take a moment to speculate about each of these techniques. What, in your opinion, are the advantages and disadvantages of each?

Meaning Emphasis Approaches

Meaning emphasis approaches take as their basic philosophy the idea that since understanding, deriving meaning from print, is the goal of "real" reading (reading done by fluent readers, not beginning readers), the way to start reading instruction, and for that matter, to continue reading instruction, is to have meaning as the focus from the first. Thus, going back to our hoary old feline example, in meaning emphasis materials, the students would not simply learn how to recognize the word "cat" in print. They would read about that cat doing something. The differences in the group of approaches labeled meaning emphasis would be in *what* the student would read.

In whole word approaches, the unit of instruction, as the name implies, is the word. The basic point of departure for various schemes within this approach is the specific group (corpus) of words chosen to teach. Typically, the words are chosen on the basis of their frequency of occurrence in the language, with the most frequent words (plus some that are needed to build a story) taught first *as units*.

Very simply stories which contain, say, twelve different words are used. The teacher teaches the twelve words to the children so that they can recognize them at sight (Sometimes referred to as the "sight word" approach). Then the students read the story.

The classic whole word approach or sight word approach was exemplified by the old Scott-Foresman series featuring Dick and Jane. To your adult eyes, there may not seem to be a great deal of meaning in those stories, but the fact is, they contained at least the rudiments of fiction-character, action, and some sort of conflict. Dick and Jane and countless imitators (Jack and Janet, Alice and Jerry) were based on the simple fact that the most frequent 2500 or so words in our language account for something over 90% of the words we ever encountered in print. Mastery of that fairly small corpus would ensure a high percentage of success in reading. Not only that, mastery of the corpus would form a basis from which students could generalize in order to pronounce words they had not been taught. Knowing "might," "light," "sight," "fun," "find," and "fill," a student could be expected to be able to figure out the word "fight." It may be a wee flaw in reasoning to assume that 90% word recognition is sufficient for comprehension and that generalization will take place.

The Language Experience approach, which is a total Language Arts approach is, from strictly a reading point-of-view, a whole word approach. What distinguishes it from the published whole word approach is that the students select for themselves the words they will learn and then they write for themselves the stories which are formed from those words.

Actually, Language Experience is a class of approaches. Some advocate the use of child-generated experience stories as a total Language Arts curriculum for the elementary school. Some advocate Language Experience as a useful tool in conjunction with other approaches. Some merely suggest Language Experience as a means of introducing beginning readers to the words in print. Whatever the point of view, the basic idea is the same. It is a whole word approach in which the individual child has a personal stake since s/he chose the words to be learned.

Staying with the feline example (relentlessly) the children being instructed with the Language Experience approach might discuss in class what they know about cats, have a cat in class, visit a cat ranch, or see a film about cats, and then, write a story about cats. The stories would then become the basis for instructing the students in reading the words they used to write about cats.

Literature Approaches

Literature approaches to beginning reading instruction do not really exist in anything like a pure form in any modern program. It is, in fact, doubtful that they ever existed in a pure form except in some isolated instances. Still, the idea of the literature approach is important here since much of what goes into a modern basal system is influenced by the ideas behind a literature approach. Those ideas are, chiefly, these: Children will learn to read and appreciate good literature by learning to read from good literature.

In some cases the "good" literature (classics, well-known fairy tales) was rewritten in a simpler form for children. The literature became the vehicle for instruction and the actual instruction in word recognition could run the gamut from synthetic phonics to whole word instruction. Still, the point was that the literature served to teach and motivate with an emphasis on meaning.

In its most extreme form, literature (not rewritten) was read over and over again until all the students could read it fluently. Considering the number of times a less able student might read something, it is hard to know whether the student learned to read or simply memorized the material. That, and the extreme boredom inherent in reading the same piece, no matter how good or even great it is, over and over again probably contributed to the historically rapid demise of this seldom used approach. Nonetheless, the idea of the motivating value of well-written material has found its place in modern basal systems. Those systems typically include, to the greatest extent possible, good and well-recognized children's literature.

Modern Basal Systems

Something over 90% of the reading instruction in this country is done from a published basal reading system. These systems, as with the approaches already discussed, can be arranged along a continuum from code emphasis to meaning emphasis. They are, however, eclectic—that is, selections are chosen from various sources. In other words, the modern basal follows no one system, such as purely analytic phonics. Instead, the selections include what is best from the continuum. As with anything thought to be eclectic, the notion of what is best is crucial. That is why the published basals are arranged along a continuum from code emphasis to meaning emphasis. Within a particular basal you will find examples of analytic phonics, synthetic phonics, whole word approach, and language experience. This lack of purity of approach is intuitively sensible. If we were locked into a synthetic phonics approach, how would we deal with words like "have," "love," and "of?" We would be better served teaching those words as whole words. If we were locked into a whole word approach, would we not be better served in teaching words like "rate," "mate," "date," "fate," and "gate," by pointing out the obvious phonics generalizations in each of those words? That is exactly the reasoning behind modern eclectic basals—some aspects of the reading program are best taught by one method, others by another method. Some examples of modern eclectic basal materials follow. Can you spot which approach is being used in each instance?

Administrative Concerns

Individualized reading programs are *not* approaches to teaching reading. They are ways of managing instruction. Some are formal: that group of published programs known collectively as management systems. Some are less formal: that group of techniques known collectively as individualized reading programs. But whether formal or informal, they share a basic goal: to allow each student to progress at his/her own rate. The differences lie in how that goal is met.

Management Systems. Management systems work, typically, in a non-graded fashion. At no point is a child thought to be a third-grade reader, fourth-grade reader, or whatever. Instead, children are tested and, based upon the results of the testing, are directed to various skill groups and levels of material. If, for example, a second-grader is tested and found to be a very efficient reader, s/he then would work in materials appropriated to his/her skill level. By the same token, a child tested and found deficient in some crucial skill would be directed to a group working on that skill or in that skill area. Thus, in any small group in a school using a management system, one would be likely to find, within that group, children of varying ages.

Two things that are obviously crucial to the success of any management system; one is the strength of the placement tests used. They must be detailed enough to assess accurately the strengths and weaknesses of the child. The second is the strength of the skill group instruction and the materials used for that instruction. It is easy to see that a child is not helped by simply discovering an area of deficit. Instruction must successfully remediate the deficient area. Naturally enough, these two crucial elements form the basis for both the stated strengths and weaknesses of management systems.

There is an overarching concern within management systems. They must have as their basis, a stated hierarchy of skills. As noted previously, any such hierarchy is arbitrary. Or, at least arbitrary in the sense that there is, among experts in the field, no single agreed upon hierarchy. Whether the writer agrees or disagrees with the hierarchy of skills forms the third basis for assessment of the strengths and weaknesses of management systems.

Individualized reading. Broadly speaking, the elements of individualized reading programs are these: a large number of books from which the child may select, the individual conference with the teacher, and the teacher's record of those conferences.

By allowing children to choose for themselves what they will read, two things are assumed. One is that the child will select materials at the right reading level. The other is that the students will be highly motivated. Once the books have been chosen and read, the children then confer with the teacher.

The individual conference with the teacher is critical since it is within that conference that the teacher assesses the child's comprehension and, after listening to the child read, assigns him/her to various skill groups as needed. The instruction within the various skills groups is eclectic. That is, teachers choose whatever approach they think is best for teaching that skill.

Note that in individualized reading, as in the management system, the quality of the assessment (test or conference) and the quality of the subsequent small group or individual instruction are absolutely crucial to the success of the program. To the extent that either of those is weak, the program is weak.

The Success of Reading Instruction

Before launching into an examination of the strengths and weaknesses of the various approaches and techniques discussed, it seems appropriate to discuss the overall success of reading instruction.

First of all, in spite of what you may have read in the popular press or seen on television, we are *more* successful today at teaching reading than we have been at any time in the past.

Consider this: About 85% of the people we attempt to teach to read succeed at some reasonable level. That is, they become *at least* functional readers. Roughly half of the remaining 15% also become functional readers *with special help.* About half of the remaining few who don't learn the skill at some acceptable level in school do learn it as adults. That leaves roughly 3-4%. Small in percentages but very large in actual numbers, those who are unable to learn to read are a part of a true modern tragedy. Still, the overall success rate, while certainly not acceptable to reading specialists, is much higher than what one might think if they only listen to the television or read the newspaper. Progress has been made towards building a totally literate society, but there is still a long way to go.

Pros and Cons of the Various Approaches

What are the strengths and weaknesses of the various approaches and techniques discussed in this chapter? Since what you have read is a very short overview of a very complex topic (reams have been written about every point discussed here), only general strengths and weaknesses will be discussed herein.

Code emphasis approaches are often criticized on what their adherents consider their main strength: systematic teaching of the code. The pro side of the argument is, simply, that a person who cannot decode rapidly, even automatically, cannot hope to comprehend. In other words, unless a reader has some way of rapidly assigning sound (aloud or in the head) to a series of letters s/he has no way of making sense of what is on the page—no way of understanding. The critics of code emphasis suggest that by emphasizing the code there is a danger of creating readers who can only "bark at print." That is, since written messages only have meaning in context, the decoding of single words does not ensure comprehension. Besides, they point out, fluent readers recognize words immediately and automatically. They do not decode in the sense of sounding out words. The strength, competency at decoding, is seen as both a plus and a minus of the code emphasis approach.

In the cases of those approaches which either control the symbols presented to the child or augment the alphabet in order to achieve one-to-one symbol sound correspondence, the chief strength—consistency—is also the chief source of criticism. They create an artificial language. In the case of the controlled symbol presentation system, the stories are stilted, and the child encounters words in and out of school that do not conform to the system of symbol control. In the case of the augmented symbol system, the child encounters materials, daily, that are not written in the special alphabet that s/he is learning. Plus, the student must eventually learn how to transfer information from the special alphabet to the normal alphabet.

What do you think about the various code emphasis approaches?

Meaning emphasis approaches suffer the following criticism. English, in spite of its obvious symbol to sound inconsistencies, is an alphabetic language. The various letters and letter combinations do symbolize sounds. To teach reading as though those correspondences do not exist is to ignore one of the main strengths of the language. Again, the rebuttal is similar.

The language is simply not symbol to sound regularly enough. The teaching of "rules" or "generalizations" about the written language brings with it the obligation to teach exceptions to the generalizations. Since some of the most frequently taught generalizations have 50% or lower utility (they work half or less than half the time) the process is too confusing. In addition, meaning does not reside in single words. Since the comprehension of meaning is the point of reading, it is better to teach by emphasizing meaning. Again, fluent readers read whole words—they do not decode.

The basis for the criticisms and the kudos due to administrative systems (management systems and individualized reading programs) have to do with the strengths and weaknesses of three areas of such programs. Those areas are (1) the assessment used, (2) the followup to that assessment, and (3) the hierarchy of skills stated or implied in such programs. The chief strength is thought to be their allowance for individual differences, which leads to greater individual progress. The chief weaknesses are thought to be in the assessment and the followup to assessment.

One more criticism: In any totally individualized program, either formal or informal, there may be a lack of group discussion and interaction which children need in order to gain further understanding. Through discussion of a movie you have seen or a book you have read, you can gain further insight into your experience. Students also need to have the benefit of group interaction. Note that in administrative systems there is nothing that precludes group interaction. However, it may be overlooked unless the teacher weaves group discussion into the reading time.

Most modern approaches, whether basal, language experience, or management are eclectic. Most cluster toward the center of the decoding - the whole word continuum and borrow from both as needed.

Years of extensive research have not revealed a single best method for teaching reading. The research backs this point: the teacher's comfort with, and thorough understanding of the approach and the materials seem to correlate well with the children's success at the skill of reading. In other words, a teacher who likes and thoroughly understands the approach and materials s/he is using is more likely to be successful than a teacher who does not.

INTERMEDIATE READING

There is no clear line of demarcation between beginning reading and intermediate reading. There is no magic age or grade-level where students suddenly metamorphose into intermediate readers from beginning readers. There is a basic difference between the two concerns. Beginning reading is chiefly concerned with helping students to learn the skill of reading. Intermediate reading is chiefly concerned with helping student expand their reading skills. The cliche to describe this change is "reading to learn" as opposed to "learning to read."

The intermediate grades, fourth through sixth, are characterized by a greater emphasis on content subjects such as science and social studies, and increasing the level of sophistication in the process subjects, such as math and reading. The teaching of reading at the intermediate level begins to focus on content area reading, vocabulary growth, study skills, and comprehension.

Intermediate grade reading involves taking the students beyond recognizing in print, words they already have in their speaking and listening vocabularies. At this point in their instruction, vocabulary acquisition becomes even more important.

Intermediate grade reading involves a broadening of the conception of what literacy is. This broadening conception embraces such concerns as graphic literacy, discerning fact from opinion, and increasing emphasis on applicative comprehension.

As intermediate grade reading program will include systematic vocabulary instruction, practice in reading maps, charts, and graphs, work with persuasive prose, reading in order to do something, such as following a recipe, running a science experiment, doing a math problem, figuring out a bus schedule, creating an effect in art, and so on.

Each of these areas will be discussed further. Please be aware that we are presenting an overview of a topic about which entire volumes have been written. What you are reading is highly condensed.

Systematic Vocabulary Instruction

As we discussed in Chapter 5 Language Development, vocabulary growth depends on the following:

(1) Instruction that is direct, not incidental;
(2) Instruction that is long term, not intermittent,
(3) Instruction that is purposive, not just an adjunct;
(4) Instruction that is whole-curriculum based, not just a Language Arts unit;
(5) Instruction that is related to all the Language Arts, not just spelling, or reading, or writing, or listening, or speaking; and
(6) Instruction that reaches outside the school walls for examples and reinforcement, not instruction that implies that vocabulary is only a school concern unrelated to non-school existence.

Part of the magic of language study is that the language changes and grows. Words that seem essential to one generation often come to seem quaint to the next. The job of conveying these aspects of language and, particularly of vocabulary study, falls to the Language Arts teacher. The larger job of systematic vocabulary instruction should concern all teachers.

Additional techniques within intermediate reading instruction that have an impact on vocabulary growth are context-clue utilization and understanding of affixes and roots. Basal readers intended for use in the intermediate grades include some systematic instruction in these areas. Still, these are components of an ongoing vocabulary program and are, therefore, a concern of the total curriculum.

Graphic Literacy

Before you begin the following discussion, with a classmate or on your own, rate yourself on the following scale. Your answers should reveal two things: How you feel about the strength of your own skills and possible areas in which you might want to improve.

Instruction in interpreting and understanding graphs, charts, and tables is essential to intermediate reading. This task is accomplished in different ways in various reading and language arts curricula. Some examples from basal reading series follow. In some school districts there are in-district curricula designed for this purpose. Whatever approach is used where you teach, here are some important things to know about graphic literacy.

FIGURE 13-1 Self-Rating Scale: Applied Graphic Literacy Skills

SA Strongly Agree
A Agree
U Undecided
D Disagree
SD Strongly Disagree

SA A U D SD

1. I have no trouble discerning fact from opinion in persuasive writing.
2. I have no trouble discerning fact from opinion in expository writing (such as news stories).
3. I generally can understand bar graphs.
4. I generally can understand line graphs.
5. I generally can understand pie graphs.
6. I generally can understand tables.
7. Following simple directions is no problem for me (such as easy recipes).
8. Following direction is no problem for me (such as more complex recipes, putting a model together).
9. Following complex directions is no problem for me (such as preparing an income tax return, applying for a grant, and so on).
10. Airplane, train, ferry and bus schedules are easy for me to figure out.

Scoring: Assign five points to "Strongly Agree," four points to "Agree," three points to "Undecided" answers and so on.

A score of 50 indicates a high level of confidence in your ability to understand graphs and charts.

A score of 30 indicates an overall average level of comfort.

A score of 10 indicates a high level of discomfort.

Thus, the more points you score indicates a higher level of your confidence in reading and understanding various graphs.

The ability to interpret and understand such material proceeds from simple to complex. Typically, such instruction begins with the students working with information about themselves or about where they live. For example, a bar graph depicting age in months or years of the entire class is a good introduction to understanding bar graphs. Or, a pie graph showing how total square footage of the school is divided among classrooms, hallways, bathrooms, offices, lunchroom gymnasium, and so on is a good technique for relating that kind of graph to students' experiences. A line graph depicting rainfall or snowfall over the period of time students have been in school directly taps student experience. Many will remember that particularly rainy, snowy, cold, warm, whatever winter from two or three years ago. The point is that such instruction uses simple graphs that directly relate to students' experiences. What they learn is not new information, but how information is graphically represented. Once they learn how information is presented, then they are capable of learning new information from the various graphs they will encounter in science, social studies, and math.

Persuasive Writing

Children are bombarded with persuasive writing that they hear on television. Such material is carefully, even meticulously prepared and presented. In publications intended for children, the same is true—meticulously prepared persuasive writing abounds. Of course, we are talking about advertising. Being a critical reader (or listener) of such material requires the ability to separate fact from opinion and the recognition of techniques employed—often called propaganda techniques.

Within the broad file of Language Arts, unfortunately, instruction is often splintered and solitary. What we mean is, the composition classes wherein students write to persuade are too often not coordinated with reading instruction in persuasive materials. In addition, reading persuasive writing and attempting to create it are too often discrete units: taught once —then forgotten.

Applicative Comprehension

Applicative comprehension is a broad term that is used to indicate a level of understanding that requires readers to act on what they have read. At the simplest level, such comprehension is indicated by the reader's successful following of easy directions. At a more complex level, such understanding might be indicated by a reader successfully completing a long series of difficult tasks, a series which might well include many decision points. For example, if you have ever tried to follow the directions for restoring an old piece of furniture, you probably found directions within directions: "If this happens, do the following," or "if such and such happens, refer to Section

C," and so on. Another example of a task requiring a high level of applicative comprehension is following a multi-part recipe. In such recipes you have to first prepare a sauce, next prepare the main ingredient, and finally blend the two together according to more instructions.

Applicative comprehension as a reading skill within Language Arts tends to focus on written directions for various school activities. In fact, "following directions" is the standard title for such instruction. This instruction serves a purpose beyond school requirements—that of preparing one for a lifetime of applicative comprehension.

Reference Skills

Instruction in the use of reference texts is not the sole domain of intermediate grade reading instruction. But, it is a topic that receives fairly heavy emphasis at this level.

Reference text use depends upon the following skills: ability to alphabetize (beyond first-letter of word), ability to use table of contents and index, and the ability to use guide words. Those skills are usually taught in conjunction with dictionary use. The use of such references source, using cross references, and experience in choosing from among related topics listed.

In published basal material and in curriculum guides, these skills are taught throughout the upper primary and intermediate grades in progression from fairly simple to fairly complex. Reference skills are useful throughout a person's life, not just in school. For purposes of reinforcing and extending these skills, it is worthwhile for students to be taught that telephone books, auto repair manuals, catalogs, and other examples are reference books, too. Successful use of those references depends upon mastering the same skills used in the more school-oriented references.

We have written this overview of the content of intermediate reading for three reasons. First, we wanted to illustrate that the teaching of reading does not stop at the end of the child's primary years. Second, we wanted to illustrate how reading instruction in the intermediate years becomes increasingly crucial to and supportive of the other school subjects. Third, we wanted to illustrate how reading instruction relates to, supplements, and is integrated with the other parts of the Language Arts curriculum at the intermediate level.

READING TO STUDENTS

Why Teachers Should Read to Students

The goal of reading is comprehension. The goal of reading instruction is to produce fluent readers: fluent comprehenders. One activity that can help attain that grand goal is frequent reading to and discussion with students.

For beginning readers and older readers, oral reading by the teacher serves as a good model, is an enjoyable shared experience, and allows good discussion of the material read.

Particularly important is that a carefully led discussion serves as a kind of model for reading comprehension. A good discussion with active participation from students will reveal points-of-view and levels of understanding that a solitary reader could never attain.

Discussing What Has Been Read

First of all, keep in mind that your students may not have had much experience at participating in the kind of free discussion we are going to describe here. Here is how to do it. Choose a topic *you* like:

1. Choose carefully what you are going to read to your class. First, make sure it is something that you enjoy and that you think your students will enjoy. Second, at least, for the first few times you try this activity, choose something short. Third, read it yourself two or three times. You will be the expert. You will have to know the story very well.
2. Free discussion is just that. There is no test and no formal assessment, no evaluation of participation
3. Students must clear their tables and listen.
4. Only the teacher reads. The students listen. They do not follow along in a book.
5. The teacher prepares questions in advance of the lesson. The questions are at various levels, but are actually prompts to get the discussion going. The teacher's role is to add questions, offer alternative points of view, buttress sagging arguments, and so on, as the discussion proceeds.
6. Levels of questions. Refer to the brief description of the following taxonomy of questions. This taxonomy is not intended to be exhaustive of the question types you might pose. It is only indicative of the range of questions and the requirements to answer questions. Study it a bit, and for your discussion prepare a number of questions at each level. Remember, your questions are only prompts to the discussion. They should not be followed slavishly.
7. A free discussion is over when it is over. Initially, students not used to the free discussion idea will probably be a bit reluctant to participate. However, when they see that the discussion really is free, they will get involved. So, at first, you will probably have fairly short answers, few participants and finish fairly quickly. Later, after a few sessions, you will probably have to set a time limit for the discussion.

The Standal Taxonomy of Questions

The range of questions discussed below is not intended to serve as a psychological model of comprehension or even as an exhaustive review of question types. Rather, it is intended to serve as a guide to the broad range of questions that can be asked, to suggest some ways to respond to questions, and to relate discussion questions to reading/listening purpose.

1. Literal level. Literal level questions are *textbound*. They ask for an answer that is stated directly in the text. For example, in a story about a boy pulling a little yellow wagon and going to the store to buy milk, bread, and eggs, what he bought, what he carried his purchase home in, and his sex are only literal level questions relative to whatever else takes place in the story.

As the story unfolds, if we find out that there is a search for a boy and his red wagon, then the color of our hero's wagon becomes important. If the story unfolds in the direction of what use was made of the grocery items, then the color of the wagon is not as important. Therefore, literal level questions should be chosen on the basis of their importance to the entire story. Unfortunately, many literal level questions that are essentially irrelevant are posed every day.

Responses to literal level questions are either right or wrong. Handling right responses is easy. An enthusiastic "yes" or "very good" is all that is needed. Handling wrong responses are a bit more difficult. You do not want to discourage the student from trying and, at the same time, you must not accept wrong answers. A good way to handle a wrong response is to simply say "no" or "that's not it" and *give some positive reinforcement for the effort.*

2. Inferential questions. Inferential questions are text-plus questions. The plus is the ability of the reader/listener to put together two facts (literal level) or more in order to infer from them something not directly stated in the text. For example, adding into the previous example the time of day the boy went to buy groceries, might be an inference worth making if it is important as the story unfolds.

Responses to inferential questions are more likely to be on target or off target than they are to be clearly right or wrong. A good inferential question usually requires a tag such as "Why do you think that?" or simply "Why?" The strength of an answer to an inferential question lies in the strength of the facts marshalled to support it. Still, where an answer is fact-based, it can not be wrong. It can be weak or off target or lousy reasoning, but it can not be wrong. Therefore, such responses should not be labeled incorrect. They should be accepted as "a point of view" or "an interesting way of looking at it."

3. Higher-than-inferential questions. H-T-I Questions, for lack of a better name, are text-plus-plus questions. The first plus is the same as that of inferential questions. The second plus involves the reader/listener's individual experience, feelings, and thinking about the story. As with the other categories, H-T-I questions are better than others. The classic H-T-I question, and one which students come to loathe is "What did you learn from this story?" A better use for this level of involvement in a story is one which allows the readers/listeners to unite their own feelings, experiences, and thoughts with those of the characters in the story. For example, asking students whether they have had experiences or feelings similar to those described in the story allows them to think about the story from their own unique perspective.

As with inferential question responses, H-T-I responses, when they are based on the story, are not simply right or wrong. However, since H-T-I questions elicit experiences, feelings, and thoughts, it is extremely important that the responses be treated with a great deal of respect. Sometimes, by the way of example, students will seem to be unduly harsh in their judgments of a character's actions. They will be quick to label the character as a fool or coward. No matter how harsh or unfair the judgments are, it is the student's right to feel that way and to respond that way. No one's response to an H-T-I question should be belittled by the teacher or by any student. They can be explained further, expanded upon, but they can not be put down.

What is a reasonable mix of questions for a discussion? That depends upon what you want from the discussion. If there is a theme to the piece and you want to get at that, then designing literal and inferential questions that elicit the information necessary for recognition of the theme is all that is required. Enough is enough. If what you want is a broad exploration of students' reactions to the story, then a broad variety of questions at the literal and inferential level is necessary. You can not predict what students' reactions will be during the discussion, so you must make up H-T-I questions as the discussion progresses. The mix of questions can not be separated from the goals of the discussion. Think carefully about what you want and design your questions accordingly.

SUMMARY

The importance of reading in school and in life cannot be overstated. Reading is crucial as a means of learning, both in school and out.

Faced with the task of instructing students in groups, educators have developed a range of approaches for teaching reading and for administering the reading program. That range includes a variety of approaches emphasizing instruction in decoding, a variety of approaches emphasizing meaning, and formal and informal techniques for managing the reading instruction enterprise. Each approach and technique has its adherents who tout its strength and its critics who point out its weaknesses.

Reading instruction at the intermediate grade levels shifts in focus from learning the skill to broader applications of the skill. Among the broader applications are reading in science, social studies, math, and other content and process subjects. Reading in those subjects requires vocabulary growth, graphic literacy, applicative comprehension, use of reference materials, and critical reading of persuasive prose.

In the final analysis, it may be the individual teacher's comfort with and knowledge of the approach that contribute most to pupil success.

ACTIVITIES

1. What might be good sources for examples of persuasive writing?
2. What things in your students' background experience might be represented on a bar graph? A line graph? A pie graph?
3. Following written directions can be very difficult. In your own experience, what are the most difficult directions you have followed successfully?
4. The Murphy's Law of direction writing is: "If it can be misinterpreted, it will be." Discuss with a classmate examples of misinterpreted directions with which you are familiar.
5. Spend a few minutes in small groups discussing the methods used to teach you how to read and what you liked and disliked about the process.
6. Review strengths and weaknesses of the various approaches and techniques discussed in this chapter. In your opinion, which approach seems to have the most going for it? Why? With which would you feel most comfortable?
7. What is the "wee flaw" in the reasoning behind the whole word approach referred to on page 257?

REFERENCES

ALLINGTON, R. L. (1984). "Oral Reading." In P. D. Pearson (Ed.), *Handbook of Reading Reasearch*, (pp. 829–864). New York: Longman.

ANDERSON, R. C., et. al. (1985). *Becoming a Nation of Readers: The Report of the Commission on Reading*. Urbana, IL: University of Illinois, Center for the Study of Reading.

DISHAW, M. (1977). *Descriptions of Allocated Time to Content Areas for the A-B Period*. San Francisco: Far West Regional Laboratory for Educational Research and Development. Beginning Teacher Evaluation Study Tech. Note IV–11a.

FIELDING, L. G., WILSON, P.T., and ANDERSON, R. C. (in press). "A New Focus on Free Reading: The Role of Trade Books in Reading Instruction." In T. E. Raphael and R. Reynolds (Eds.), *Contexts of Literacy*. New York: Longman.

HEINTZE, R. A., and HODES, L. (1981). *Statistics of Public School Libraries/Media Centers, Fall 1978*. Washington, D.C.: National Center for Education Statistics.

14

EVALUATION STRATEGIES

PURPOSES OF EVALUATION

Evaluation serves two major purposes in language arts instruction. One purpose is to *provide knowledge of results of instruction* to students, parents, the teaching staff, even the nation. Within that context, the reporting of results is done at the individual pupil level and at the aggregate level which includes whole classes, grade levels, schools, districts, and so on. Both individual results and aggregate results are inevitably compared to grade or age-level norms. Thus, an individual who is eight or in third grade has his/her achievement compared to others of similar age or grade. We can then conclude that his/her achievement is "average," "above average," or whatever.

The other purpose of evaluation is to *diagnose learning*. It is one thing to know how well someone is doing academically. It is another thing to do something about it. Doing something about a student's achievement or lack of it is where diagnosis enters the picture. A pre-test given to students at the outset of a unit might serve the purpose of dividing certain portions of the unit instruction into three student ability levels: remedial, instructional, and enrichment. Formal test results might mean anything from recomending a student for a gifted-talented program to merely passing him/her on to the next grade level.

EVALUATION STRATEGIES

Evaluation is a continuous process as the following graphic illustrates:*

EVALUATION		
Knowledge of Results	Test scores Grades Report Cards	Checklists Anecdotal Records Parent Conferences
Diagnosis	Recommendation on basis of test scores Cumulative Folder Promote/Retain	Teacher Judgment Remediation Assignment to Groups Enrichment

FORMAL AND INFORMAL EVALUATION

Often, when the term "evaluation" is used in an instructional setting, we tend to think of formal tests. There are, in fact, many alternatives to testing. We will explore these alternative strategies following a look at some formal measures.

Formal measures. As children grow older and progress through the grades, they become increasingly accustomed to formal testing. Formal

**Language for Daily Use*, Harcourt, Brace Jovanovich, 1983, p. T25.

tests have value, particularly when they are normed, in that they can be used to make comparisons of a given student against the level of achievement s/he should be capable of attaining at a certain age or grade.

Pretests. At the *pretest level,* you are able to determine what skills or concepts students have acquired prior to formal instruction.

The formal tests found in teacher's editions of language arts tests have been developed in the context of grade-level expectation. They are developed by publishers to be used by teachers in testing that which is taught in a specific commercial program. Standardized tests such as the *Iowa Tests of Basic Skills* or the *California Achievement Tests* have well established national norms and are less content specific than the tests produced for a given commercial program. No doubt if merit pay systems become widespread, standardized test results will be used as one of the criteria for salary increments. Such usage of tests will, of course, spark great controversy.

Studies of effective instruction indicate rather conclusively *the value of frequent monitoring of achievement.* This provides learners with both an incentive to learn and knowledge of results. These are two important psychological factors in the learning process. At the very least, formal tests should be employed at the end of each unit of instruction, prior to the close of each reporting period, at mid-year, and at the school's year's end. The use of such a formal testing sequence will ensure you that you have adequate documentation on which to base report card grades as well as recommendations which you will need to make with regard to promotion and retention.

It is important to keep in mind that a clear and logical pattern ought to emerge in your sequence of (1) objectives for student learning, (2) instructional strategies, and (3) assessment of student learning. Such an approach has been cited in studies of effective instruction as a "tightly coupled curriculum." Strong evidence exists to indicate that such a tight coupling of objectives, instruction, and evaluation yields consistently higher results in achievement. In a tightly coupled curriculum, the processes of setting instructional objectives, teaching students through the use of a variety of strategies, and diagnosing and assessing learning are a continuous process.

Here is an illustration of how this continuous process works. In the following excerpt, you will find that *pretest items* are written to capture *learning outcomes* that represent *behavioral objectives. The behaviorial objectives guide the* learning activities *of the unit, which are then captured by the unit* posttest.

PRETEST

Record scores on individual Record Form and Class Record form. Note how the students score on items as related to stated measurement objectives, and group the students according to needs.

PRESCRIBE APPROPRIATE ASSIGNMENTS

Below 50%	50-79%	80% and above
Follow easy Rx in TE	Follow average Rx in TE	Follow challenging Rx in TE

UNIT TEST IN STUDENT'S EDITION

Below 50%	50-79%	80% and above
Reteaching Models and further Practice from More Practice Review Handbook. Additional Practice. Oral Activity, Workbook, or Extra Practice Masters.		Enrichment activities from Unit Activities. Additional Practice. Extension, or Enrichment Masters.

POSTTEST

Record scores on Individual Record form and Class Record Form.

FIGURE 14-1 Excerpts From Unit on Action Verbs. From Language for Daily Use. Harcourt, Brace, Jovanovich, 1983, Level 3.

SAMPLE OBJECTIVES

1. The student identifies action verbs in sentences. (test items 1,8)
2. The student identifies present and past tense verbs in sentences. (test items 2, 9)
3. The student identifies the correct present tense verbs that agree with singular and plural subjects. (test items 3, 10)

(pretest – posttest examples)

The unit posttest results will tell you which students have attained an acceptable level of performance and which students are in need of remedial help.

Informal evaluation strategies. Formal testing is a necessary and integral component of the teaching/learning process in language arts. Objective and essay tests provide students, parents, teachers, and other interested parties with both diagnostic and reporting criteria. Without formal tests, it would be extremely difficult for you to assign and justify student grades or other indicators of progress.

Formal testing does, however, have its limitations. One problem with formal tests is that young children are often not "test-wise." They simply do not understand the purpose or value of tests. One could argue that this is to their credit, but that is another issue. They also have not yet learned that tests, particularly objective tests, tend to follow formats that one must master in addition to the content that has been taught. Thus, trick question, two-part items, and so on are simply beyond their level of sophistication. The statement, heard often in one form or another from younger children, "I know that, but I didn't get it right," is patently true. For the child, learning has been largely a naturalistic process. There have been few interventions (potty training is an exception!). He or she learned to eat, crawl, walk, speak, laugh, and cry without the benefit of formal instruction and formal evalution. Thus, for the young child who takes learning for granted, a formal test is truly a discrepant event. All this argues for other, less formal means of addressing learning outcomes. Here are a few simple strategies that, when systematically employed, will give you a great deal of data on the progress of your students.

Class discussion. A simple, non-threatening evaluation strategy is a class discussion focused on several key points of instruction which you are attempting to make through your lesson activities. If, for example, your class has been studying dictionary skills, you may want to begin the discussion by saying, "What are some of the things you can use a dictionary for? Let's see if we can list them on the board."

Keep the discussion brief, but be sure to make a check in your grade book beside the names of those students who participate actively. Over time, you will have a record of each student's involvement. You will want to talk individually with those students who do not tend to participate. Keep in mind that involvement in group discussion itself is a skill you need to cultivate, and that it becomes increasingly difficult if it is not developed early in life.

"I learned" statements. Perhaps once a week you should collect "I Learned" statements from your students. You merely ask them to write down something they have learned during a given class period or during a week. Here is an example written by Hannah:

> I learned that you should tell three things when you describe something. What it is, what you use it for, and I can't remember the third thing.

I learned statements are useful to the teacher because they provide mosaic of what the entire class learned about a topic. Do not be too surprised if the students' comments are somewhat at variance with your instructional objective for a lesson. What is taught and what is learned are not always the same.

Summary sheets. To utilize the summary sheet evaluation strategy, place students in small groups and ask them to review a topic of current study. For example, you might provide each group with the question, "What are some important things to keep in mind when you write a letter?" The students discuss the question, and one person in each group is assigned the role of recorder. For young children, you may wish to let each group summarize its discussion while your record key points on the chalkboard. In addition, to its function as a review of what has been learned, the summary sheet strategy also serves to develop speaking, listening, and reporting skills.

Interviews. A time-consuming but invaluable (in terms of one-to-one contact with your students) evaluation technique is the personal interview. Interviews need not be lengthy, and they can be conducted any time the opportunity presents itself. To conduct an interview, you merely ask a student for a few minutes of his or her time and begin by asking how things have been going, how he or she feels about language arts, whether there has been something that is difficult, and so on.

Artifacts. It is easy to overlook the commonplace. Your students will draw pictures, write letters, practice their handwriting, compose stories and poems, and complete many other assignments during any given reporting period. Merely keep certain examples of each students work in a folder which can be sent home with parents at conference time. The folder with its several assignments will give you something tangible to discuss with parents at conference.

Checklists. A checklist is based on a master sheet of your instructional objectives. Each student's name appears on the checklist and provision is made for noting to what extent he or she acquired the objectives. See Figure 14-2.

ACTIVITIES FOR THE ELEMENTARY METHODS CLASS

1. Evaluate "The Christmas Mouse" written by a hypothetical fifth-grade student using the checklist for paragraph skills.
2. Think of another language skill, such as specific word choice or spelling, and create a checklist for a specific grade level that could be used in evaluating that skill.
3. Devise questions that you would use to evaluate expressive work such as a creative drama activity or a poem. Devise them with a specific grade level and activity in mind.
4. For help with activity 3 re-read the sections on evaluation in Chapters 8 and 9 and the section on evaluating creative drama in Chapter 6.

FIGURE 14-2 Checklist for Paragraph Skills

	Ida	Bruce	Mason	Ruth	Jo
Identifies main idea	X	/	X	X	/
Identifies topic sentences	X	/	/	X	/
Identifies irrelevant details	X	/	/	X	O
Identifies supporting details	X	O	X	X	O

O = No evidence
/ = Some evidence
X = Good evidence

Christmas Mouse

Once upon a time there was a mouse named Noisy. He lived in a big house. It was christmas Eve and Noisy was waiting for Santa to slide down one of the chimneys. But Noisy had a big problem he didn't know wich chimney to run to. Then he thought of another big problem he also had with his little feet he couldn't run fast enough to get there even if he did now witch chimney to run to He thought and thought then he remberd the ceiling is made of glass. He could look up and see witch chimney to run to. But in the meintime Santa had already come down the chumney and started his work. Just then in came Noisy. He was so busy looking at the ceiling that he pumped into Santa.

REFERENCES

AHMANN, J. S., and M. D. GLOCK. *Evaluating Student Progress: Principles of Tests and Measurements*, 6th ed. Boston: Allyn and Bacon, 1981.

BLOOM, B. S., T. J. HASTINGS, and G. F. MADAUS. *Handbook on Formative and Summative Evaluation of Student Learning*. New York: McGraw-Hill Book Company, 1971.

GRONLUND, N. E. *Measurement and Evaluation in Teaching*, 3rd ed. New York: Macmillan Co., 1976.

Language for daily use. Level 3. (1983). Orlando, Fla: Harcourt, Brace, Jovanovich.

LYMAN, H. B. *Test Scores and What They Mean*, 2nd Ed. Englewood Cliffs, N. J.; Prentice-Hall, 1971.

STUFFLEBEAM, D. I., et al. *Educational Evaluation and Decision Making*. Itasca, Illinois: F. E. Peacock Publishers, 1971.

TENBRINK, T. D. *Evaluation: A Practical Guide for Teachers*. New York: McGraw-Hill Book Company, 1974.

TERWILLIGER, J. S. *Assigning Grades to Students*. Glenview, Ill.: Scott, Foresman, and Company, 1971.

WITTROCK, M. C., and D. E. WILEY, eds. *The Evaluation of Instruction: Issues and Problems*. New York: Holt, Rinehart and Winston, 1970.

Epilogue

OVERVIEW OF RESEARCH IN THE LANGUAGE ARTS

Kindergarten children talking earnestly in groups of four about the favorite toys they have brought to school. Third graders engaged in a lively discussion about a film they have just seen. Fifth graders putting the finishing touches on the covers of the books they have written about their families. A fourth grader telling a friend about a book he has just read. Three third graders gathered around a computer trying to figure out the next step in a program they are designing. Second graders rehearsing the parts in a radio play they will perform and record later. A group of third-graders listening intently to their teacher's reading of a well-known children's book. First graders in pairs helping one another write captions for pictures they have just drawn. All of these events have two things in common. They represent children using the language arts and they are the focus of research in the language arts.

Research in the language arts goes on in a wide variety of settings, not all of them schools, and uses a full spectrum of research modes, from classic experimental research design to structured observation of language use in a range of settings, to careful analysis of writing both by and for children and, of course, much more. There is a great richness in this diversity of subject of study and mode of inquiry into those subjects. Unfortunately, that richness can only be hinted at in this discussion.

Language arts research is traditionally categorized as reading, writing, speaking, or listening research. Spelling is rarely given its own category, being considered, if at all, under the category of writing. However, if there is one dominant trend in the research of the last few years, it is to avoid this implied compartmentalization and, instead, to try to understand particular uses of language, not only for themselves but also for the way in which they relate to the whole. In fact, a great deal of research effort is directed to specifying more carefully the relationships between and among the various language arts as, for example, the research on the reading-writing connection. We, too, wish to avoid the implicit, if not explicit, separation of the language arts in this discussion. Thus, the overview of research that follows emphasizes the interactive nature of the language arts and language arts theory, research, and instruction.

Children produce language all the time. One of the most interesting and important areas of research on language production is within the study of the composition process. What is most impressive in this area of research is the recognition of the writer's need to talk about his or her writing. (The composition chapter in this text, for example, emphasizes broad exploration through child-child and teacher-child discussion within the stages of the composing process.) A host of carefully done studies in a variety of research modes has changed the way we think about writing and the teaching of writing. For example, the composing process is no longer thought of as linear. No longer does one expect to find research-based composition instruction suggesting a step-by-step process of composing. What one does find is the recognition of stages, which are travelled through and returned to again and again. Composition researchers refer to this as the recursive nature of composition. That simply means that there are stages or processes within the composition process itself that are recoursed, gone through again and again.

The amount of attention, both theoretical and research attention, given to the composing process has greatly increased in the last few years. Research articles and books by Donald Graves and his colleagues have, in a very real way, revolutionized the way we think about writing and the teaching of writing. (See, for example, X, Y, and Z.) What once had been instruction oriented to forms and final product has now become instruction focused on the learners and the processes they use to write about topics that interest them to audiences interested in them.

This revolution, properly reflected in our own chapters, on writing in particular, but evident throughout the book, has brought writing and writing processes into the forefront of all the language arts: reading, writing, speaking, and listening. The research clearly suggests that each of these is essential to and interrelated with the learning of each of the others. Did you, for example, notice how much reading, listening, and speaking there was in the chapters on writing?

Another important finding from recent research is that skilled writing is within the reach of virtually all students. Properly nurtured and thoughtfully taught, it seems that we all have something to say and can learn to say it in ways that others can understand and appreciate.

The nature of the composition process as explicated by these researchers makes clear the point that language production, writing, and speaking, go on together. Thinking aloud, bouncing one's ideas off another, rereading aloud, trying different words aloud, and many other instances of oral language within the composing process research make it clear that writing, at least for a beginning writer, is anything but the lonely and solitary task it is frequently thought to be.

This unity of the language arts is a theme of this book. Even while the focus of a chapter is on a particular language skill, that skill is never isolated from the rest of the language arts.

Reading, for example, has been thought of as the most basic of the basic skills, the first R, even as *the* language art. That stance is not taken here. The research, particularly the research in schema theory, demonstrates the need for readers to talk and write and listen to others talk about what they've read. It is interesting to note that some of the most thorough comprehension research in recent years uses not just reading but discussion and written response to increase reading comprehension. Apart from the skill of decoding, it is clear that our understanding of what we read is enhanced when we can talk about it and write about it.

For younger children, children just being initiated into the world of the literate, the importance of shared experiences to discuss and write about and read about cannot be overstated. That old bugaboo for all writers but particularly the young writer, spelling, has come to be thought of quite differently—different enough that even the youngest writer/readers are being encouraged to get their thoughts and responses and impressions on paper in any way they can. Invented spellings, close, and then closer approximations to conventional spellings, are not just tolerated but encouraged by the wise language arts teacher who knows that they represent developmental levels and not carelessness or mistakes. Chapter 11, Spelling should free you, the language arts teacher, to capitalize on this burgeoning ability as it can serve the learning of all the language arts.

Grammar, the mainstay of the back to basics advocates, is another area of the language arts that has been positively influenced by the research on the composing process. It is apparent that mastery of the formalities of grammar, apart from any application for them, is unlikely. If mastered, it is quickly forgotten. If mastered and retained, useless. Again and again, we see what must be the quintessential fact of life for the language arts teacher. Language is for use. Its use is communication. The skills that serve that use are the essential skills to be taught and the way to teach those skills is *through* their use, not apart from their use.

There remains much to be discovered about the ways in which language is learned and used. That research will go on in a variety of modes and from a variety of perspectives and it will guide us, as professionals, in the ways language is taught and evaluated. While we dare not be satisfied that we know what there is to know and that we teach as well as we can teach, it is both safe and reasonable to say that we know a great deal and that knowledge informs our thinking about language and our teaching of language. It is that knowledge, along with our experiences as teachers and learners, that has guided us in the writing of this book.

INDEX